MOUNTAIN BIKE!
Florida

MOUNTAIN BIKE!

Florida

A GUIDE TO THE CLASSIC TRAILS

SECOND EDITION

STEVE JONES

Menasha
Ridge
Press

Library of Congress Cataloging-in-Publication Data
Jones, Steve, 1954-
Mountain bike! Florida: a guide to the classic trails /
Steve Jones.—2nd ed.
p. cm.
Includes index.
ISBN 0-89732-340-8
1. All terrain cycling—Florida—Guidebooks.
2. Bicycle trails—Florida—Guidebooks.
3. Florida—Guidebooks. I. Title: Florida. II. Title.
GV1045.5.F6 J65 2000
796.6'3'09759—dc21   00-048723

Photos by the author unless otherwise credited
Maps by Brian Taylor at RapiDesign
Cover Photo by Dennis Coello
Cover and text design by Suzanne H. Holt

Menasha Ridge Press
P.O. Box 43673
Birmingham, Alabama 35203
www.menasharidge.com

All trails described in this book are legal for mountain bikes. But rules can change—especially for off-road bicycles, the new kid on the outdoor recreation block. Land-access issues and conflicts between cyclists, hikers, equestrians, and other users can cause the rewriting of recreation regulations on public lands, sometimes resulting in a ban of mountain bike use on specific trails. That's why it's the responsibility of each rider to check and make sure that he or she rides only on trails where mountain biking is permitted.

CAUTION

Outdoor recreational activities are by their very nature potentially hazardous. All participants in such activities must assume the responsibility for their own actions and safety. The information contained in this guidebook cannot replace sound judgment and good decision-making skills, which help reduce risk exposure, nor does the scope of this book allow for disclosure of all the potential hazards and risks involved in such activities.

Learn as much as possible about the outdoor recreational activities in which you participate, prepare for the unexpected, and be cautious. The reward will be a safer and more enjoyable experience.

To Fender and the piece of three-legged gator in all of us.

If I remember the sunflower forest,
it is because from its hidden reaches man arose.
The green world is his sacred center.
In moments of sanity he must still seek refuge there.

—Loren Eiseley

CONTENTS

CENTRAL FLORIDA RIDES—ORLANDO AND BEYOND   155

SOUTHEAST FLORIDA RIDES   187

SOUTHERN GULF RIDES   225

AMERICA BY MOUNTAIN BIKE! · Map Legend

Ride trailhead

Primary bike trail

Direction of travel

Optional bike trail and trailhead

Other trail

Hiking-only trail

Interstate highways (with exit no.)

US routes

State routes

County or local roads
Jeffers Rd.

Unpaved, gravel or dirt roads (may be 4WD only)

Forest Service roads

Cities
Tallahassee

Towns or settlements
Blue Spring
St. Marks

Dam

Lake

Intermittent stream

Perennial stream

0 1/2 1
MILES
Approximate scale in miles

True North

CLEAR SPRINGS WILDERNESS AREA
Public Lands*

State Border

Airport

Archaeological or historical site

Boat ramp

Campground (CG)

Cattle guard

Cemetery or gravesite

Church

Cliff, escarpment or outcropping

Drinking water

Falls or rapids

Fire tower or lookout

Food

Gate

House or cabin

Lodging

Mine or quarry

Mountain or butte

Mountain pass

Mountain summit
3312 (elevation in feet)

Observatory

Park office or ranger station

Picnic area

Power line or pipeline

Rest rooms

Spring

Stable, corral, or ranch

Swimming area

Transmission towers

Tunnel or bridge

*Remember, private property exists in and around our national forests.

FLORIDA · Ride Locations

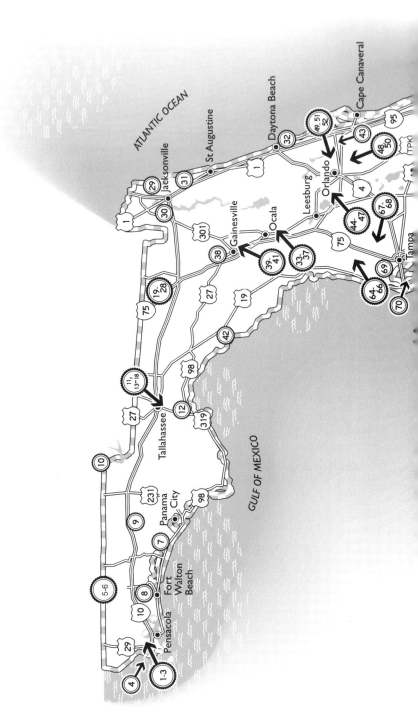

LIST OF MAPS

ACKNOWLEDGMENTS

There are so many people to thank at the end of a big project like this. Editor Dennis Coello and publisher Molly Burns hatched the idea in the first place, so it is to their credit that you see this guide at such an exciting time for off-road biking in Florida.

Next in line for a tip of the helmet are the many public officials who conceive and carry out policy designed to attract not just more bikers into the woods, but all the other people who need places to go with no walls. Of course, most of the encouragement for trail building comes straight from local bike clubs, stores, and people who organize and supply the muscle power required to blaze a trail. If it weren't for these dedicated people who have made riding off-road a priority, this guide would be considerably slimmer. Join a club and build a trail—you can tell your grandkids all about it.

My family and friends have been especially helpful in providing whatever they could to make this book possible. Mike did some cyberdigging for me and uncovered some great trails. Neel and his family put me up for the week I was in Tallahassee, and my Aunt Myrtle allowed the use of her condo for a couple of weeks. Thanks also to Brian for taking care of Betsy. Pam and Jared have my thanks for more things than I can remember. They not only took care of the chores on the home front while I was away, but they have also served as diligent copyeditors, careful cartographers, and loyal cheerleaders. Thanks.

FOREWORD

Welcome to *America by Mountain Bike!*, a series designed to provide all-terrain bikers with the information they need to find and ride the very best trails around. Whether you're new to the sport and don't know where to pedal, or an experienced mountain biker who wants to learn the classic trails in another region, this series is for you. Drop a few bucks for the book, spend an hour with the detailed maps and route descriptions, and you're prepared for the finest in off-road cycling.

My role as editor of this series was simple: First, find a mountain biker who knows the area and loves to ride. Second, ask that person to spend a year researching the most popular and very best rides around. And third, have that rider describe each trail in terms of difficulty, scenery, condition, elevation change, and all other categories of information that are important to trail riders. "Pretend you've just completed a ride and met up with fellow mountain bikers at the trailhead," I told each author. "Imagine their questions, be clear in your answers."

As I said, the *editorial* process—that of sending out riders and reading the submitted chapters—is a snap. But the work involved in finding, riding, and writing about each trail is enormous. In some instances our authors' tasks are made easier by the information contributed by local bike shops or cycling clubs, or even by the writers of local "where-to" guides. Credit for these contributions is provided, when appropriate, in each chapter, and our sincere thanks goes to all who have helped.

But the overwhelming majority of trails are discovered and pedaled by our authors themselves, then compared with dozens of other routes to determine if they qualify as "classic"—that area's best in scenery and cycling fun. If you've ever had the experience of pioneering a route from outdated topographic maps, or entering a bike shop to request information from local riders who would much prefer to keep their favorite trails secret, or know how it is to double- and triple-check data to be positive your trail info is correct, then you have an idea of how each of our authors has labored to bring about these books. You and I, and all the mountain bikers of America, are the richer for their efforts.

You'll get more out of this book if you take a moment to read the Introduction's explanation of the trail listings. The "Topographic Maps" section will help you understand how useful topos will be on a ride, and will also tell you where to get them. And though this is a "where-to," not a "how-to" guide, those of you who have not traveled the backcountry might find "Hitting the Trail" of particular value.

In addition to the material above, newcomers to mountain biking might want to spend a minute with the glossary, page 275, so that terms like *hard-pack, single-track,* and *waterbars* won't throw you when you come across them in the text.

Finally, the tips in the Introduction on mountain biking etiquette, and in the Afterword on land-use controversy, might help us all enjoy the trails a little more.

All the best.

Dennis Coello
St. Louis

PREFACE

Many people have drawn their picture of Florida based on what flashes outside the windows of an air-conditioned car. Speed: 70 mph. Destination: sand, sea, and palm trees. That pretty well sums up what I had seen before heading out to do the research for this guide. I was prepared to find little more than featureless rides in trackless, bug-choked swamps. I was ready to spin on the sandy hips of this 65,000-square-mile peninsula while I bunny-hopped gators and armadillos. But what I found for the adventurous off-road biker in this, the oddest-shaped state in the union, makes the Magic Kingdom an understatement.

So I kissed my wife and son good-bye and took off for the Panhandle, already knowing, I thought, what I would find. Sometimes referred to as L.A., or Lower Alabama, this part of Florida is thick and tangly — and it also has the highest elevation in Florida. I reasoned that if I started somewhere near the Blackwater River and Paxton, where the elevation reaches 345 feet above sea level, it would be all downhill from there. By the time I reached Fort Walton Beach, I was convinced that a little elevation goes a long way. After staying in the Tallahassee area for a week, I knew I had underestimated Florida's off-road potential. Sand be damned, I was having fun!

By then, I hadn't even seen the one-of-a-kind trails along the banks of the Suwannee River yet, and I was already calling home and telling people I met, "You would not believe the great trails in Florida!" Single-track, double-track, paved, dirt, grass, sand, even rocks formed the various surfaces I rode in America's Sunshine State. I pedaled swamps, sure — for the most part staying dry. I learned to enjoy riding in sand (I was told I would). I learned to identify and appreciate the difficulty of rolling over gatorbacks — not the reptile, but the palmetto roots exposed across the trail. And there were more than a few sections of trails out there that I simply could not ride because . . . they were too steep. Ocala, Bellview, Gran Canyon, Croom, Oleta, and Spruce Creek—these are places where hot-dog out-of-state "mountain bikers" learn that Florida is not always on the level.

But the lower-key off-road rider can find plenty, too, in the way of straight and flat. I've ridden and reported in this guide on some of the state's better rides in the panoramic, rails-to-trails category. For a larger listing of these destinations, I recommend *Florida Rail-Trail Bicycling* by Joan Scalpone. I was also directed to many fine trails in the Orlando area by the Florida Freewheelers Bicycle Club's *A Guide to All-Terrain Biking in Central Florida*, whose proceeds go to trail construction and education.

While I do not suggest you load the mountain bikes solely for an off-road trip to the Keys, you will find places along this 140-mile stretch (including Key West) where you can ride off-road. Also, I do not suggest—providing you have the choice—arranging a summer trip to cycle the interior of the Everglades. But go to the Everglades and ride, even if you can only arrange to do so in the summer. With a few extra precautions (see the chapter on weather), each and every month is a pleasure to ride in.

You probably would guess that, with all the water in and around Florida, boating is its top recreational activity. But number two? Biking, of course. On-road, off-road, races (Florida is ranked tenth in number of National Off-Road Biking Association members, i.e., racers), night rides, club rides, and solos—you name it and Floridians (and their guests) are out there having the ride of their lives on the trail of their choice. I've put together nearly 80 complete trails for you to choose from, with several more that are either in the late or early planning or physical development stages. I hope after reading a few, you will put the book down and say, "Enough! Let's ride!"

PEOPLE

The first Floridians presumably made their way here from the same direction you arrived in Florida—the north. They lived more or less peacefully with each other for thousands of years, with an occasional ritual raid on a neighboring tribe to ensure a subsequent fertile and productive year. Their existence was tied to the seasons, moving inland to hunt deer and turkeys, and to the sea to catch the great runs of fish and harvest huge beds of mollusks.

And then the white men came. By the time the natives figured out they weren't interested in fresh fish or clams—but wanted to know where they were hiding all their gold and fountains of youth—there were precious few natives left for the Spanish priests to convert. But convert they did. They also went through the motions of making treaties with the American government,

Florida's early inhabitants were as tough as the cypress used for this sculpture near Panama City Beach.

only to see them broken before the parchment reached the Suwannee River. Most gave up their rights to the land peacefully, but there were some native Floridians who were not willing to give up or give in.

The young United States government had set its sights on western expansion, and a temporary oversight left the rugged peninsula alone to those settlers who were independent, strong, and lucky enough to survive the Indians and the elements. Eventually, the policy of removal and genocide made its way down to the exotic tropical outposts in Florida until the last handful of Indians remained inside the great "river of grass," the Everglades.

Commands came from Washington to remove the last tribes and send them to Oklahoma. And, as the saying goes, it was much easier said than done, for the Miccosukee and Seminoles decided they preferred a nomadic life in the swamp—even if they had to spend most of their time fighting Zachary Taylor—over living in Oklahoma. So fight they did—and run—disappearing many times with little or no trace except for the dead soldiers and settlers left in their wake.

Incredibly, the government eventually conceded the Second Seminole War and awarded the Indians their space in Florida, where today museums and airboats are run by descendants of the people who defeated a nation. And you can, of course, ride your bike in the areas where these battles took place and the Indians lived on the run for so many years. One can't help but admire and respect the skill it took to survive in such an apparently inhospitable environment like the Everglades—especially in the summer.

But little contact will be made with these proud people by the off-road biker in Florida. Over twelve million people call Florida home—primarily the sons and daughters of Crackers and Conchs (you've probably heard of Crackers, but Conchs are those who have Carribean ancestors), along with immigrants from nearly every country in the world. Many immigrants, especially those now living in south Florida, arrived from Cuba. Others have ties to big northern cities like New York and Boston, holdovers from Florida's first days as a winter retreat for the wealthy.

All this has created a curious blend of cultures, fairly dilute by the time it hits the single-track. But inside the stores, it's different. On any given day in any given big-city Florida bike shop, an hour spent browsing will bring a carousel of cultures spinning past the checkout counter. You will also see a cross-section of Florida along its highways, especially the interstates.

Life on Florida's asphalt can be a bit unnerving for the unprepared. I knew I had to drive by a new set of rules when I began seeing bumper stickers like "Horn Broke—Watch For Finger" and "Keep Honking—I'm Reloading!" inside the back windows of cars. I drove nearly 10,000 miles in Florida, however, without incident. One of my friends, though, tells me I have a mug that discourages antagonistic behavior directed my way. I guess all those years spent scowling at teenagers as a teacher in public schools was good for something after all.

Although it may be more of an indication of the people attracted to off-road cycling than to the general population, I had nothing but the best treatment from whomever I met. Of course, the nicest ones were the bikers and shop owners who quickly and willingly agreed to set up rides and tell me where to go for the best in Florida biking. But there were others. One older lady met me going in the opposite direction on a desolate dirt road as I was searching vainly for a trailhead. Forgetting I was in the twentieth century, I slowed down and stuck my arm out the window. I waved and came to a complete stop as her car rolled by, then stopped and backed up to me. After I asked my question and got my answer, I told the lady that I had not expected her to stop. She said, "We're friendly people around here." They sure are.

The words of Flannery O'Connor came to me one evening around 10 P.M. as I was staring at the headlights of an approaching pickup on a deserted forest service road. My car, unused to the sandy conditions that can suddenly crop up on Florida backroads, was firmly stuck on a pedestal of sand. I believe I uttered, "A good man is hard to find," as visions of Misfit and his wayward gang came to mind. As the truck pulled up and stopped behind my car, one of the riders got out—quart bottle of beer in tow—and asked, "You stuck, Bro? You need some help?"

After I told him I believed I had just finished digging my way out, and thank you kindly, I got in, eased out of the rut, and pulled over to let those good old boys by. As they passed, another stuck his head out the window and reminded me, "Just keep it out of those ruts and you'll do fine." About then I thought of the words of Tennessee Williams regarding the beauty brought on by "depending on the kindness of strangers."

Although some might argue it was just plain luck that "Bro" hadn't already drunk the extra quarts in the huge cooler riding in the back and being guarded by a large German shepherd, time after time I was presented with the kindness of strangers who helped me on my way. And so while I believe that Florida's off-road biking trails are among the finest anywhere, the greatest assets this state possesses are its people, who acted—at least while I was around—like they never met a stranger.

FLORA AND FAUNA

Much of Florida's mystique comes from its exotic native collection of plants and animals, many of which can best be seen astraddle the saddle of a mountain bike. Along with the alligators and palm trees, the grainy terrain in between the Gulf of Mexico and the Atlantic is home to creatures that slither, nest, hop, buzz, gallop, and burrow in the state's 65,000 square miles.

Part of the reason so many living things congregate on this peninsula can be seen bubbling up from the limestone caverns and flowing—imperceptibly at times—to the seas surrounding it. Water. Without it, life on earth ends. When it is abundant like it is in Florida, all forms of creation come to eat and raise their young.

Another attraction Florida has for the world's wildlife is its long growing season. No need to hibernate or break the cycle of procreation here in the mostly tropical climate. Birds flock here to escape the sleet and ice of their northern summer feeding grounds. Insects and fish thrive from January to December in the air and water, thus ensuring an adequate supply of food for the winged visitors.

I did most of my trail research in summer, when the waters rise and spread, taking much of the wildlife to more remote regions. Still, I saw more wildlife than I have anywhere else. True, some of that was sighted on the asphalt tracks of Interstate 95 and the sandy sofas along the surf, but my favorites were found in the marshes, swamps, and sloughs.

After I found this overturned gopher tortoise and righted it, the endangered reptile returned to its burrow, cohabited by many Florida fauna.

Early morning and late afternoon are the best times to glimpse raccoons foraging in the rich muck for clams and mussels. Land crabs crawl through the wiregrass, and the armor of the armadillo can more often be heard than seen clacking against the stiff fronds of saw palmetto as it makes its way to another pawful of grubs. Certain sections of Florida have become the last refuge for the gopher tortoises, whose burrows (both abandoned and occupied) supply an important haven for many forest animals. A mural at the Munson Hills trailhead in Tallahassee portrays this important link in a healthy longleaf-wiregrass ecosystem. One thing's for sure: after seeing what may be hiding in a gopher tortoise hole, you won't stick your hand down there, no matter how many double-dog-dare-you's your buddies may taunt you with.

Topside views of Florida's animals will keep you busy enough. Many people are uncomfortable with the possibility of riding over a six-foot-long reptile with rattles. Although this could happen, the diamondback rattlesnake is in decline, and I saw nary a one in all the miles I spent on the trail. In fact, I saw only three snakes total—that is, if you exclude the rides out into the Everglades, where I saw (and heard) one every mile or so. Reptiles prefer the cooler Florida weather and stay in the shade during the heat of midday, so my late-morning and midday rides in summer made it unlikely that I would have much contact with our scaled cousins.

Gators are another story. Besides the farms and shows where you can get an eyeful of the beasts, the once threatened alligator has made a comeback in Florida. Seeing one is probable, and you need to know some facts before you have any sort of encounter with them. First of all, they're fast. My son told me he was confident he could outrun one should the need present itself . . . until I told him gators have been clocked at 30 mph. Thankfully, they're shy and will run away if they can. The five-footer floating on the surface of Wekiwa Springs disappeared considerably faster than its land speed after I surprised it. If you should happen upon a small gator, don't stop and admire its cute shape. Baby gators stay around their momma for several years, and she is not the least bit shy about thrashing an intruder she perceives as a threat to her sons and daughters.

Insects—amazing in their myriad forms—can be, for the most part, enjoyed, after you take a few precautions. Butterflies bob up and down in the humid swamp air, dancing in colors so striking you'll be hard-pressed to stay focused on riding a straight line on the trail. Skeeterhawks, or dragonflies as they're sometimes called, probably exist nowhere in greater concentration than in some parts of Florida. Spiders string webs high in boughs of live oaks, where they help prevent the weight of the six-legged population from sinking Florida back from whence it came.

The list of insects found in Florida is long, and chances are you'll see a new species every day if you look. But some of the peskier representatives may keep you too preoccupied to notice. Mosquitoes head my list of irritating bugs. Although I seldom suffer a subsequent itch, the bite of the salt marsh mosquito can take away the fun of a rest stop. Repellent's effectiveness drops in the humid conditions where you'll be meeting up with these gals (the males don't bite but boy, do they breed!). Since I spent much of my time in Florida camping, I got plenty of practice dealing with the blood suckers. Here's my strategy for the trail: keep riding. Mosquitoes do not keep up with even a casual speed. In camp, however, I turned in as soon after sundown as I could, and I stayed inside until the sun had been up for an hour or so.

Deer- and horseflies are another story. The tinier "yellow flies," as they are sometimes called, are seldom more than a nuisance. But they can be considerably more painful than a mosquito. I discovered they liked to swarm around my helmet as I was riding and draft in the eddy behind my ears. There it seems they have some archetypal timing mechanism allowing them to achieve a simultaneous penetration of dermis. Most get squashed, but it is obvious from the numbers that enough survive encounters with warm-blooded animals to perpetuate the species ad infinitum. Horseflies grow nearly big enough in Florida to saddle up. One such black monstrosity—the size of a large man's thumb—landed on the hot hood of my car and began probing for a weak spot. If it had found one, it could've taken a quart of oil with one good bite.

But most things that fly in Florida are nothing but joys. Songbirds twitter all day long, but are especially active in the morning. I was surprised to hear the friendly whistle of the rufous-sided towhee, a common resident in the north Georgia woods by my home, wherever I went in Florida. But most birds I heard and saw are uncommon in the mixed hardwood forests of Appalachia. Egrets, herons, gallinules, pelicans, moorhens, eagles, osprey, black vultures, cranes, wood storks, spoonbills, and hundreds of others come to Florida, which makes the state a mecca for birdwatching—a multimillion-dollar industry. And don't forget the snowbirds, a term locals use to describe the influx of people who come south for the winter.

Some of the plants and trees are familiar to those who live in other southeastern states. Oaks, maples, pines, and gums all can be found in the upland forests of Florida. But the palm tree (more specifically, the sabal palm) is what best defines the Sunshine State's landscape. Its graceful fronds spread a dappled shade over what is invariably a thicket of saw palmetto, named for its tendency to cut unprotected flesh. Vines and air plants grow among the trees, creating a jungle setting where you would hardly blink an eye should you see Tarzan making his way through the high canopy.

Grasses and shrubs give way to each other in a succession of prairie to forest. The tall sawgrass of the Everglades and other aquatic plants provide both food and hiding places for birds, mammals, and amphibians. It is a curious feature in this land of little elevation that as many as seven different ecosystems can be viewed in areas where the ridges begin a hundred feet above sea level (or more) and then gently slope to the sea.

At first thought, Florida's land suggests a featureless plain of marsh and pine forest. But it only takes a few rides in places like the Ocala National Forest, Manatee Springs State Park, or Oleta River State Park to show how mistaken this view is. Florida is a land of many terrains, supporting some of the world's most fascinating plants and animals. It won't take you long to figure out what fun it is to see it all from your bike.

WEATHER

Florida's nickname—the Sunshine State—is well chosen because summer here is nine months long. This is one reason bicycling is such a popular recreation. Many racers train in Florida when the rest of the country is iced over and chattering. Those who can afford to live here in winter, basking in tropical rays and yanking mangoes and guavas, enjoy bushels of all types of citrus grown in the frost-free climes. To the snowbirds, it appears that Florida has only one season, which is hot. But to the millions of people living in Florida year-round, this sandy peninsula sticking into the sea has meteorological rhythms as unique as its landscape.

The vast Florida sky allows constant observation of distant, developing weather.

The less complicated season, to be sure, is winter. From Orlando south, each day from late November to early May nearly repeats itself in a dry and warm pattern. Blue skies become streaked with high white clouds, and temperatures seldom drop below 60 degrees. But they can drop. My earliest experience with a Florida winter came when my family took a Christmas camping trip around the state. Our memories of that time are shaped by the cold front that made its way to Naples, causing us to keep our bathing suits and flip-flops packed up with the sunscreen. It can happen.

By luck of the draw, my lot as bike guide author was to explore this winter paradise . . . in the summer. I shelved all my arguments for delaying the research for cooler months and checked the batteries for my handheld fan. This was especially tough since the summers in north Georgia where I live are relatively cool. But I was going to Florida and getting to ride my bike. How bad could it be?

My first trip south began in mid-May while the tulips in our garden were still blooming. Florida, on the other hand, was harvesting its first crop of heat

. . . and stacking it tall. Thunderstorms crackled in the afternoon, cooling things off to the lower 80s. Mornings broke wet and heavy with dew, causing me to remember Florida's most often quoted observation about summertime weather: "It's not the heat [that's so bad], but the humidity." I resisted the truth in this statement for as long as I could, but by September—Florida's hottest month—I had been given all the evidence I could stand. It *is* the humidity.

The moisture rolling in from the Gulf of Mexico and the Atlantic Ocean collides in Florida's rainy months—May through September—dumping in the neighborhood of fifty inches in five months, which made me wonder if I should mount pontoons on my bike. But with all the sand on the single-track I was riding, the rain turned out to be a blessing in disguise. In fact, toward the end of the trip, I began anticipating those cooling afternoon showers, packing a bottle of soap with me and lathering up. I got to where I could time the length of the showers pretty well, and I had to rinse the soap out of my eyes with a water bottle only once.

But it was those radical lightning strikes that kept me on my toes. I observed a particularly nasty-looking thunderstorm forming over the Everglades one afternoon at about 4 p.m. Making my way from Fort Myers to West Palm Beach on a tight schedule, I drove straight into a black mountain of water, wind, and electricity. As the roiling insides of the thunderhead swallowed the sun, I noticed staccato strikes dancing cloud-to-cloud so close together that it looked like a laser show.

But compared to the rain that battered me and my small car, the lightning bolts were birthday candles. The sky and side of the road disappeared into a gray, gauzy underbelly of water. I understood after that day how rainfall serves as the sole water source for the countless lakes, sloughs, strands, and branches whose presence makes an argument for changing Florida's name to "the Water State."

Although Florida seldom has to worry about extended cool weather, it does have a season that focuses the entire state's attention on the sometimes deadly combination of sea and air: hurricanes. These monster storms have ripped across this land ever since it rose out of the sea and are usually confined to late August, September, and October. But wouldn't you know it? As my wife, son, and I were making our way south in July (partly a precaution for avoiding one of these storms), we stopped at a Burger Doodle and saw the morning paper's headline—HURRICANE HAMMERS CARIBBEAN! HEADED TOWARD U.S.

As it turned out, Hurricane Bertha stayed offshore in the Floridian latitudes, electing to make landfall in North Carolina. Although we could see the big swells rolling onshore, the weather remained dry and unremarkable on Florida's east coast. But Florida is not always this lucky. The last big hurricane to hit south Florida was Andrew in late August 1992. And the Panhandle region had a rough year for hurricanes in 1995. By late October, the hurricanes usually quit forming, although squirrely Hurricane Gilbert occurred in November 1994.

If you have the choice, load your bikes and ride Florida's off-road trails in the fall and winter. But if you're like me and can't be choosy, don't postpone a trip because of the heat. Pack along extra water and sunscreen, pick some trails that are noted for their shady single-track, and plan to ride near the bookends of day—dawn and dusk. And if you get caught out on the trail in the teeth of a Florida summer day when the heat index is breaking 110 degrees, choose a smaller gear and drink plenty of water. Enjoy—you'll probably have the whole trail to yourself.

THE LAND

A long time ago, Florida rose from the shallows between what are now the Gulf of Mexico and the Atlantic Ocean. The separation between dry land and the surrounding sea has never been much. Even now, the greatest distance between one coast and the other barely exceeds 150 miles; its highest elevation is slightly more than the length of a football field. America's largest collection of freshwater lies in between. Rivers, lakes, and springs make up the most familiar of wet spots, but creeks, branches, sloughs, strands, marshes, and swamps swell the number to make Florida appear to be—at times—more water than land. In fact, over 4,300 square miles of inland

Cabbage palm fronds erupt from a large gatorback, which can eat up a front tire.

waters can be found in Florida. You'll get used to riding when it's wet, and you'll quickly learn when it's too wet to ride.

The other consequence of the sea—sand—challenges the off-road biker in Florida's dry season, becoming loose and giving little grip. Florida's "grades," as they are called, can come awfully close to giving a mountain-type workout. Higher speeds are required to keep moving at all, demanding leg strength, subtle balance, and a sure grip on the handlebars. Only a strong rider can pedal at all when the sandy ruts get loose to a depth of more than a couple of inches.

Although it's possible to acquire a comparable workout on a climb, no places exist in Florida to glide down a long, steep drop. Gone are the sustained, euphoria-creating descents that whip your jowls back and forth. There are, however, plenty of short and steep sections offering highly technical workouts. Mostly the remnants of former limestone and phosphate mining, these pits should only be ridden by those wanting to execute "combat moves."

It's easy to think of Florida as a place where trails could only be flat and straight—and there are plenty of those. But bikers coming here will soon discover the high degree of technical skill required to ride some off-road mileage. Gatorbacks (the exposed root system of a cabbage palm or saw palmetto—several inches high and just as wide) lie across the trail in what can be a frustratingly difficult obstacle course, at least without front suspension. Tight turns and narrow widths are signatures of the modern single-track being built by Florida's bike clubs and associations.

When I stopped by bike shops and talked to local riders about the diversity of Florida's trails, I said, "People are not going to believe that all this is in Florida!" They all smiled and said, "We know."

I think it's time you find out what they're smiling about.

Steve Jones

Advanced

4 Chickasabogue Park	58 Markham Park
8 Timberlake Trail	60 Oleta River State Park
15 Redbug Trail	64 Croom Trails, Withlacoochee
17 Fern Trail	State Forest
18 Magnolia Trail	80 North Port
29 Hanna Park	81 Boyett Park
33 Hardrock Ocala MTB Park	82 Gran Canyon
34 Bellview-Santos Trailhead	

Adventure Trails

7 Eastern Lake Trail	68 Green Swamp Trails
9 Dutch Tiemann Trail	75 Fakahatchee Strand Preserve
16 Phipps Park	76 Bear Island
27 Holton Creek	79 Long Pine Key Trail
43 Tosohatchee State Reserve	

Beginners

2 Fort Pickens Trail	30 Cary State Forest
10 Chattahoochee State Park, Alabama	31 Guana River State Park
11 St. Marks Trail	34 Bellview-Santos Trailhead
12 Wakulla Springs State Park	39 Gainesville-Hawthorne State Trail
13 Munson Hills	44 Wekiwa Springs State Park
14 Paper Trail	50 Bull Creek Wildlife Management Area
19 Gar Pond	54 DuPuis Reserve
22 Little Shoals, Deep Creek Conservation Area	55 Lake Trail, Palm Beach (Trail of Conspicuous Consumption)
23 Stephen Foster State Folk Culture Center	59 Hugh Birch State Park
24 The Spirit of the Suwannee	61 Shark Valley
25 Camp Branch	69 Morris Bridge Park
26 Allen Mill Pond	71 Myakka River State Park
28 Twin Rivers Wildlife Management Area	72 Sanibel Island
	77 Gold Head Branch State Park

Double-track

3 Big Lagoon Cookie Trail	20 White Springs and Bridge-to-Bridge Trails
6 Blackwater River State Forest	22 Little Shoals, Deep Creek Conservation Area
7 Eastern Lake Trail	
9 Dutch Tiemann Trail	23 Stephen Foster State Folk Culture Center
10 Chattahoochee State Park, Alabama	24 The Spirit of the Suwannee
12 Wakulla Springs State Park	25 Camp Branch
16 Phipps Park	

Family

Long

Loops

Out-and-Backs

Paved Paths

Scenic

32 Spruce Creek Preserve
34 Bellview-Santos Trailhead
36 Alexander Springs Loop
37 Clearwater Lake Loop
38 O'Leno State Park
40 Chacala Trail, Paynes Prairie State Preserve
43 Tosohatchee State Reserve
44 Wekiwa Springs State Park
46 Rock Springs Run State Reserve
49 Little-Big Econ State Forest
50 Bull Creek Wildlife Management Area

51 Environmental Center at Soldier Creek
53 Jonathan Dickinson State Park
60 Oleta River State Park
61 Shark Valley
64 Croom Trails, Withlacoochee State Forest
68 Green Swamp Trails
72 Sanibel Island
73 Ding Darling Trail
74 Loop Road
75 Fakahatchee Strand Preserve

Short

1 University of West Florida
2 Fort Pickens Trail
3 Big Lagoon Cookie Trail
10 Chattahoochee State Park, Alabama
14 Paper Trail
15 Redbug Trail
17 Fern Trail
22 Little Shoals, Deep Creek Conservation Area

25 Camp Branch
26 Allen Mill Pond
41 Cone's Dike
49 Little-Big Econ State Forest
56 Quiet Waters Park
59 Hugh Birch State Park
63 Bridal Trails, Key West
73 Ding Darling Trail

Single-track

4 Chickasabogue Park
5 Conecuh Trail
8 Timberlake Trail
9 Dutch Tiemann Trail
13 Munson Hills
14 Paper Trail
15 Redbug Trail
17 Fern Trail
18 Magnolia Trail
29 Hanna Park
32 Spruce Creek Preserve
33 Hardrock Ocala MTB Park
34 Bellview-Santos Trailhead
36 Alexander Springs Loop

37 Clearwater Lake Loop
46 Rock Springs Run State Reserve
51 Environmental Center at Soldier Creek
56 Quiet Waters Park
57 Southern Trail
58 Markham Park
60 Oleta River State Park
64 Croom Trails, Withlacoochee State Forest
79 Long Pine Key Trail
80 North Port
81 Boyett Park
82 Gran Canyon

Technical

1 University of West Florida
4 Chickasabogue Park
15 Redbug Trail

17 Fern Trail
18 Magnolia Trail
29 Hanna Park

Traffic

INTRODUCTION

TRAIL DESCRIPTION OUTLINE

Each trail in this book begins with key information that includes length, configuration, aerobic and technical difficulty, trail conditions, scenery, and special comments. Additional description is contained in 11 individual categories. The following will help you to understand all of the information provided.

Trail name: In some instances, trails are named by the author. In others, trail names are as designated on United States Geological Survey (USGS) or Forest Service or other maps, and/or by local custom.

At a Glance Information

Length/configuration: The overall length of a trail is described in miles, unless stated otherwise. The configuration is a description of the shape of each trail—whether the trail is a loop, out-and-back (that is, along the same route), figure eight, trapezoid, isosceles triangle, decahedron . . . (just kidding), or if it connects with another trail described in the book. See the Glossary for definitions of *point-to-point* and *combination*.

Aerobic difficulty: This provides a description of the degree of physical exertion required to complete the ride.

Technical difficulty: This provides a description of the technical skill required to pedal a ride. Trails are often described here in terms of being paved, unpaved, sandy, hard-packed, washboarded, two- or four-wheel-drive, single-track or double-track. All terms that might be unfamiliar to the first-time mountain biker are defined in the Glossary.

Note: For both the aerobic and technical difficulty categories, authors were asked to keep in mind the fact that all riders are not equal, and thus to gauge the trail in terms of how the middle-of-the-road rider—someone between the newcomer and Ned Overend—could handle the route. Comments about the trail's length, condition, and elevation change will also assist you in determining the difficulty of any trail relative to your own abilities.

Scenery: Here you will find a general description of the natural surroundings during the seasons most riders pedal the trail and a suggestion of what is to be found at special times (like great fall foliage or cactus in bloom).

Special comments: Unique elements of the ride are mentioned.

Category Information

General location: This category describes where the trail is located in reference to a nearby town or other landmark.

Elevation change: Unless stated otherwise, the figure provided is the total change in elevation as measured from high point to low point. Total gain, that is, the cumulative total feet in which the trail ascends, is difficult to measure accurately, but suffice it to say that it generally exceeds the simple difference between high and low points. In an effort to give you a sense of how much climbing is involved in a particular ride, brief but general descriptive phrases are used in conjunction with elevation change.

Season: This is the best time of year to pedal the route, taking into account trail conditions (for example, when it will not be muddy), riding comfort (when the weather is too hot, cold, or wet), and local hunting seasons.

Note: Because the opening and closing dates of deer, elk, moose, and antelope seasons often change from year to year, riders should check with the local Fish and Wildlife Department or call a sporting goods store (or any place that sells hunting licenses) in a nearby town before heading out. Wear bright clothes in the fall, and don't wear suede jackets while in the saddle. Hunter's-orange tape on the helmet is also a good idea.

Services: This category is of primary importance in guides for paved-road tourers and is far less crucial to most mountain bike trail descriptions because there are usually no services whatsoever to be found. Authors have noted when water is available on desert or long mountain routes and have listed the availability of food, lodging, campgrounds, and bike shops. If all these services are present, you will find only the words, "All services available in . . ."

Hazards: Special hazards like hunting season, rattlesnakes, alligators, bears, ticks, poison oak, earthquake, lightning, other trail users, and vehicular traffic are noted here. Other hazards which are considered a regular part of a ride, such as steep cliffs, boulder stair-steps, or scree on steep downhill sections are discussed in the "Notes on the trail" section.

Rescue index: Determining how far one is from help on a particular trail can be difficult due to the backcountry nature of most mountain bike rides. Authors therefore state the proximity of homes or Forest Service outposts, nearby roads where one might hitch a ride, or the likelihood of other bikers being encountered on the trail. Phone numbers of local sheriff departments or hospitals have not been provided because phones are almost never available. If you are able to reach a phone, the local operator will connect you with emergency services.

Land status: This category provides information regarding whether the trail crosses land operated by the Forest Service, the Bureau of Land Management, or a city, state, or national park; whether it crosses private land whose owner (at the time the author did the research) has allowed mountain bikers right of passage; and so on. A note regarding fees for land usage: There is no standard by which user fees are charged. Some land agencies charge a fee to park within designated areas, others charge a fee regardless of where you park your car. Some areas are free year-round, others only during the off-season or during the week. Some parks charge a day-use fee, regardless of whether you park a car or not. Most national forests do not charge a day-use fee, nor do most BLM districts. State parks almost always charge a day-use fee at the very least.

Note: Authors have been extremely careful to offer only those routes that are open to bikers and are legal to ride. However, because land ownership changes over time, and because the land-use controversy created by mountain bikes still has not completely subsided, it is the duty of each cyclist to look for and heed signs warning against trail use. Don't expect this book to get you off the hook when you're facing some small-town judge for pedaling past a "Biking Prohibited" sign erected the day before you arrived. Look for these signs, read them, and heed the advice. And remember, there's always another trail.

Maps: The maps in this book have been produced with great care and, in conjunction with the trail-following suggestions, will help you stay on course. But as every experienced mountain biker knows, things can get tricky in the backcountry. It is therefore strongly suggested that you avail yourself of the detailed information found in the USGS (United States Geological Survey) 7.5 minute series topographic maps. In some cases, authors have found that specific Forest Service or other maps may be more useful than the USGS quads, and they tell how to obtain them.

Finding the trail: Detailed information on how to reach the trailhead and where to park your car is provided here.

Sources of additional information: Here you will find the address and/or phone number of a bike shop, governmental agency, or other source from which trail information can be obtained.

Notes on the trail: This is where you are guided carefully through any portions of the trail that are particularly difficult to follow. The author also may add information about the route that does not fit easily in the other categories. This category will not be present for those rides where the route is easy to follow.

ABBREVIATIONS

The following road-designation abbreviations are used in the *America by Mountain Bike!* series:

CR	County Road	I-	Interstate
FR	Farm Route	IR	Indian Route
FS	Forest Service road	US	United States highway

State highways are designated with the appropriate two-letter state abbreviation, followed by the road number. Example: FL 6 = Florida State Highway 6.

RIDE CONFIGURATIONS

Combination: This type of route may combine two or more configurations. For example, a point-to-point route may integrate a scenic loop or an out-and-back spur midway through the ride. Likewise, an out-and-back may have a loop at its farthest point (this configuration looks like a cherry with a stem attached; the stem is the out-and-back, the fruit is the terminus loop). Or a loop route may have multiple out-and-back spurs and/or loops to the side. Mileage for a combination route is for the total distance to complete the ride.

Loop: This route configuration is characterized by riding from the designated trailhead to a distant point, then returning to the trailhead via a different route (or simply continuing on the same in a circle route) without doubling back. You always move forward across new terrain but return to the starting point when finished. Mileage is for the entire loop from the trailhead back to trailhead.

Out-and-back: This is a ride where you will return on the same trail you pedaled out. While this might sound far more boring than a loop route, many trails look very different when pedaled in the opposite direction.

Point-to-point: A vehicle shuttle (or similar assistance) is required for this type of route, which is ridden from the designated trailhead to a distant location, or endpoint, where the route ends. Total mileage is for the one-way trip from the trailhead to endpoint.

Spur: This category shows a road or trail that intersects the main trail you're following.

Ride Configurations contributed by Gregg Bromka

TOPOGRAPHIC MAPS

The maps in this book, when used in conjunction with the route directions present in each chapter, will in most instances be sufficient to get you to the trail and keep you on it. However, you will find superior detail and valuable information in the USGS 7.5 minute series topographic maps. Recognizing how indispensable these are to bikers and hikers alike, many bike shops and sporting goods stores now carry topos of the local area.

If you're brand new to mountain biking you might be wondering, "What's a topographic map?" In short, these differ from standard "flat" maps in that they indicate not only linear distance but elevation as well. One glance at a topo will show you the difference, for contour lines are spread across the map like dozens of intricate spider webs. Each contour line represents a particular elevation, and at the base of each topo a particular contour interval designation is given. Yes, it sounds confusing if you're new to the lingo, but it truly is a simple and wonderfully helpful system. Keep reading.

Let's assume that the 7.5 minute series topo before us says "Contour Interval 40 feet," that the short trail we'll be pedaling is two inches in length on the map, and that it crosses five contour lines from its beginning to end. What do we know? Well, because the linear scale of this series is 2,000 feet to the inch (roughly 2 ¾ inches representing 1 mile), we know our trail is approximately ⁴⁄₅ of a mile long (2 inches

× 2,000 feet). But we also know we'll be climbing or descending 200 vertical feet (5 contour lines × 40 feet each) over that distance. And the elevation designations written on occasional contour lines will tell us if we're heading up or down.

The authors of this series warn their readers of upcoming terrain, but only a detailed topo gives you the information you need to pinpoint your position on a map, steer yourself toward optional trails and roads nearby, and see at a glance if you'll be pedaling hard to take them. It's a lot of information for a very low cost. In fact, the only drawback with topos is their size—several feet square. I've tried rolling them into tubes, folding them carefully, even cutting them into blocks and photocopying the pieces. Any of these systems is a pain, but no matter how you pack the maps, you'll be happy they're along. And you'll be even happier if you pack a compass as well.

In addition to local bike shops and sporting goods stores, you'll find topos at major universities and some public libraries, where you might try photocopying the ones you need to avoid the cost of buying them. But if you want your own and can't find them locally, contact:

USGS Map Sales
Box 25286
Denver, CO 80225
(888) ASK-USGS (275-8747)
http://mapping.usgs.gov/esic/to_order.html/

VISA and MasterCard are accepted. Ask for an index while you're at it, plus a price list and a copy of the booklet *Topographic Maps*. In minutes you'll be reading them like a pro.

A second excellent series of maps available to mountain bikers is put out by the United States Forest Service. If your trail runs through an area designated as a national forest, look in the phone book (white pages) under the United States Government listings, find the Department of Agriculture heading, and run your finger down that section until you find the Forest Service. Give them a call, and they'll provide the address of the regional Forest Service office, from which you can obtain the appropriate map.

TRAIL ETIQUETTE

Pick up almost any mountain bike magazine these days and you'll find articles and letters to the editor about trail conflict. For example, you'll find hikers' tales of being blindsided by speeding mountain bikers, complaints from mountain bikers about being blamed for trail damage that was really caused by horse or cattle traffic, and cries from bikers about those "kamikaze" riders who through their antics threaten to close even more trails to all of us.

The authors of this series have been very careful to guide you to only those trails that are open to mountain biking (or at least were open at the time of their research), and without exception have warned of the damage done to our sport through injudicious riding. We can all benefit from glancing over the following International Mountain Bicycling Association (IMBA) Rules of the Trail before saddling up.

1. *Ride on open trails only.* Respect trail and road closures (ask if not sure), avoid possible trespass on private land, obtain permits and authorization as may be required. Federal and state wilderness areas are closed to cycling.

2. *Leave no trace.* Be sensitive to the dirt beneath you. Even on open trails, you should not ride under conditions where you will leave evidence of your passing, such as on certain soils shortly after rain. Observe the different types of soils and trail construction; practice low-impact cycling. This also means staying on the trail and not creating any new ones. Be sure to pack out at least as much as you pack in.

3. *Control your bicycle!* Inattention for even a second can cause disaster. Excessive speed can maim and threaten people; there is no excuse for it!

4. *Always yield the trail.* Make known your approach well in advance. A friendly greeting (or a bell) is considerate and works well; startling someone may cause loss of trail access. Show your respect when passing others by slowing to a walk or even stopping. Anticipate that other trail users may be around corners or in blind spots.

5. *Never spook animals.* All animals are startled by an unannounced approach, a sudden movement, or a loud noise. This can be dangerous for you, for others, and for the animals. Give animals extra room and time to adjust to you. In passing, use special care and follow the directions of horseback riders (ask if uncertain). Running cattle and disturbing wild animals is a serious offense. Leave gates as you found them or as marked.

6. *Plan ahead.* Know your equipment, your ability, and the area in which you are riding—and prepare accordingly. Be self-sufficient at all times. Wear a helmet, keep your machine in good condition, and carry necessary supplies for changes in weather or other conditions. A well-executed trip is a satisfaction to you and not a burden or offense to others.

For more information, contact IMBA, P.O. Box 7578, Boulder, CO 80306, (303) 545-9011.

Additionally, the following Code of Ethics by the National Off-Road Biking Association (NORBA) is worthy of your attention.

1. I will yield the right of way to other non-motorized recreationists. I realize that people judge all cyclists by my actions.

2. I will slow down and use caution when approaching or overtaking another and will make my presence known well in advance.

3. I will maintain control of my speed at all times and will approach turns in anticipation of someone around the bend.

4. I will stay on designated trails to avoid trampling native vegetation and minimize potential erosion to trails by not using muddy trails or shortcutting switchbacks.

5. I will not disturb wildlife or livestock.

6. I will not litter. I will pack out what I pack in, and pack out more than my share if possible.

7. I will respect public and private property, including trail use and no trespassing signs; I will leave gates as I found them.

8. I will always be self-sufficient and my destination and travel speed will be determined by my ability, my equipment, the terrain, and present and potential weather conditions.

9. I will not travel solo when bike-packing in remote areas.

10. I will leave word of my destination and when I plan to return.

11. I will practice minimum impact bicycling by "taking only pictures and memories and leaving only waffle prints."

12. I will always wear a helmet when I ride.

Worthy of mention are the following suggestions based on a list by Utah's Wasatch-Cache National Forest and the *Tread Lightly!* program advocated by the U.S. Forest Service and Bureau of Land Management.

1. *Study a forest map before you ride.* Currently, bicycles are permitted on roads and developed trails which are designated bikes permitted. If your route crosses private land, it is your responsibility to obtain right-of-way permission from the landowner.

2. *Stay out of designated wilderness areas.* By law, all vehicles, including mountain bikes are not allowed.

3. *Stay off of roads and trails "put to bed."* These may be resource roads no longer used for logging or mining, or they may be steep trails being replaced by easier ones. So that the path returns to its natural state, they're usually blocked or signed closed to protect new vegetation.

4. *Keep groups small.* Riding in large groups degrades the outdoor experience for others, can disturb wildlife, and usually leads to greater resource damage.

5. *Avoid riding on wet trails.* Bicycle tires leave ruts in wet trails. These ruts concentrate runoff and accelerate erosion. Postponing a ride when the trails are wet will preserve the trails for future use.

6. *Stay on roads and trails.* Riding cross-country destroys vegetation and damages the soil. Resist the urge to pioneer a new road or trail, or to cut across a switchback. Avoid riding through meadows, on steep hillsides, or along stream banks and lakeshores because the terrain is easily scarred by churning wheels.

7. *Always yield to others.* Trails are shared by hikers, horses, and bicycles. Move off the trail to allow horses to pass and stop to allow hikers adequate room to share the trail. Simply yelling "Bicycle!" is not acceptable.

8. *Control your speed.* Excessive speed endangers yourself and other forest users.

9. *Avoid wheel lock-up and spin-out.* Steep terrain is especially vulnerable to trail wear. Locking brakes on steep descents or when stopping needlessly damages trails. If a slope is steep enough to require locking wheels and skidding, dismount and walk your bicycle. Likewise, if an ascent is so steep that your rear wheel slips and spins, dismount and walk your bicycle.

10. *Protect waterbars and switchbacks.* Waterbars, the rock and log drains built to direct water off trails, protect trails from erosion. When you encounter a waterbar, ride directly over the top or dismount and walk your bicycle. Riding around the ends of waterbars destroys their effectiveness and speeds erosion. Skidding around switchback corners shortens trail life. Slow down for switchback corners and keep your wheels rolling.

11. *If you abuse it, you lose it.* Mountain bikers are relative newcomers to the forest and must prove themselves responsible trail users. By following the guidelines above, and by participating in trail maintenance service projects, bicyclists can help avoid closures that would prevent them from using trails.

12. *Know your bicycle handling limitations.*

You get the drift. So that everyone can continue riding our bikes through some of our country's most beautiful places, I urge you to follow the codes above and not be the "one bad apple" that spoils it for the rest of us.

HITTING THE TRAIL

Once again, because this is a "where-to," not a "how-to" guide, the following will be brief. If you're a veteran trail rider, these suggestions might serve to remind you of something you've forgotten to pack. If you're a newcomer, they might convince you to think twice before hitting the backcountry unprepared.

Water: I've heard the questions dozens of times. "How much is enough? One bottle? Two? Three?! But think of all that extra weight!" Well, one simple physiological fact should convince you to err on the side of excess when it comes to deciding how much water to pack: A human working hard in 90-degree temperature needs approximately ten quarts of fluids every day. Ten quarts. That's two and a half gallons—12 large water bottles or 16 small ones. And, with water weighing in at approximately 8 pounds per gallon, a one-day supply comes to a whopping 20 pounds.

In other words, pack along two or three bottles even for short rides. And make sure you can purify the water found along the trail on longer routes. When writing of those routes where this could be of critical importance, each author has provided information on where water can be found near the trail—if it can be found at all. But drink it untreated and you run the risk of disease. (See *giardia* in the Glossary.)

One sure way to kill the protozoans, bacteria, and viruses in water is to boil it. Right. That's just how you want to spend your time on a bike ride. Besides, who wants to carry a stove or denude the countryside stoking bonfires to boil water?

Luckily, there is a better way. Many riders pack along the inexpensive and only slightly distasteful tetraglycine hydroperiodide tablets (sold under the names Potable Aqua, Globaline, and Coughlan's, among others). Some invest in portable, lightweight purifiers that filter out the crud. Unfortunately, both iodine *and* filtering are now required to be absolutely sure you've killed all the nasties you can't see. Tablets or iodine drops by themselves will knock off the well-known *giardia*, once called "beaver fever" for its transmission to the water through the feces of infected beavers. One to four weeks after ingestion, giardia will have you bloated, vomiting, shivering with chills, and living in the bathroom. (Though you won't care while you're suffering, beavers are getting a bum rap, for other animals are carriers also.)

But now there's another parasite we must worry about—*cryptosporidium*. "Crypto" brings on symptoms very similar to *giardia*, but unlike that fellow proto-zoan it's equipped with a shell sufficiently strong to protect it against the chemical killers that stop giardia cold. This means we're either back to boiling or on to using a water filter to screen out both *giardia* and crypto, plus the iodine to knock off viruses. All of which sounds like a time-consuming pain, but really isn't. Some water filters come equipped with an iodine chamber to guarantee full protection. Or you can simply add a pill or drops to the water you've just filtered (if you aren't allergic to iodine, of course). The pleasures of backcountry biking—and the dis-pleasure of getting sick—make this relatively minor effort worth every one of the few minutes involved.

Tools: Ever since my first cross-country tour in 1965 I've been kidded about the number of tools I pack on the trail. And so I will exit entirely from this discussion by providing a list compiled by two mechanic (and mountain biker) friends of mine. After all, since they make their livings fixing bikes, and get their kicks by riding them, who could be a better source?

These two suggest the following as an absolute minimum:

tire levers	spare tube and patch kit
air pump	Allen wrenches (3, 4, 5, and 6 mm)
spoke wrench	six-inch crescent (adjustable-end) wrench
chain rivet tool	small flat-blade screwdriver

On the trail, their personal tool pouches contain these additional items:

channel locks (small)
air gauge
tire valve cap (the metal kind, with a valve-stem remover)
baling wire (ten or so inches, for temporary repairs)
duct tape (small roll for temporary repairs or tire boot)
boot material (small piece of old tire or a large tube patch)
spare chain link
rear derailleur pulley
spare nuts and bolts
paper towel and tube of waterless hand cleaner

First-Aid kit: My personal kit contains the following, sealed inside double Ziploc bags:

sunscreen
aspirin
butterfly-closure bandages
Band-Aids
snakebite kit

gauze (one roll)
gauze compress pads (a half-dozen 4" × 4")
ace bandages or Spenco joint wraps
Benadryl (an antihistamine, in case of allergic reactions)
water purification tablets/water filter (on long rides)
Moleskin/Spenco "Second Skin"
hydrogen peroxide, iodine, or Mercurochrome (some kind of antiseptic)
matches or pocket cigarette lighter
whistle (more effective in signaling rescuers than your voice)

Final considerations: The authors of this series have done a good job suggesting that specific items be packed for certain trails—rain gear in particular seasons, a hat and gloves for mountain passes, or shades for desert jaunts. Heed their warnings, and think ahead. Good luck.

Dennis Coello

CELL PHONES

Thinking of bringing the Flip-Fone along on your next off-road ride? Before you do, ask yourself the following questions:

- Do I know where I'm going? Do I have an adequate map? Can I use a compass effectively? Do I know the shortest way to civilization if I need to bail out early and find some help?

- If I'm on the trail for longer than planned, am I ready for it? Do I have adequate water? Have I packed something to eat? Will I be warm enough if I'm still out there after dark?

- Am I prepared for possible injuries? Do I have a first-aid kit? Do I know what to do in case of a cut, fracture, snakebite, or heat exhaustion?

- Is my tool kit adequate for likely mechanical problems? Can I fix a flat? Can I untangle a chain? Am I prepared to walk out if the bike is unridable?

If you answered "yes" to *every* question above, you may pack the phone, but consider a good whistle instead. It's lighter, cheaper, and nearly as effective.

If they start searching for you, but dusk is only two hours away, and you have no signaling device and your throat is too dry to shout, and meanwhile you can't get the bleeding stopped, you are out of luck. I mean *really* out of luck.

And when the battery goes dead, you're on your own again. Enough said.

Jeff Faust
Author of Mountain Bike! New Hampshire

THE FLORIDA PANHANDLE— WEST OF THE APALACHICOLA

In 1540, as part of his New World expedition, Hernando de Soto sailed along the Gulf of Mexico's coast and into Pensacola Harbor. Instead of finding an area where a civilization could easily be established, the Spanish and the rest of the world discovered a remote coastal region whose "vast howling wilderness" kept it thinly settled until the eighteenth century.

The Emerald Coast now, however, has had its beachfront thoroughly developed with countless vacation attractions. The desire to own a piece of this magical strand caused land prices to rise so quickly in the 1950s that the stretch between Pensacola and Panama City was nicknamed "Miracle Strip." Forty years later, it hasn't slowed down a bit. Hotels, restaurants, and condos are still popping up faster than ghost crabs out of their burrows at low tide.

Occasionally, however, things have to be rebuilt. Storm surges from giant hurricanes wash away buildings and roads. Sustained winds of 115 mph move onto land, spawning tornadoes whose winds reach over 200 mph. House code improvements have been reflected in fewer buildings damaged by wind, but the large number of fallen trees sometimes left on local biking trails can mean weeks of work to reopen them.

Although Pensacola, Fort Walton Beach, and Panama City represent a hundred miles of some of Florida's most extensive seaside development, north of Pensacola—in Blackwater River State Forest—some of the state's most undisturbed land has been opened to off-road cycling. Another state forest—Pine Log, located north of Panama City—allows biking on its primitive double-track and even remoter single-track. It is in these places that the true character of Florida remains.

Bikers coming to Fort Walton Beach can get a taste of an urban single-track that seems far removed from anything you would imagine in Florida.

The trail at Timberlake lies on property owned by the U.S. government and is maintained as a wildlife management area on Eglin Air Force Base, the western hemisphere's largest military compound.

The Gulf of Mexico has 150 miles of protected barrier coast managed as the Gulf Islands National Seashore; approximately a third of that lies in Florida, from Destin in the east to Perdido Key in the west. Its off-road trails are open to foot travel only due to the sensitive nature of the sugar sand dunes, but bikers can ride the paved road servicing Santa Rosa Island and be only a few whitecaps away from the surf.

Although the slot leading to Pensacola Bay has changed dramatically in the more than 400 years since de Soto arrived with his men, places north of the coast still keep alive the memory of what the entire panhandle of Florida must have looked like back then. It is a land living between ticks of the geologic clock, where early travelers explored and where the modern one can rediscover . . . by bike, of course.

Sources of additional information:

Cycle Sports
3423 North 12th Avenue
Pensacola, Florida 32503
(850) 434-8100

Bob's Schwinn
431 Bryn Athyn Boulevard
Mary Esther, Florida 32569
(850) 243-5856 or 244-0319
fax (850) 244-1651

RIDE 1 · University of West Florida

AT A GLANCE

Length/configuration: 5-mile series of loops: 3 horseshoe trails at the end of an out-and-back

Aerobic difficulty: Moderate

Technical difficulty: Challenging; when trail is firm after a rain, this single-track allows for high speeds and provides challenging narrow chutes for the best urban rider

Scenery: Scrub oak forest, wild woody area

Special comments: Easy access and beautiful wilderness make this ride appealing anytime of the year; nearby Thompson Bayou makes for frequent and varied wildlife sightings

FL

Northwest of Pensacola in the wooded area surrounding the University of West Florida, fairly technical single-track makes up a five-mile series of loops at the end of a short out-and-back. Some places open up enough so that

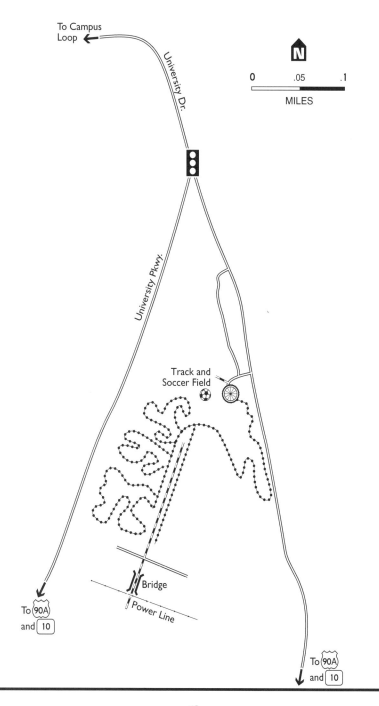

To Campus Loop

University Dr.

University Pkwy.

N

0   .05   .1

MILES

Track and Soccer Field

Bridge

Power Line

To 90A and 10

To 90A and 10

you can relax and enjoy the wilderness, but not many. Most of your attention will be focused on clearing the frequent, narrow slots between trees.

The University of West Florida owns the land managed by the state of Florida as a wilderness area. Its success can be seen in the frequent and varied sightings of wildlife on the protected shoreline along Thompson Bayou. Two other creeks make their way into the swamp north of campus where the Escambia River twists its way into the bay. It is even said a three-legged alligator named Fender has claimed the campus wetlands as his territory—although the beast is seldom seen. Such is the stuff of legend and myth.

The trail at the University of West Florida (UWF) has already made the top ranks of Florida's off-road destinations. Enough acres to expand an already lengthy ride, combined with the energy and enthusiasm of local bikers who built and are maintaining the route, make it likely that the University of West Florida trail system will become the top trail in Florida's central time zone. Since the first edition of this guide, five more trail areas have been developed: three of them are adjacent to the power line and run between Pate Street and Greenbrier Boulevard.

General location: On the University of West Florida campus in Pensacola, Florida, 1 mile west of Escambia Bay and US 90.

Elevation change: For the most part, the single-track is either gaining or losing the 50 or so feet vertical change found along the creek banks and estuary.

Season: My experience on this trail came on one of the hottest mornings of the year. The yellow flies were aggressive, and I hopped over snakes stretched across the trail. Thirty yards of deep, soft sand had formed in the dry season, making pedaling even more difficult. When it cools off, the bugs abate, and the rain firms up the sandy spots, you've got one of the more challenging and scenic year-round urban rides anywhere.

Services: With Pensacola being a university town and the U.S. Navy's air base down the road, there should be no difficulty finding the service to fit your need. The student center has rest rooms, parking, and phones.

Hazards: Due to the extremely narrow chutes on this single-track and the popularity of the trail among UWF's student body, the biggest danger comes from hitting someone head-on at a high rate of speed. I usually reserve ringing my bell to warn hunters of my whereabouts, but regularly ringing your bell on this ride—especially if it's a busy weekend—would be a welcome courtesy and safety precaution.

Rescue index: Despite its wild interior, this trail sits in a heavily populated area, and a quick rescue could be effected easily. You'll notice the University of West Florida's safety campaign advising to partner up and "Just 2 It."

Land status: This is land owned by the University of West Florida and managed by the state of Florida as a wilderness area.

Maps: A map of the campus can be picked up at the information center on University Drive. It does not show the bike route, however. The map in this guide has been drawn based on firsthand information and interviews with local riders.

Finding the trail: Entering University Parkway, take a right at the light toward the sports complex. Take the second paved right into the parking lot for the track and soccer field. Locate the small, paved parking area closest to the track. A single-track leads into the woods on your left as you face the track.

Source of additional information:

> University of West Florida
> University Parkway
> Nature Trail Information
> Pensacola, Florida 32501
> (850) 474-2000

Notes on the trail: The first half mile twists and turns through a young scrub oak forest, rising and falling a couple of times before opening up along the fence on the other side of the track, which you can see from the trailhead. Begin looking for (and taking) the single-tracks off to the right. Each 1 represents 1 end of the 3 horseshoe loops into the woods, reconnecting to the main double-track trail along the fence and power line.

Another series of single-track can be easily ridden to by taking the double-track until it turns into an asphalt road in a quiet subdivision. As you approach the bridge, look off to the right. The power line right-of-way leads to single-track loops into the forests on both the right and left. Both the land status and trail direction are more difficult to determine in this area, although by keeping the power line as a reference, no major confusion over direction should occur; however, this land may be slated soon for development. Who knows? With some quick thinking, this section of single-track could become an extension of the already protected area on campus.

RIDE 2 · Fort Pickens Trail

AT A GLANCE

Length/configuration: 3 miles one way from Fort Pickens Visitor Center to the beach at Battery Langdon

Aerobic difficulty: Low; terrain is flat

Technical difficulty: Easy

Scenery: High and hilly sand dunes (not part of the trail), seaside vegetation, campsites, and picnic area

RIDE 2 · Fort Pickens Trail

Special comments: A section of the oyster shell–covered double-track winds through Blackbird Marsh, home to almost 300 different bird species; site of historic Civil War structures

America's early coastal defenses called for building numerous forts positioned on barrier islands. Florida's westernmost island, Santa Rosa Island—part of Gulf Islands National Seashore—has a nineteenth-century military base where today's visitors can mount a patrol by pedal. Approximately three miles one-way of double-track layered with oyster shell (six miles total out-and-back) begin by the Fort Pickens Visitor Center, go through the camping loops (200 sites) and Blackbird Marsh, and end at the beach at Battery Langdon.

Intended to repel invading sea forces by blowing ships out of the water, the forts' cannons were made obsolete (in some cases even before they were installed) after rifling increased the range of shipboard guns to five miles. The forts themselves have seen little military action, having served primarily as P.O.W. camps in the Civil War.

These structures have seen their share of meteorological warfare, usually in the form of hurricanes, even surviving the force of Hurricane Opal, which on October 10, 1995, produced wind speeds greater than 155 mph and a tidal surge 15 feet high. The storm destroyed roads and many buildings along the coast, but the stalwart Fort Pickens stayed tightly locked on its limestone shelf.

General location: West of Pensacola Beach, inside the Fort Pickens Area.

Elevation change: Some of the sand dunes are big enough to be tall hills, but since you can't ride on them, the rest of the elevation change is a couple of feet, max.

Season: The shell surface helps with traction, even when conditions are dry.

Services: Pensacola carries all goods and services several times over. The Fort Pickens Area has camping facilities, showers, and rest rooms.

Hazards: Hikers also share this popular path. Be alert to sudden, inexplicable actions by our fellow bipeds.

Rescue index: This is a popular destination with easy access . . . normally. Fort Pickens Road remained closed 7 months for repairs after Hurricane Opal struck shore. The overall effectiveness of the Hurricane Evacuation Plan was highly questionable during 1995's fall storm season. Thousands of motorists were stranded in slow-moving traffic jams as the hurricane hit. Should you be planning a trip here during tropical storm season, you should pay special attention to the weather predictions.

Land status: This is land managed by the National Parks Service, which requires either a $6 per car entrance fee, or a $3 per person entrance fee (good for 7 days).

Maps: A free map of Gulf Islands can be picked up at entrance stations and visitor centers throughout the park.

Finding the trail: Cross Pensacola Bay on US 98 and cross the toll bridge (FL 399) to Pensacola Beach. Follow signs to Fort Pickens and park by the fishing pier. The trail begins between the Gulf and the Fort Pickens Visitor Center.

Source of additional information:

Gulf Islands National Seashore
Superintendent
1801 Gulf Breeze Parkway
Gulf Breeze, Florida 32561
(850) 934-2600

Notes on the trail: The first section of the white, shell-covered trail—approximately 1 mile—connects the Visitor Center on the west end of Santa Rosa Island to the picnic area at Battery Worth. After riding through the large camping area (loops B, C, D, and E), the trail splits Blackbird Marsh, where over 280 different kinds of birds have been spotted. While I rode there, a flock of brown pelicans flew over me, flapping their wings in time like one great bird, stopping in time to glide above a sunburned sea. As I watched them disappear into the black line of coast, I felt the rhythm of flight in my legs.

RIDE 3 · Big Lagoon Cookie Trail

AT A GLANCE

Length/configuration: 5-mile loop

Aerobic difficulty: Low; flat terrain

Technical difficulty: Easy; soft sand is the biggest challenge

Scenery: Longleaf pines, yaupon shrubs, and palmettos; much of the ride is lagoonside so egrets and dolphins are often spotted

Special comments: Once the plan to cover this too-sandy double-track in wood chips and bark is complete, this ride will be fun for the whole family; enjoy the frequent benches and resting spots along the way

FL

After talking to Mary Fortney at Bicycle Doctor, I was prepared to find an off-road biking opportunity at Big Lagoon State Recreation Area (SRA). But I wasn't sure what it would be. The ranger at the entrance cleared things up when he told me I could ride the loop at the end of an out-and-back

RIDE 3 · Big Lagoon Cookie Trail

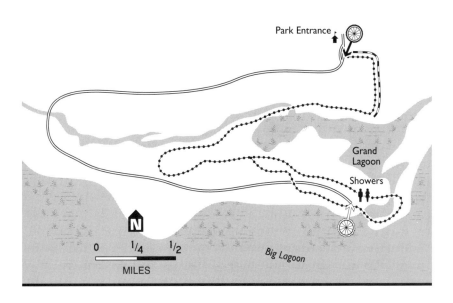

Cookie Trail's sugar-sand double-track makes for a challenging ride, especially where the bark on the trail has worn thin.

around Big Lagoon—approximately five miles total length of double-track. He cocked his head and grinned a big Florida panhandle smile and said, "It's sandy in places."

Saying it's sandy in Florida is like saying it's cold in Alaska. If a native tells you to watch out, then prepare for the extreme. Despite the slippery conditions, Cookie Trail stands as perhaps Girl Scouting's most significant contribution to Florida off-road biking. Where the wide trail has been covered with pine straw and bark, traction is sufficient. Future troop projects call for completely covering the trailway with a layer of wood chips, but until then, long loose stretches of sugar-fine sand will even make pushing the bike a challenge in places.

The 700 acres of Big Lagoon SRA preserve a salt marsh that has more in common with the Gulf of Mexico a scant half-mile away than it does with the land it protects. Still, longleaf pines and wire grass grow among yaupon shrubs and palmettos. Low-growing flowers colonize the habitat of burrowing lizards that tunnel through the sandy dunes. White egrets stalk the water's edge, looking to stab themselves a meal. And, since the lagoon is open to the sea, dolphins can sometimes be seen slowly swimming to the surface, then exploding into the air.

General location: Big Lagoon State Recreation Area is located 10 miles southwest of Pensacola, barely east of the Alabama-Florida line on Perdido Key.

Elevation change: Dune ridges and the swales in between make up the only elevation change.

Season: A good rain—more likely in the winter months—will pack the sand enough to make riding easier. Very little shade is found on the trail, making the summer months more physically demanding.

Services: The recreation area has camping with showers. Nearby Pensacola has a full range of services.

Hazards: Loose sand can quickly unbalance you. Other than that, this trail has only ubiquitous reptiles to contend with. The trail, however, is wide enough to allow for clear views should any evasive action need to be taken. Straying off into the hip-deep shrubs would quickly bring you in contact with diamondback habitat. Stay on the trail.

Rescue index: Your signals for assistance would likely be answered quickly. Although I rode this trail in the heat of a very hot day, I still passed someone else using the trail.

Land status: A state recreation area managed by Florida's Department of Environmental Protection, Department of Recreations and Parks.

Maps: Ask for the map of the Cookie Trail when you pay your entrance fee.

Finding the trail: Take US 98 west to County Road 293. Turn left (south), passing Bronson Field on the right and coming to a stop sign. The entrance is plainly marked straight across the intersection. Pay your fee and pick up the map before parking in the lot to the left of the entrance station.

Source of additional information:

Big Lagoon State Recreation Area
12301 Gulf Beach Highway
Pensacola, Florida 32507
(850) 492-0794

Notes on the trail: When the trail receives its riding surface of pine chips and bark, it will serve as an enjoyable ride for the whole family. It's an easy trail to follow with red blazes prominently lining the double-track hiking path. Despite its short length, plan for a longer trip, making use of the benches and meditation stations along the way. Push through the sandier sections and remember, "If you aren't hiking, you aren't biking!"

While you're in the area, leave the park on your bike and ride north on CR 293. Look for some jeep track on the left (western) side heading into the slash pine woods. Several miles make a loop around Bronson Field on the edge of Perdido Bay. Other roads diverge south around Tarklin Bayou.

RIDE 4 · Chickasabogue Park

AT A GLANCE

Length/configuration: 15 miles of various loops

Aerobic difficulty: High; short steep hills leave even the most advanced rider huffing and puffing

Technical difficulty: Moderate to challenging; the 3 single-track trails vary in difficulty—Beach Loop is the most difficult and exposed and protruding tree roots hazard each trail

Scenery: Trails vary: pine forest ridges, tributaries, and coastal wildlife sightings on Cemetery Loop; Chickasaw Creek on Indian Loop; and an interstate overpass and a beautiful view from the creek's backwaters on Beach Loop

Special comments: One of the most scenic trails in the northern Gulf Coast; recommended for intermediate-advanced riders; per a riding schedule, certain sections of trails are closed off at specific times of year

The 15 miles of single-track looping through Chickasaw County's recreation park may be in Alabama, but it ranks as the most technically demanding and scenic bike trail system anywhere along the northernmost Gulf Coast. Off-road bikers from Biloxi, Montgomery, and Pensacola drive an hour to the tiny park, located north of Mobile Bay, and crank it up Turtle Ridge and roar down Dead Man's Run.

It's no wonder, then, that you'll most likely find bikers riding early and staying late. Even on early weekday mornings, the lot across from the sports field will have at least one vehicle parked with an empty bike rack. Unlike some trails, which have been worn down to eroding ruts and disrepair, Chickasabogue has been regularly improved by the addition of substantial boardwalks across the wetter areas.

Such an environmental awareness goes to show that the county and the park's regular riders do not take lightly the old boughs hanging over the trail from live oaks and tall longleaf pines. The sparse understory of much of the forest gives the effect of a cavern whose floor catches the dappled light sparkling on the last dew of morning.

The noise of Interstate 65 seldom fades from the background of blue jays squawking and crows cawing. Although this may, for some, detract from the otherwise primitive and secluded character of the trail, I seldom thought about it as I huffed up Bakers Ridge or caught my breath looking at Chickasaw Creek

RIDE 4 · Chickasabogue Park

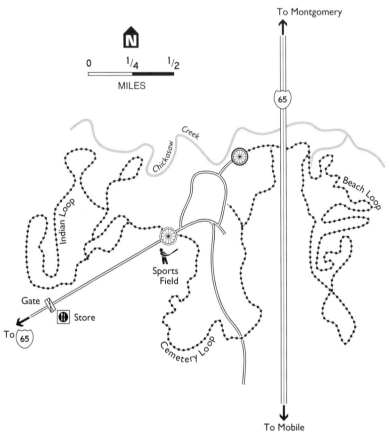

moving in a black oxbow. Chances are you'll only remember this trail for the good things that keep others coming back and biking.

Since the first edition of this guide, several sections of trail have been reworked and expanded, resulting in a net gain of five more miles of tight, winding single-track. Most of the additional mileage has been added to the Beach Loop.

General location: It's found about 12 miles north of Mobile, Alabama, off I-65.

Elevation change: The hills aren't long, but they are steep. Being able to climb them will rank you in at least the advanced-intermediate class.

Season: The sandy clay soils allow the trail to hold up well to the heavy traffic it receives. With the addition of bridges across the bogs and low-lying areas, Chickasabogue has become an all-season destination.

Services: Mobile is a major port of entry; expect to find all goods and services nearby. The park has camping, rest rooms, and showers. A small store at the entrance carries some basic biking supplies and tubes, etc.

Hazards: Although it is unlikely, hikers could be on the trail. Yield to them. A more likely hazard is that you'll spend too much time on this trail, thereby risking unemployment.

Rescue index: It is an easy place to walk out of, and to receive help if you can't walk.

Land status: This land is managed and owned by the good people of Chickasaw County, Alabama.

Maps: Ask for the free biking and hiking map of Chickasabogue Park . . . after you pay the nominal ($1) entrance fee.

Finding the trail: Take Exit 13 from I-65 and head west, following the conspicuous signs to Chickasabogue Park. Turn left onto Shelton Beach Road at the first light west of the interstate. A flashing yellow light marks the intersection where you turn left onto Whistle Road. A final left onto Aldock Road goes through a quiet residential neighborhood before entering the park. After paying your entrance fee, look for the parking lot on the left across from the sports field. If it's full, park across the street.

Source of additional information:

Chickasabogue Park
760 Aldock Road
Mobile, Alabama 36613
(334) 452-8496

Notes on the trail: Although there are three different trails, a modification in the riding schedule combines them into either a "red" riding month or a "yellow" riding month. Observe where the trail has been opened by moving portable gates, and stay off the closed sections. As always, when in doubt, stay out.

CEMETERY LOOP

This trail is listed as a moderate challenge for the average mountain biker. It starts off running along the ridges of pine forests and some hardwoods before dropping off into the draws of tributaries flowing into Chickasaw Creek. Just like flying a plane, the landing into and taking off from these draws provide the most need for concentration. Exposed roots will rattle a rigid-forked bike.

The back side of the trail leads to a cemetery within close earshot of the interstate on the other side of a stand of small pines. As I was meditating on mortality under the magnificent old live oak shading the headstones, I heard the boom of a truck recap blowing out and dove for cover.

The last part of the loop comes in behind the sports field, which you cross; then head toward the parking lot. Yield the trail to people and fly balls, frisbees, and the other accoutrements of recreation. You may just want to watch it all on the bench by the small pond—that is, before heading out to the rest of the single-track.

INDIAN LOOP

Indian Loop and Cemetery Loop share the same trailhead by beginning at the parking lot across from the sports field. The trails are well marked at this point, so you should not have any trouble finding the extremely tight single-track that begins Indian Loop. I can't imagine anyone wanting or being able to go very fast on the first half-mile or so of this trail. It nearly loops back on itself in quite a few places. Exposed roots three or four inches high, along with muddy spots, require finesse instead of speed. The trail changes character after the first mile or so, when it dead-ends into a sandy section. A right turn leads to Chickasaw Creek. You can build up a good head of steam in this section, but be aware that the thicker sandy spots can quickly write a surprise ending to your forward progress.

This is the trail where all sorts of coastal wildlife can be seen if you pay attention: deer, foxes, beavers, rabbits, and other animals are frequently sighted on this trail. Also, as you make your way closer to the water's edge, you may also encounter various representatives of the reptilian and amphibian race, most of which only want to get out of your way. The two possible exceptions to this rule are the cottonmouth and alligator. Both of these are used to getting their way, so don't try to mimic what you saw in an old movie and wrestle with either one. Save your energy for the trail.

BEACH LOOP

This is by far the most difficult loop of the three. Pick up the beginning at the cemetery and head for the noise of the interstate. There are few trails in Florida where you go under interstate overpasses, but that is what's required here. It isn't as bad as it sounds, although I confess to having an uneasy feeling when I thought of what could happen if someone going 70 mph above me tossed out a bottle or some other missile. I stopped underneath and listened to tires sing for a few minutes before heading down the trail.

The backwaters of Chickasaw Creek offer an especially beautiful, relaxing view, and you should plan some time to take it in before climbing above the creek. Once you start the descent from Turtle Ridge, the extra challenging section begins and doesn't let up for about 2 more miles, when the flatter piece begins near the interstate. Expect steep climbs (never mind that they are relatively short) up slopes that would be tough enough without having to pick your slots between the large roots supporting live oaks, sweet gums, and pines.

RIDE 5 · Conecuh Trail

AT A GLANCE

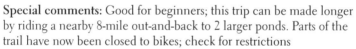

Length/configuration: 10-mile loop

Aerobic difficulty: Low; no long climbs as you ride from wetland to wetland

Technical difficulty: Easy; the flat terrain and wide single-track trail make this a relaxing ride for all

Scenery: Bogs, ponds, and savannas dot this 80,000-acre forest, which is filled with unusual plants (including 23 species of carnivorous flora!)

Special comments: Good for beginners; this trip can be made longer by riding a nearby 8-mile out-and-back to 2 larger ponds. Parts of the trail have now been closed to bikes; check for restrictions

This ten-mile loop of wide single-track through Alabama's Conecuh National Forest provides an easy day trip under most conditions. Those conditions were changed considerably in fall 1995 when Hurricane Opal tore across the panhandle. Barely 35 miles inland, the Conecuh (whose name means "land of cane") was hit with numerous tornadoes in addition to the storm's sustained winds of over 75 mph. Many of the large pines, maples, and sweet gums fell across the trail, blocking it for months afterward.

Originally begun as a hiking-only trail in 1976 by the Youth Conservation Corps, the Conecuh Trail was only recently opened to mountain biking. Despite having the "rollingest" hills around (Florida's highest elevation is approximately 25 miles southeast), no long climbs exist between the numerous wetlands, marked most often by ponds, or sinks, as they're called a few miles south in Florida.

A quiet approach to these clearings will seldom disappoint the alert wildlife watcher. Ducks, egrets, and herons stalk and paddle among turtles basking on logs. An extremely furtive approach to one of these sites could catch a mink among the brush or a gator laid out on the surface of the water, eyes up and watching for a side order of frog legs.

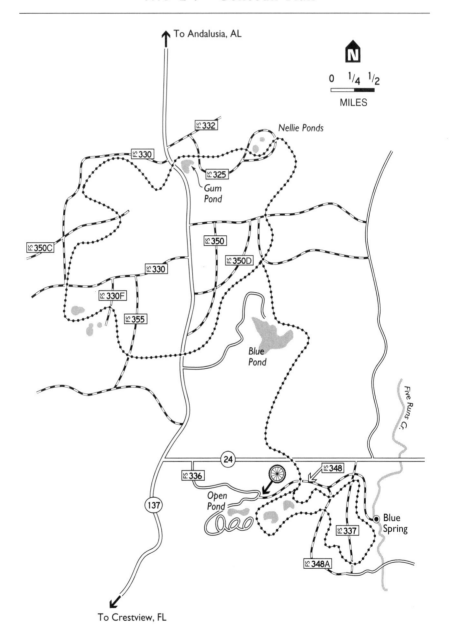

The bogs, ponds, and savannas inside this 80,000-acre forest also support a wide variety of unusual plants. Pitcher plants, sundews, bladderworts, and butterworts make up a total of 23 species of carnivorous flora that use a variety of strategies to lure insects into their digestive systems. The bladderworts use a triggering mechanism located in the hairs sticking above the surface of a pond. When a small fly lands on the hairs, a nearby "bladder" opens rapidly, sucking the meal into a sticky gut.

General location: The national forest lies adjacent to the Florida border, 90 miles from Pensacola.

Elevation change: The trail seldom gains ground higher than 300 feet above sea level, or dips below 240 feet, though the total elevation gained in a round trip is 120 feet.

Season: The summer brings lush growth to the occasional wildlife opening you must cross. It is more than a little unnerving to pedal in shin-high grass which may be hiding who-knows-what. There are, however, ways around these sections: use one of the 15 Forest Service roads that intersect with the trail.

Services: Basic supplies can be picked up in Wing, Alabama, 8 miles south of the southern trailhead on AL 137. The trailhead is near camping, showers, and rest rooms.

Hazards: Hunters will be present in season. Avoid riding in the early mornings or late afternoons at those times. The trail may be blocked in several places due to storm damage.

Rescue index: Conecuh Trail is among the most remote described in this guide. Acquiring adequate assistance quickly could be a problem. Plan on self-sufficiency.

Land status: This land is managed by the Department of Agriculture as a national forest.

Maps: An excellent map of the Conecuh Trail—complete with contour lines—may be purchased from the National Forest District Ranger's Office in Andalusia, Alabama.

Finding the trail: Leave Crestview, Florida, northbound on FL 85. Approximately 15 miles from Crestview, turn left onto FL 2. When FL 2 dead-ends, turn right onto FL 189 at Blackman, Florida. The Alabama border lies less than 5 miles away, where the highway changes numbers and becomes AL 137. Ten miles later, just after passing Forest Service Road 350, look on the right for parking and the trailhead.

Source of additional information:

National Forest District Ranger Office
Route 5, Box 157
Andalusia, Alabama 36420
(334) 222-2555

Notes on the trail: Begin riding counterclockwise from the southern trail-head, where you'll cross 4 Forest Service roads before coming to Nellie Ponds. Two more service roads are crossed before you come to Gum Pond and AL 137, the halfway point. Three more miles lead to Mossy Ponds, around which occur the most dramatic elevation changes anywhere on the trail—70 feet are lost in less than a half-mile. After the descent, the trail turns east for the 2 flat remaining miles.

An additional 8 miles can be tacked on by taking an out-and-back to Blue Pond (a mile away) and then Open Pond (3 miles farther). In order to work these into the ride, turn right onto the single-track just before its intersection with FS 355.

RIDE 6 · Blackwater River State Forest

AT A GLANCE

Length/configuration: 14-mile loop of service roads plus 6-mile lake trail

Aerobic difficulty: Low, especially after a rain when the double-track's rolling clay terrain makes for little difficulty in climbing its moderate hills

Technical difficulty: Easy

Scenery: Expanses of longleaf pine forest and wire grass; Coldwater and Dixon Creeks

Special comments: Good place for riders of all abilities; an ancient cemetery, a memorialized tree, and nearby canoe rentals make this an adventurous spot

A 14-mile loop on sandy, red clay double-track service roads explores the rolling terrain between Coldwater and Dixon creeks. In drier weather, the sand almost becomes more challenging to ride than it's worth, but when the surface packs down after rains, even beginners should have little difficulty climbing the small hills.

The forest's approximately 190,000 acres join the Conecuh National Forest's 91,000 acres immediately to the north (in Alabama) for an unbroken expanse of longleaf pine and wire grass ecosystem—the world's largest example. This relatively undisturbed land is among the last places where the endangered red-cockaded woodpecker and gopher tortoise breed and multiply.

Other, more common sightings of deer and armadillos occur in an intensively managed forest system. For that reason, you are likely to observe a "prescribed burn" occurring in one or more sections of forest. Therapeutic in nature, the fires help the wire grass bloom and control longleaf pine needle blight, a disease of young longleafs.

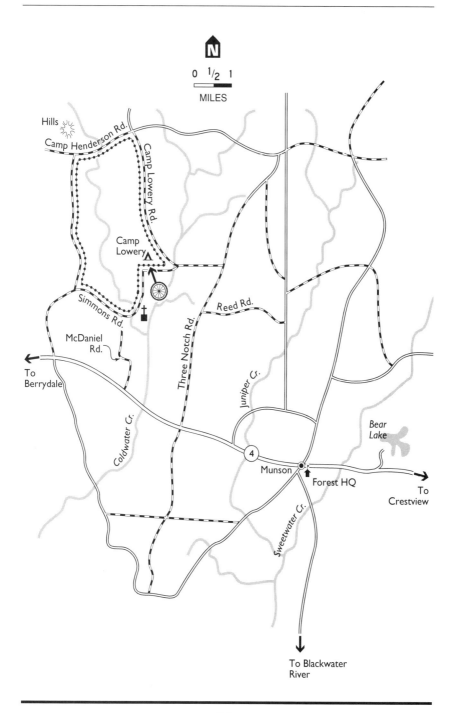

Numerous bike routes and configurations can be put together in Black-water State Forest, but for a different adventure incorporating the river, try some paddling down this popular river. Blackwater Canoe Rental can provide anything needed in the way of a shuttle or boating supplies.

General location: The entrance to Blackwater River State Forest is located approximately 25 miles northeast of Milton, Florida, via FL 191 — 10 miles south of the Alabama border.

Elevation change: Although elevation changes do occur inside the forest (between 10 and 290 feet above sea level), little of it happens at so great a rate as to require "weenie gear climbs."

Season: Hunting season is late fall, early winter, and early spring. Bikers should wear bright orange when riding, especially in remote areas. Consult the Florida Fish and Wildlife Conservation Commission for season dates. Otherwise, plan for times after the sand has been packed down by heavy rains. Riding in loose sand is only fun for short sections.

Services: Munson is a small community located at the intersection of FL 191 and FL 4 where you can acquire the basics. Look to Pensacola, 45 minutes to the south, or Milton, 20 minutes away, for a wider selection.

Hazards: Hunting season and vehicles (year-round unless you choose to stay only on closed roads) present the most dangerous hazards. Loose sand is another, but coming to a sudden stop in sand usually does less harm than wrecking on rock or pavement. Hunting with dogs is not allowed south of FL 4, so hunting is of less concern there.

Rescue index: Some roads through the forest get more traffic than others, but the closely packed gridwork of routes ensures fairly easy recovery in case of mishap.

Land status: This land is managed by Florida's Department of Agriculture and Consumer Services.

Maps: The forest office in Munson has a free 17-by-11-inch map of Black-water River State Forest.

Finding the trail: From the intersection of FL 191 and FL 4, head west for 4 miles, where the second paved road to the right (Three Notch Road) bears a sign for Stump Springs Church. Just after 4 miles, take the dirt road to the left and arrive at Camp Lowery bridge, a canoe put-in for Coldwater Creek and also a primitive camping area. It is also the beginning of the ride. Park in the areas provided.

Sources of additional information:

Blackwater Canoe Rental
Highway 90 East
Milton, Florida 32583
(850) 623-0235

Blackwater Forestry Center
11650 Munson Highway
Milton, Florida 32570
(850) 957-6140

Sunrise at Bear Lake inside Blackwater River State Forest—where all you need is some time.

Notes on the trail: Begin the 14-mile loop by heading west on Simmons Road. The first 3 miles go along the ridges between Dixon and Coldwater creeks. On the final descent to Dixon Creek, a graveyard from the area's earliest days makes an interesting stop. Take a right at the next intersection. McDaniel Road leads left and to FL 4, 2 miles away. The first half of the ride is marked at the next intersection, just past Dixon Creek's western ridge. Take a right to the ride's most curious sight. You'll easily notice the large knoll on the left, balled up like a fist. Motorized vehicles have been discouraged from driving up to its summit by placement of large pine poles anchored deep in the ground. A large white cross has been placed high on a tree trunk. It'll give you something to think about on the rest of the loop, which is completed by taking a right that intersects Camp Lowery Road 2 miles away.

Blackwater State Forest has opened a 6-mile mountain bike trail around Bear Lake. There's a map at the kiosk at Bear Lake. *Note:* Wiregrass, Jackson, and Sweetwater Trails are for hiking only.

RIDE 7 · Eastern Lake Trail

AT A GLANCE

Length/configuration: 9-mile loop of logging roads

Aerobic difficulty: Low; flat terrain

Technical difficulty: Easy, provided the sandy double-track has been packed down by a good rain

Scenery: Twists through pine forest, and then through marshes behind sand dunes which line the Gulf of Mexico; small creeks and grasses; Eastern Lake

Special comments: A great place to watch herons swoop down near the creeks

It was on my very first off-road ride in Florida that I heard, after plowing through a 20-yard sandy swale, "You'll get used to riding in the sand in Florida." If you want to get used to it in a hurry, take your bike to Eastern Lake Bike Trail, a nine-mile loop of old double-track logging roads. However, the Florida Division of Forestry recently completed a $20,000 grant to improve the trail surface here with clay—a much harder surface that's easier to pedal—so this should be a smoother ride in the future.

Located one to two miles away from the Gulf of Mexico, these roads command ground (or I should say sand) 35 feet above sea level on the 15,000 acres of Point Washington State Forest. South Walton Conservation and Development Trust's Conservation and Recreation Task Force (that's SWCDTCRTF, for short) selected the pine forest as the site for a new off-road biking trail.

The trail winds through marshes behind long, white knuckles of dunes rising along the Gulf of Mexico. As it gets closer to Eastern Lake, Gulf waters gleam through the broken row of trees on the horizon. Herons—great blue, Louisiana, and green-backed—swoop over grasses growing along small creeks. Raccoons knock dry stalks and leaves together as they run in the marsh, sounding eerily like what my imagination suggested, at the time, was an alligator.

General location: Find Eastern Lake approximately 22 miles east of Destin, 1 mile south of US 98.

Elevation change: Some occasional changes occur, but nothing dramatic.

Season: I would recommend trying this after flooding rains have subsided. The extremely sandy nature of this terrain makes for tedious traveling if it's dry and loose.

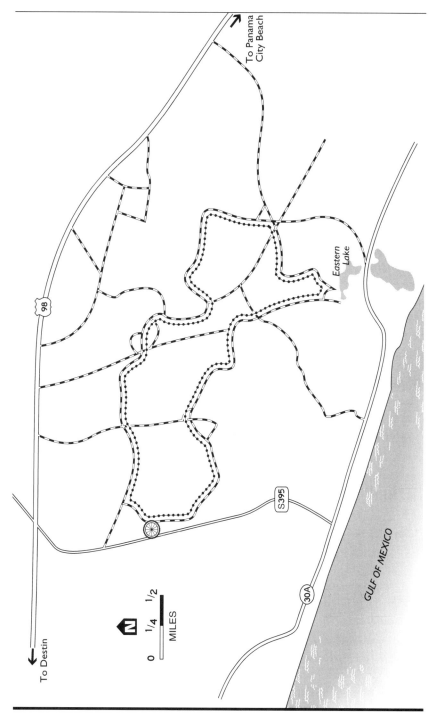

It's best to ride Eastern Lake's double-track down the middle, where the grass locks the slippery sand together.

Services: All services can be found nearby or in Fort Walton Beach and Panama City, each approximately 30 miles west and east, respectively, of the trailhead.

Hazards: Nothing specific, but the sweeping statement issued by the state of Florida, "Natural conditions are present which are dangerous," applies.

Rescue index: This is fairly remote traveling, considering its location near Miracle Strip Parkway. And it could take a miracle to get to you quickly. Plan accordingly.

Land status: This land is managed by Florida as a public state forest.

Maps: A map of Eastern Lake Bike Trail, Point Washington State Forest can be picked up during normal business hours at Point Washington Tower, located a couple of miles east of the trailhead, to the left of US 98. The cypress-shingled information station has a detailed map posted behind glass and available brochures.

Finding the trail: Leave Fort Walton Beach headed east on US 98. About 25 miles down the highway, you'll notice US 98's intersection with US 331 coming from the left (north). Three miles after this landmark, turn right onto County Road 395. The trailhead is plainly marked—with parking lot—a little over a mile on the left.

Sources of additional information:

Thomas Beitzel
Division of Forestry
Chipola River District
715 West 15th Street
Panama City, Florida 32401
(850) 747-5639
(850) 872-4879 (fax)

Point Washington State Forest
Point Washington Tower
5865 Highway 98
Santa Rosa Beach, Florida 32459
(850) 231-5800

Notes on the trail: A short connector leads to the loop proper, which can be ridden in any direction. Taken in a clockwise direction, the first intersection—a dead end—heads back to CR 395 to the left, with a right turn to the loop. Go straight across the next 2 intersections. Turn right at the next intersection, which is a dead end. Another road comes in from the right shortly; pass it by and turn right at the next intersection. Take the next left, circling for nearly 2 miles as you make the approach to Eastern Lake. Bear right at the next intersection, turn right at the next crossroads, and straight at the next one. The next 3 miles take you closest to the lake. The return to the trailhead is completed by going straight at the next intersection and turning left at the dead end. The last 2 miles have no turns.

RIDE 8 · Timberlake Trail

AT A GLANCE

Length/configuration: 10-mile loop if you ride all trails

Aerobic difficulty: Moderate

Technical difficulty: Moderate to challenging; all trails are single-track, and several have sand and root-infested hills; the first 4.5 miles of main trail is a set of steep switchbacks

Scenery: Lotus blooms float on Timberlake in the springtime, and alligators, turtles and herons are regulars in this area

Special comments: An annual recreation permit ($3) is required

Eglin Air Force Base set aside a portion of its 728 square miles north of the Emerald Coast for single-track mountain biking. I got to ride it with Robin Wilkes of Bob's Bikes one May evening as storm clouds threatened. He explained, "Most people are really surprised when they walk in and ask where they can ride off-road near Fort Walton, and they wind up here." Large knuckles

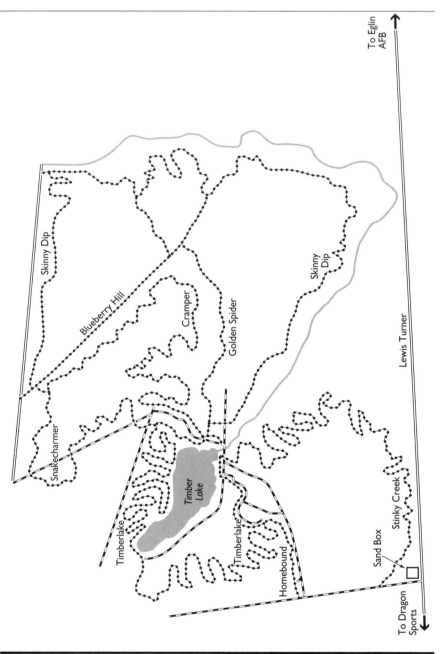

The trail gets narrow at Timberlake, a technical single-track loop near Fort Walton Beach.

of land formed live oak hammocks. Lotus blooms floated on Timberlake's surface, and turtles poked their heads above the reflection and watched the ones wearing shells on their heads.

"We like to take beginners out here," Robin said, "even though there are some places they have to push. After they're finished, they're sure they want to do more of this." With that, we took off through a narrow gap of single-track, switchbacking easily to gain the ridge.

A light green moss covered large areas under blackjack oak and yaupon shrubs like bumpy shag carpet. Birds flitted in front of us. A loud clap of thunder caused us to pick up the pace a bit as rain began to fall. "Do you mind getting wet?" Robin asked me. I told him, "No, but I don't want to sizzle from a bolt of 10,000 volts."

"I believe it's moving off," Robin reassured me and we took off. It wasn't too long before I heard two more explosive sounds. I asked, "Uh, Robin, were those sonic booms?" Eglin has a total of 21 runways nearby and very fast jets use them regularly, so I wasn't totally unprepared to hear the sound barrier broken. Still, I was glad when Robin confirmed my foreigner's suspicion. We finished the ride in a thickening dusk to the sound of bullfrogs warming up for a night of croaking.

General location: Timberlake is located just north of Fort Walton Beach, Florida, east on FL 189 near its junction with FL 85.

Elevation change: Most people can ride the hills here. There are, however, at least 2 places where riders unfamiliar with the trail may have to push up—like I did. A rather dramatic drop of about 3 feet occurs as the single-track crosses the service road. Although the hills are short, they will test your legs and lungs.

Season: I rode this trail during a dry time. The sand was as loose as it probably gets and was only very thick in short stretches. Again, wet weather tends to make this type surface easier for tires to grip.

Services: Fort Walton Beach is the largest urban area on the Emerald Coast, surpassing both Panama City and Pensacola. All services are available there. Primitive camping is allowed at Timberlake by registration with Jackson Guard in Niceville about 6 miles north.

Hazards: Traffic may be present at the trailhead and as you return to the parking area from Homebound. Also, other bikers will be using this trail, and some will be coming head-on. Stay in control and ring your bell. Stop and scout the slots you need to take on the initial run through the steep and rooty sections of the lake's north shore.

Rescue index: This is an urban route allowing for quick and easy access.

Land status: This land is part of Eglin Air Force Base. You must acquire an annual recreation permit ($5) in order to ride Timberlake Trail. New permits are available beginning October 1 from the Jackson Guard in Niceville. The fine for riding without a permit is $35, payable in Federal Court in Pensacola.

Maps: Current maps are available at Dragon Sports, approximately 1 mile west on FL 189.

Finding the trail: From US 98, turn north onto FL 189 (Beal Parkway). After about 5 miles, the road curves to the right. Proceed about 2 miles and look for a dark brown, wooden sign for Timberlake Campground. Park at the corner.

Sources of additional information:

For annual recreation permit by mail write to:
Eglin Natural Resources Division
107 Highway 85 North
Niceville, Florida 32578

For ride information, write or call:
Emerald Coast Cyclist Club
P.O. Box 592
Niceville, Florida 32588
24-hour hotline: (850) 864-7166

Enclose a $5 check or money order (no cash) along with a photocopy of some I.D. (driver's license preferred) showing current address (zip, too), full name, and date of birth. It will take three weeks to process your request.

Notes on the trail: You'll take the Stinky Creek Trail to the lake. From there, depending on your ability, choose from various trails that loop back to the lake. Skinny Dip is one of the most difficult, with logs to bunny hop and a set of switchbacks with logs to climb. After the switchbacks, you'll gradually climb to the top of Blueberry Hill. You'll choose between Snakecharmer and Cramper Trails to return to the lake. Snakecharmer is easy and runs slightly downhill, wiggling like a snake. Cramper offers a great downhill, snaking around trees and over logs and traversing the hill, some logs, and some dips—it's a fast, exciting single-track. Either trail returns you to the lake near the pavilion.

But that's not all. Golden Spider Trail heads back out into the woods. It's an easy trail until it joins Blueberry Hill, which is a quarter-mile climb; it's not steep but will test your aerobic capacity. Blueberry Hill then links to Snakecharmer or Cramper—your choice.

The final loop is Timberlake Trail, the original trail around the lake. It begins as a twisting, flat trail, crosses a dry creekbed, then becomes technical before returing to the pavilion. As you begin Timberlake, you'll see the exit trail called Homebound. It's exactly that and will return you to the parking area. It's an easy trail, but watch out for coral snakes and pygmy rattlers in summer.

If you ride all trails, you'll log about 10 miles, but additional trail development is underway, with stream crossings to access the area east of the creek.

RIDE 9 · Dutch Tiemann Trail

AT A GLANCE

Length/configuration: 20 miles total of loops and service roads; 5-mile single-track through woods

Aerobic difficulty: Low to moderate; gently rolling hills in places

Technical difficulty: Easy to moderate; sand and hills in unexpected places

Scenery: Deep woods, longleaf pine forest, lakes lined with Spanish moss–covered cypress trees

Special comments: Several paddle-pedal combinations and secluded camping available along Pine Log Creek

The first thing most people think about when they hear "Panama City" is white, sugar-fine beaches—no place to ride a bike off-road. But less than 15 miles north of this famous resort city, in Pine Log State Forest, a system of single-track allows for over five miles of deep woods exploration, making a loop up and down gently rolling slopes. Combined with service roads, more than 20 miles of loops of varying lengths can be ridden on sandy track in a longleaf pine forest just south of the Choctawhatchee River.

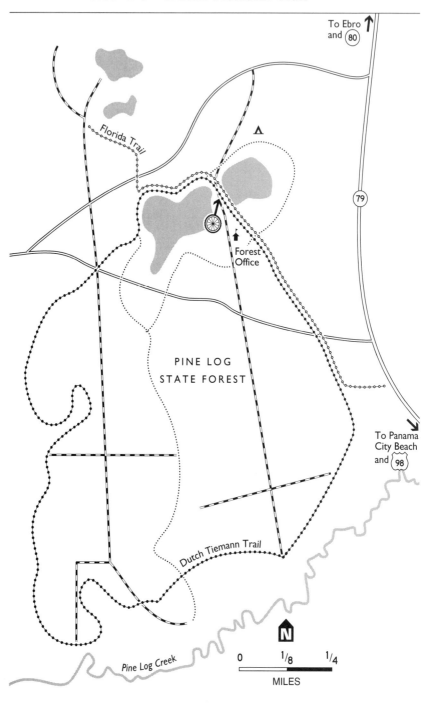

To Ebro and (80)

Florida Trail

79

Forest Office

PINE LOG STATE FOREST

To Panama City Beach and (98)

Dutch Tiemann Trail

Pine Log Creek

N

0   1/8   1/4

MILES

For those who would rather steer clear of Miracle Strip Amusement Park and the Snake-a-Torium, a quiet camping spot (20 sites available) in the Pine Log woods might serve your needs better than the popular St. Andrews State Recreation Area (176 sites). Its four small lakes—banks lined with gray-barked cypress trees sporting beards of Spanish moss—make for peaceful rides with plenty of chances to catch Florida's rich array of wildlife in action.

Those who see the natural connection between riding a bike in the woods and paddling a canoe down a stream will want to spend another day exploring one of the possible paddle-pedal combos along Pine Log Creek, a tributary of the East River which, of course, flows north and west through a large swamp along the Choctawhatchee River.

Primitive camps in the quiet backwoods along Pine Log Creek provide an even more secluded experience. After spending a summer evening around a campfire listening to the maniacal cackle of the barred owl and the thunder of gators and bullfrogs, an early morning ride will sharpen the senses and quicken the wits. It's hard to find fault with a trail like that.

Longleaf pines, like these at Pine Log State Forest, form an important link in a wire grass and pulpwood community.

General location: Pine Log State Forest is located approximately 15 miles north of Panama City Beach (and pier) on FL 79, south of the intersection with FL 20 at Ebro.

Elevation change: An occasional hill will pop up on the trail like a rogue wave at sea. Otherwise, it's basically flat.

Season: As with so many Florida off-road trails which are largely composed of sand, traction is improved after rains. This trail is in a part of the forest that is closed during hunting season; riders do not have to worry about being mistaken for a wild critter.

Services: Panama City made its reputation catering to the needs of the tourist. The forest has camping, showers, and bathrooms.

Hazards: Sandy spots, if they're long enough, make coming off the bike likely. Parts of the palmetto understory grow close to the trail. Should you have to put your foot down, make sure it lands where you can see what you're stepping on. As a state brochure pointed out, "Natural conditions may be present which are dangerous."

Rescue index: Despite a fairly remote location, easy access to the trails inside the state forest facilitates rescues.

Land status: This is a state forest managed by Florida's Department of Agriculture and Consumer Services, Division of Forestry.

Maps: Maps showing the trail system within the forest can be picked up in an information mailbox across from the forest headquarters. If the mailbox is empty, drive to the office and ask for the Pine Log State Forest Trail Map.

Finding the trail: Leave Panama City Beach and Pier and head north on FL 79. After crossing the bridge about 15 miles down the road, look for the sign for Pine Log State Forest on the left. Take the first dirt road to the right. After traveling past the lakes, look to the left for the pavilion and a place to park. Begin by riding the red-blazed trail winding around the camp area.

Sources of additional information:

Pine Log State Forest (mailing address)
715 West 15th Street
Panama City, Florida 32401
(850) 747-5639

Bonifay Forestry Center
2889 Forestry Drive
Bonifay, Florida 32425
(850) 547-7083

Notes on the trail: By beginning with the red-blazed camp loop, ride clockwise around the easternmost lake. Just before coming to the dirt road entrance, take a left onto the blue-and-orange-blazed Dutch Tiemann and Florida Trail. After crossing the main service road coming from FL 79, the orange-blazed Florida Trail splits off to the left, while Dutch Tiemann Trail continues south to Pine Log Creek, the boundary between Washington and Bay counties, which the trail follows for the next 2 miles. After crossing the Forest Service road at the upper canoe put-in, the trail turns north (right) and stays on the right side of a wet weather slough until the intersection of 2 dirt roads. The trail continues directly opposite (to the northeast) from where it comes into the intersection. The last half mile hugs the shore of the largest of the 4 lakes.

RIDE 10 · Chattahoochee State Park, Alabama

AT A GLANCE

Length/configuration: 6-mile loop of pine needle–surfaced Jeep track connecting to a fire lane

Aerobic difficulty: Consistently flat

Technical difficulty: Easy

Scenery: Pine forest; a small lake

Special comments: Great for newcomers

Almost as if by accident, the Chattahoochee State Park claims a square mile along the western banks of the great Chattahoochee River. Its small size has not kept this former Civilian Conservation Camp from providing a little something for everyone—mountain biker included. A trail system containing six miles of looping jeep track with a grass or pine needle surface connects to the four miles of fire lane on the outer perimeter of the park.

A park employee warned me that a great many diamondback rattlesnakes (a species in decline) inhabit the area. I rode past more gopher tortoise burrows than I have ever seen anywhere else. On one stretch, I counted five burrows in a half-mile section of the gray sand. Snakes of all sorts coexist with the giant turtle, but the diamondbacks especially like the large and cool cavities, where they escape the summer's midday heat. But, to my pleasure, I saw no diamondbacks.

As I was riding along the spillway to the small lake inside the park, I saw a Louisiana heron perched in the crooked bough of a pine tree. An older couple pushed out a jon boat loaded with fishing poles and bait. When I asked the man what he was fishing for, he said, "Crappie and bass if I can get 'em, but mostly anything that bites." I rode back to the car wishing I had brought along a boat, some line, and a hook, too.

General location: This Alabama state park is found on the western bank of the Chattahoochee River, where the state borders for Alabama, Georgia, and Florida come together.

Elevation change: There is no great change in elevation.

Season: The sandy soil of the jeep track had been recently plowed, making for a slower than normal pace in places, but generally the terrain is an all-season surface.

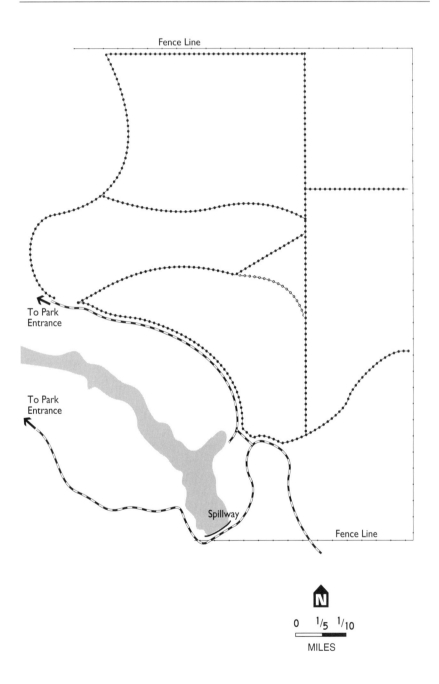

Fence Line

To Park
Entrance

To Park
Entrance

Spillway

Fence Line

N

0   1/5   1/10
MILES

Services: Marianna, Florida, is the nearest location for obtaining more than the basics. Tallahassee is the closest all-item outlet, located about an hour's drive southeast of the park. The park contains camping facilities, showers, and rest rooms.

Hazards: Vehicles are sometimes present on the main service roads that you may be crossing. Other than that, the trails are wide enough and smooth enough to provide safe and comfortable travel for 2-way traffic.

Rescue index: The park's size is 1 square mile; therefore, you are not ever too far from help, which can easily and quickly gain access to the double-track and jeep trails.

Land status: This park is managed by the state of Alabama.

Maps: The main office (on the right behind the long rock wall) has updated maps of Chattahoochee State Park on hand.

Finding the trail: Take FL 2 until you reach the sign pointing south to Three Rivers Recreation Area (just after you cross the Chattahoochee River if you're traveling west, and just before if you're headed east). Turn north onto Timberlane Road, which will turn into AL 95 after crossing the state line less than 2 miles away. The park entrance is on the right just over the border. Park at the ranger's headquarters and pick up one of the plainly marked trails coming into the dirt service road.

Source of additional information:

Chattahoochee State Park
Star Route, Box 108
Gordon, Alabama 36343
(334) 522-3607

Notes on the trail: There are fewer than 10 total miles of service roads and trails found within the park's boundaries. Although the employee I talked to seemed to think that getting lost was a possibility, I found that all roads and trails were plainly marked or cleared. By taking all right turns (or left turns), you will eventually come to the fence surrounding the park. A fire lane just this side of the fence denotes the outer perimeter of the trail system. Most of the trails lie in the north and east sections of the park. You can explore as a first-timer without too much worry that you will get lost.

TALLAHASSEE AND THE BIG BEND AREA

Florida's political center may not be its biking center, too, but it should not be automatically disqualified as a candidate for such a distinction. The campuses of Florida State University and Florida A&M provide a large demand for off-road trails. The nearby Apalachicola National Forest can satisfy some of this need, but not all of it. So the city of Tallahassee started working with area bike clubs to construct challenging single-track in local parks.

Long ago, small societies of Indians lived in the thick forests and rolling hills. Their existence was simple, and they relied on the bounty that was attracted to the shores of huge freshwater springs. Later, the white men came, tamed the land, and farmed plantations of cotton. Canals were dug and railroads built. When the time came for a capital to be chosen, the other contenders—Pensacola and Saint Augustine—never had a chance. The big money lived in the Big Bend; in one 30,000-acre area alone, over 70 plantations had been established.

When the Civil War came, Tallahassee's home guard and volunteers out-maneuvered federal troops at Natural Bridge in the headwaters of the St. Marks River and kept the city from being captured—against all odds. The government troops probably suffered logistics problems, getting bogged down in the rough country. Just east of the city in the marshes surrounding the remote rivers Wacissa and Aucilla, travel is difficult even by boat. But the off-road biker can find an extensive network of double-track service roads delving into places like Hell's Half Acre and Goose Pasture.

By setting up a central base in a state park like Wakullah Springs or inside the Apalachicola National Forest, more than a week can be spent in the area pedaling a different off-road trail each day. But go ahead and plan to stay around for at least two weeks because by the time you finish riding Tom

Brown, you'll be ready for Munson Hills again. Or will it be Redbug? Might as well make it the St. Marks and head back to Posey's for another smoked mullet sandwich.

Sources of additional information:

Capital City Cyclists
P.O. Box 4222
Tallahassee, Florida 32315-4222
(850) 847-8433 (ride hotline)
www.ccyclists.org

About Bikes
411 North Magnolia Street
Tallahassee, Florida 32308-5082
(850) 942-7506

RIDE 11 · St. Marks Trail

AT A GLANCE

Length/configuration: 16-mile one-way (32 miles out-and-back)

Aerobic difficulty: Low; flat and paved

Technical difficulty: Easy

Scenery: Giant live oaks decorated with Spanish moss shade the trail

Special comments: Probably Florida's most popular rail-to-trail conversion

For those looking to work their way up to a more challenging off-road experience, but not quite ready to tackle the technical single-track of, say, Munson Hills, St. Marks Trail offers a flexible route. The 16-mile one-way (32 miles total out-and-back), flat, paved former rail bed linking Tallahassee to the Gulf of Mexico has made itself the panhandle's most popular rail-to-trail conversion.

The slaves who did the original clearing had no idea that some 125 years later their work would be transformed into a self-propelled playground. Walkers, bladers, and bikers young and old can be seen early and late, weekday and weekend, taking advantage of this linear state park.

Although the traffic noise from FL 363 seldom disappears, from Woodville on it remains faint enough to encourage daydreams of ways gone by. One can nearly hear the talk of the men who hacked through the swamp on their way to the sea. Live oaks—some with crowns nearly 50 feet across and hundreds of years old—shade parts of the trail, sporting gray scraggly beards of Spanish moss.

It is not, however, a trail rife with wildlife . . . that is, unless you count the bipeds, some of whom are so scantily clad they would make an antebellum

RIDE 11 · St. Marks Trail

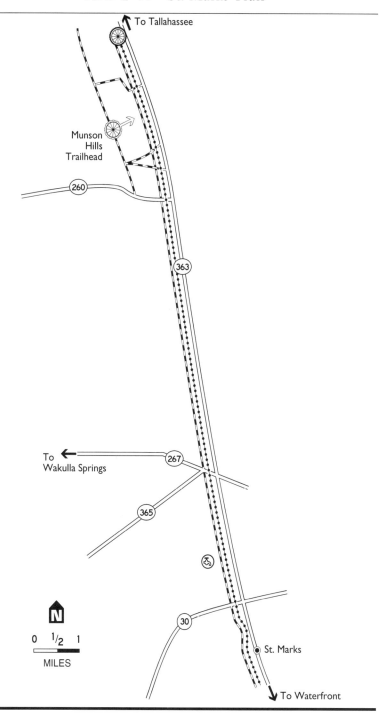

To Tallahassee

Munson
Hills
Trailhead

260

363

To ←
Wakulla Springs

267

365

30

St. Marks

N

0   1/2   1

MILES

To Waterfront

St. Marks Trail—one of Florida's paved rail beds—has this trailside water fountain approximately six miles from Posey's on the waterfront. Don't pass up either one.

matriarch swoon. I hardly had time to notice as I clicked off a mile every five minutes or so. By the time I reached Posey's on the waterfront, I had worked up a sweat and a serious appetite for a smoked mullet sandwich.

General location: Head south 10 miles on FL 363 to the intersection with Capital Circle (US 319/FL 263) and go straight another quarter mile. The parking lot is on the right.

Elevation change: It is barely perceptible, losing approximately 12 feet in the 16 miles to the river.

Season: This trail is open and easily ridden all year long.

Services: Tallahassee city limits lie just to the north of the trailhead. During normal business hours (weekdays 2–8 p.m., weekends 9 a.m.–5 p.m.), St. Marks Trail Bikes & Blades rents bikes and in-line skates, in addition to providing repairs and refreshments.

Hazards: Some intersections require full stops before proceeding, as the trail crosses major highways. Other users may not be as alert as necessary, so be quick to announce your presence and intention in a friendly voice as you overtake the slower hikers, bikers, and skaters. It is also a good idea to share the trail with a buddy. Some of the trail cuts through remote, forested areas.

Rescue index: This trail is easily accessed, so it should be easy to get assistance.

Land status: This is a Florida state park.

Maps: A map of St. Marks Trail is posted at the trailhead, and St. Marks Trail Bikes & Blades has individual maps available.

Finding the trail: Take FL 363 south to its intersection with Capital Circle (US 319/FL 263) and continue straight for another quarter mile. The trailhead is on the right at the end of the parking lot.

Source of additional information:

> Tallahassee–St. Marks Historic Railroad State Trail
> 1022 DeSoto Park Drive
> Tallahassee, Florida 32301
> (850) 922-6007

Notes on the trail: Three major intersections require stopping to ensure safe passage across: County Road 260 (just north of Woodville), FL 267 (Wakulla), and US 98/FL 30. Water and picnic tables can be located on the southern section between Woodville and Wakulla. If you don't feel you have the energy to bike the entire 32 miles, turn around wherever you feel half as tired as you want to be.

RIDE 12 · Wakulla Springs State Park

AT A GLANCE

Length/configuration: 5 miles one-way or 10 miles out-and-back

Aerobic difficulty: Low; flat terrain

Technical difficulty: Easy; this gated double-track is perfect for beginners

Scenery: 2 bridges over the Wakulla River and its springs; hickory, live oak, sweet gum, beech, cypress, and magnolia trees

Special comments: Best riding is during the spring and summer (when the trail is less soggy); $2.75 per car to enter the car and $1 if entering on a bike

Chances are good that you'll eventually wind up near this famous Big Bend resort, and although the technical riding of some of Tallahassee's single-track will not be found here, the flat five miles one way (ten miles total) of gated double-track should not be dismissed with the back of a mountain biker's glove. You'll no doubt find some of the same allure in these primitive woods that inspired gazillionaire Edward Ball to build himself a "cabin in the woods."

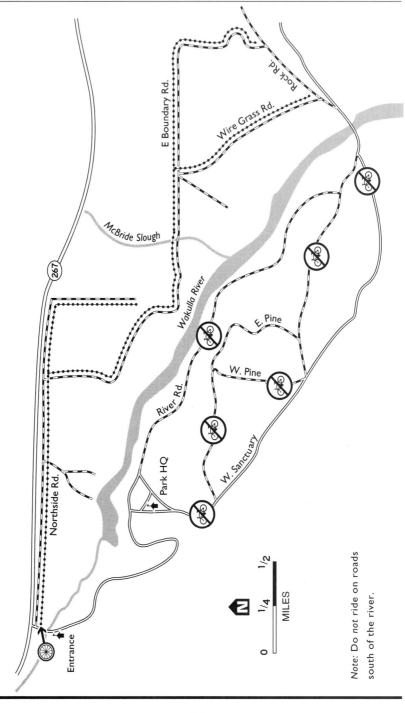

E Boundary Rd.

Rock Rd.

Wire Grass Rd.

McBride Slough

267

Wakulla River

E. Pine

W. Pine

River Rd.

W. Sanctuary

Park HQ

Northside Rd.

Entrance

N

0   1/4   1/2

MILES

Note: Do not ride on roads south of the river.

Few places so untouched by human development remain in this part of Florida, which played a role in filming some of the *Tarzan* movies here with Johnny Weismuller. Don't be surprised if you let out a blood-curdling call of the wild as you make your way saddle-bound through the towering stands of beech, cypress, and magnolias. Of course, if it's summertime and the giant painted horseflies are out looking for some tender flesh to drill, you may be screaming in earnest.

As I made my return leg to the parking lot by the entrance station, galloping along at approximately ten miles an hour, I scared up a different creature. As the yellow flies hummed behind my ears and drafted in my helmet's slipstream, I heard a rustling in the grass on my right. Thinking at first that it was an armadillo, I dropped my chin below my chinstrap and spotted a six-foot-long snake racing along beside me. Apparently, I had startled it because it peeled off and stopped after a ten-yard sprint. Later, after the pounding of my pulse subsided, I consulted a local natural history guide and determined I had been accidentally challenged by the endangered indigo "racer."

For a closer look at some of the park's more common animals, you can ride a glass-bottom boat in the river fed by the largest and deepest freshwater springs. Scads of gallinules and anhingas flock together in this birder's paradise. Bring your binoculars and snorkel for an over-and-under examination of what Tarzan left behind. Lucky us!

General location: This famous park is located approximately 15 miles south of Tallahassee.

Elevation change: There is no significant change.

Season: The fall and winter rains that visit the panhandle could make riding this trail a sloppy and soggy affair. Other than that, this trail can be enjoyed year-round.

Services: Tallahassee is Florida's capital and provides the full range of goods and services for biker and nonbiker alike. For a taste of waterfront culture as raw as the oysters they serve, head down to the mouth of the St. Marks River, where Posey's can slake the worst Gulf Coast thirsts.

Hazards: Although I didn't see one here, Wakulla Springs gets quickly associated with alligators—probably a holdover of the *Tarzan* days and "wrestlin' crocs." I would not have been surprised to have seen one strut from the Wakulla River or McBride Slough, in which case I would have either retreated or waited patiently until the unpredictable predator was again lurking under a lily pad.

Rescue index: The first half of this ride closely parallels FL 267, a fairly busy highway. The last 3 miles of this road lead into what at least feels like some remote territory. Don't forget to check in with the ranger at the gate before setting out. Otherwise, it might take a while for someone to find you on this irregularly traveled service road.

Land status: This route lies on land managed by the Florida Department of Natural Resources, Division of Recreation and Parks.

Maps: As you pay your state park user fee, ask the attendant for a park map, which represents service roads with a black, hand-drawn line. What I received was a photocopy of a topographic section showing the park and its road system, from which this book's map was made.

Finding the trail: Take FL 363 (Woodville Highway) south out of Tallahassee until it intersects with FL 267. Take a right toward the entrance to Edward Ball Wakulla Springs State Park, approximately 5 miles west. After paying the user fee ($2.75 for cars; $1 for bikers entering the park on bike), park in the lot northeast of the entrance. Ride the paved road back to FL 267. Just prior to the highway, look to the right—past the wire strung across the service road—where the trail begins.

Source of additional information:

Edward Ball Wakulla Springs State Park
550 Wakulla Park Drive
Wakulla Springs, Florida 32305
(850) 922-3633

Notes on the trail: On a weekend, the traffic noise from FL 267 will accompany you approximately 2 miles until taking the first right. Continuing straight at this point leads for about a mile to a dead end at the top of the spring feeding the tinier leg of McBride Slough. As you approach the Wakulla River—fed by giant springs covering 3 acres and generating over 14,000 gallons . . . per second—the forest changes character quickly: large stands of hickories, live oaks, sweet gums, beeches, and magnolias give way to each other. Cypress trees spread their knees in the flood plain closest to the river itself. After crossing the 2 bridges, you may have to stop at the chainlink fence on the other side of Rock Road and make the return back the way you rode. If you can continue through the gate, take a right back to the park. Allow yourself some time to explore the rest of the park, and ride the glass-bottom boat. But don't wrestle any gators.

RIDE 13 · Munson Hills

AT A GLANCE

Length/configuration: 10-mile figure eight if all loops are ridden

Aerobic difficulty: Low

Technical difficulty: Easy to moderate; a sometimes-narrow single track with a few gradual hills

RIDE 13 · Munson Hills

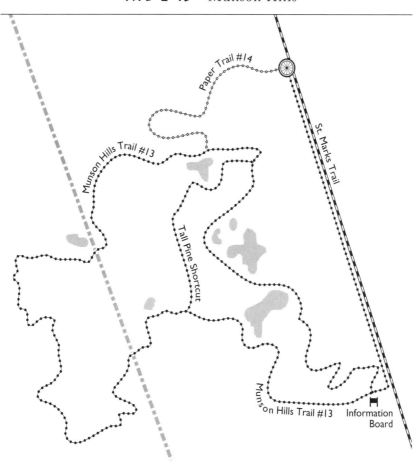

Paper Trail #14

St. Marks Trail

Munson Hills Trail #13

Tall Pine Shortcut

Munson Hills Trail #13   Information
Board

N

0   ¼   ½

MILES

and some protruding roots; can be ridden leisurely or at high speed to increase difficulty

Scenery: Long tall pines

Special comments: Something here for beginners and experts alike; 3 different routes to explore

Local riders defend this 7.5-mile loop of single-track winding through the Apalachicola National Forest as one of the best anywhere. "It's got something for everyone," claims David Gluckman, local off-road rider and author of a book-in-progress for mountain bikers over 50. "The novice can come out here and have a ball seeing what riding a bike in the dirt's all about. The expert can push it through the curves and get a demanding workout."

The yaupon and bay understory blankets the area among tall pines and occasional hardwood. Grassy areas open up around sinks—Florida ponds— where wildlife can be spotted by the surreptitious cyclist. I was rewarded by my quiet approach to the sink alongside the northern end of Tall Pine Shortcut. As I coasted to a stop on the fringe of the forest, I saw a white egret fishing the far bank shallows. While I took a drink from my bottle, I watched a mama pig—black as my grandma's frying pan—strut toward the water. Behind her, two shoats kept close, watching while mom wallowed in the mud.

During the rest of my ride, the heat of day drove all but armadillos into inactivity. Still, I kept looking for what I was sure I would see: a three-foot long, brilliantly colored coral snake. David, who had finished riding just as I was starting, said he had seen two that morning. Lucky for us. Remember, "red on black, friend to Jack" describes the arrangement of bands on a scarlet king snake; "red on yellow will kill a fellow" tells the difference between it and a coral snake, also known as the 90-second snake for the powerful neurotoxin it delivers.

General location: This off-road loop begins 1.5 miles south of the trailhead for St. Marks Trail in Tallahassee.

Elevation change: A few short, gradual climbs occur.

Season: This trail can be ridden year-round.

Services: Tallahassee, as Florida's capital and home to several universities and colleges, has a wide variety of goods and services. The trailhead for St. Marks has a store, information station, rest rooms, and water.

Hazards: Oncoming bikers should be expected . . . and alerted in a friendly voice.

Rescue index: This trail sees regular use during all times of the day throughout the year, although traffic is less heavy during summer weekday mornings. Despite being secluded and relatively remote, rescue should be quick and

The single-track at
Munson Hills bends
its way through long,
tall pines.

easy. The trail stays within 2 miles of the major asphalt, Woodville Highway
(FL 363).

Land status: This land is part of the Apalachicola National Forest.

Maps: St. Marks Trail Bikes & Blades has maps available (ask for Munson
Hills Off-Road Trail), in addition to the map posted at the trailhead's information station.

Finding the trail: Park in the large lot at the trailhead for St. Marks Trail.
Ride 1.5 miles south on asphalted St. Marks Trail. A prominent sign points to
the forest's interior and the beginning of Munson Hills' loops.

Sources of additional information:

About Bikes
411 North Magnolia Street
Tallahassee, Florida 32308-5082
(850) 942-7506

St. Marks Trail Bikes & Blades
(located at the trailhead and operated by About Bikes)
(850) 656-0001

Notes on the trail: A short connecting spur leads to the trailhead at the "kiosk," as it is sometimes called in Florida. (It's actually a bulletin board with a roof over it.) A large, custom-painted mural shows much of the flora and fauna found in a longleaf–wire grass ecosystem; a separate, number-coded drawing identifies such creations as the endangered Sherman fox squirrel and carnivorous pitcher plant.

Although no signs suggest a recommended riding direction, I began counterclockwise. It soon became obvious that the hills near Munson Slough could be easily climbed without Olympian legs. In fact, this trail can be happily ridden by most beginners. Still, the hard-core crankers come here and love it. By increasing riding speed to 10 miles an hour, the sweeping curves between pine trees demand pinpoint control to negotiate the gaps and compensate for slips in the sand by subtle, shaking hips. And if that isn't enough, just as you've cleared the trees and regained your purchase, a 4-inch root across the trail has to be hopped.

In addition to the variable skill level, at least 3 routes can be taken, depending on time—or strength—available. A 4.25-mile loop can be ridden by taking the Tall Pine Shortcut, a left turn (provided you've started out counterclockwise) conspicuously marked at the intersection with a 5-foot-tall post and sign. It dead-ends into the longer (7.5-mile) Munson Hills Loop. Take a left to complete the shortcut, or go right to finish the first leg of a 10-mile figure-eight.

RIDE 14 · Paper Trail

AT A GLANCE

Length/configuration: 1.5 miles (3 miles out-and-back)

Aerobic difficulty: Low to moderate; regular intervals of gently rolling peaks and valleys

Technical difficulty: Easy

Scenery: Young pines, hardwood forest, and yaupon shrubs

Special comments: This single-track spur can be made into a 13-mile trip by taking Paper Trail to Munson Hills

This 1.5-mile, out-and-back single-track spur (three miles total) into Munson Hills gets its name from the days when the future paper of America was carted out in longleaf pine logs. This easy ride runs through a pure stand of young pines, no doubt planted to provide the cellulose for the twenty-first century. In the quiet of an early summer morning, the tunnel

RIDE 14 · Paper Trail

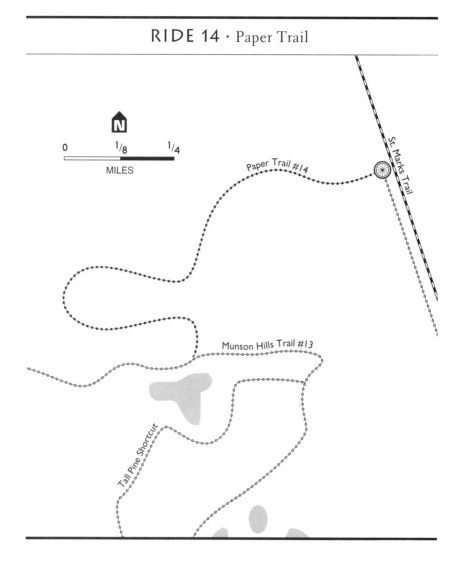

created by these trees amplifies the crunching of your tires on the sand and pine twigs.

On its final run into Munson Hills Loop, Paper Trail slithers its way among the mixed hardwood and pine forest typical of Florida's panhandle. Yaupon shrubs collect dew on their leaf tips and hang into the trail. If you're the first morning rider, you get slapped with a refreshing splash.

Before the coolness fades, you'll be on a trail that is so gently rolling it made me think what it must feel like to ride on a dolphin's back in the surf. Regular intervals of peaks and valleys occur every six to eight feet for long stretches. It's easy to coax your legs into pumping faster and faster until you're

The young longleaf pines that border Paper Trail will someday become part of Florida's annual 500-million-board-feet harvest.

catching air. Stop and regroup, however, if you begin humming the theme song for *Flipper*.

General location: This short spur is found 300 feet north of the trailhead for St. Marks Trail.

Elevation change: It's minimal, but used with great effect.

Season: The much maligned Florida summer heat and bugs do little to take away from this trail's fun. The drier months, however, do loosen the sand, especially in the curves.

Services: Tallahassee, where all things great and small can be had, lies a few minutes to the north.

Hazards: Be alert for oncoming bikers. It's cool to shout in a friendly voice, "Biker up!" Sluggish serpents sunning themselves in a blind, sandy curve could give an unpleasant surprise. Miss them if you can.

Rescue index: Should you become flatted by a fang (or worse), many fellow bikers, walkers, and rollerbladers in the nearby parking lot for St. Marks Trail would hear a sincere yell or blow on the whistle.

Land status: This is part of the Apalachicola National Forest.

Maps: An excellent map can be picked up at St. Marks Trail Bikes & Blades.

Finding the trail: Take FL 363 (Woodville Highway) south. Just past Capital Circle (US 319 and FL 261) look to the left for the large parking lot and St. Marks Trail Bikes & Blades.

Sources of additional information:

About Bikes
411 North Magnolia Street
Tallahassee, Florida 32308-5082
(850) 942-7506

St. Marks Trail Bikes & Blades
(located at the trailhead and operated by About Bikes)
(850) 656-0001

Notes on the trail: More and more people use this single-track spur to connect to the longer Munson Hills loops. A ride of more than 13 miles can be
put together by taking Paper Trail to Munson Hills. Double-track is crossed
on your way before dead-ending into Munson Hills Trail. You can, of course,
explore any of these roads, depending on your mood.

RIDE 15 · Redbug Trail

AT A GLANCE

Length/configuration: 3.5-mile loop

Aerobic difficulty: Moderate

Technical difficulty: Moderate to challenging; this
single track provides narrow chutes between trees
and several abrupt whoop-de-doos; technically satis-
fying for intermediate riders

Scenery: Tall oaks, sweet gums, and maples

Special comments: Connects to a 12-mile trail system in Phipps Park

Redbug is Southern for "chigger," the bloodsucking larva of mites. No
doubt, plenty of places exist on this 3.5-mile loop of technical single-
track where a biker could get a dose of redbug. But the itch most bikers get
comes from wanting to ride it again.

My first ride in these woods of tall oaks, sweet gums, and maples started
with what looked like a bad omen. A big-eyed man (sans goggles) rode up to
me and asked, "You haven't seen a young guy on a bike, have ya'? He's got a
bike like mine. Red helmet. Black jersey. I think he's lost."

"No," I told him. "You're the first one I've seen on the trail."

"I took off down the trail, and when I looked back, he was gone. I'm his
dad. If you see him, tell him to meet me here."

I promised him I would. But I wasn't so sure about where I was other than

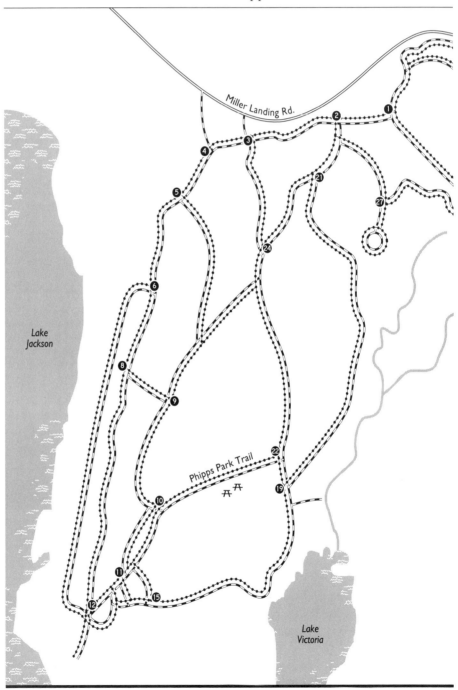

Miller Landing Rd.

Lake
Jackson

Phipps Park Trail

Lake
Victoria

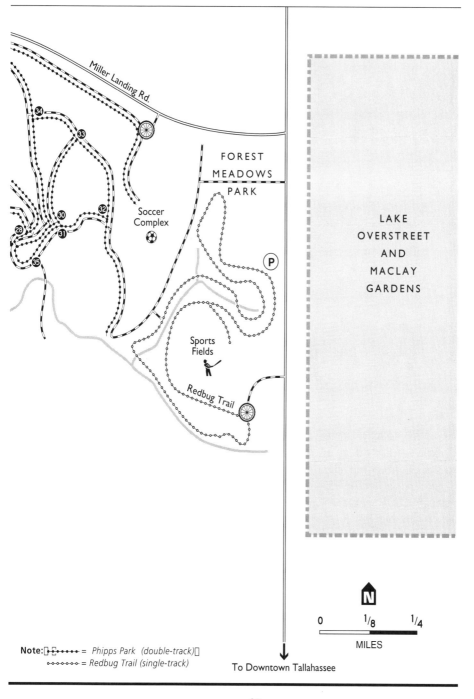

Miller Landing Rd.

34
33

FOREST
MEADOWS
PARK

Soccer
Complex

30
32
29
31
35

P

Sports
Fields

Redbug Trail

LAKE
OVERSTREET
AND
MACLAY
GARDENS

N

0   1/8   1/4

MILES

Note: = *Phipps Park (double-track)*
= *Redbug Trail (single-track)*

To Downtown Tallahassee

These two bikers
satisfy their itch to ride
on Redbug Trail.

being across from a softball diamond inside the Meridian Youth Sports Complex. I had taken, as mountain bike guide authors are prone to do, the bass ackwards approach to getting to where I was.

Quickly orienting myself, I found one of the trailheads and plunged through a parting in the pines along the edge. The wind stopped and a blanket of humidity hit me, fogging up my glasses. I could feel my tires skidding over the exposed roots and slipping in the sandy curves.

I was wondering whether the trail would allow head-on riders enough room to pass when I met two coming my way. "Biker up!" the leader called back to her buddy. As she passed me, she said, "One biker back."

"Thanks," I said and rode on to the stream in the middle of the loop. As I made my approach, I heard the unmistakable whine of a weedeater laying some brush low. At the bridge I stopped and waited for the weedwhacker to appear.

It was only a moment before a woman stepped out from behind a yaupon and took a drink from her canteen. She was a member of the local hiking club cleaning up for the National Trail Day celebration to be held the following weekend. I thanked her biker-to-hiker for contributing to such a fun trail.

General location: Meridian Youth Sports Complex, home to Redbug Trail, is located 5 miles north of downtown Tallahassee.

Elevation change: It occasionally changes abruptly, but nothing more than a biker with intermediate skills can handle.

Season: This is a trail to ride year-round.

Services: Downtown Tallahassee lies 5 miles to the south. If you can't find what you need there, you aren't looking.

Hazards: Other bikers may be heading your direction. Keep your bike under control. Sufficient speeds can be generated along the whoop-de-doos to catch air aplenty. Make sure you're expecting them and that your experience matches your speed.

Rescue index: Trail accessibility makes for easy rescues.

Land status: This is the Phipps-Overstreet Greenway, land managed jointly by the city of Tallahassee and the Northwest Florida Water Management District.

Maps: I picked up my map of Elinor Klapp–Phipps Park at About Bikes in Tallahassee. I did not find a place where I could pick one up inside the park, but you can write or call the park office and have them send you one.

Finding the trail: From downtown Tallahassee, head north on Thomasville Highway (FL 61). Almost immediately, take the left turn onto FL 155, Meridian Road, and follow it for approximately 5 miles. Signs for the park will be on the left. Look for one of the trailheads on the southern side of the tennis courts.

Source of additional information:

Elinor Klapp–Phipps Park
3540 Thomasville Road
Tallahassee, Florida 32308
(850) 891-3975

Notes on the trail: Beginning at the tennis courts, Redbug descends to a creek along a rooty chute of trees, but not before several places to launch your bike over some whoop-de-doos. The single-track is well marked with signs and blazes, virtually assuring you will not stay lost . . . for long. You can connect to the longer multi-use trail system (12 miles) inside the interior of Phipps Park by riding the service road south to the gate.

RIDE 16 · Phipps Park

AT A GLANCE

Length/configuration: 12 miles of loops; variations can be made with smaller figure-eight rides

Aerobic difficulty: Low; terrain rises and falls very gradually

Technical difficulty: Easy

Scenery: Tropical savannas, ponds, and wide-open views of Lake Jackson

Special comments: Trail's multi-use double-track is an ideal place for newcomers to off-road

The 12 miles of looping multi-use double-track developed inside Talla-hassee's Phipps Park give more of an adventure than a technical workout. For that reason, this trail system is a good place to take along the less-seasoned cyclists to give them a taste of what lies out there in the off-road world. Provided you are familiar with the trail (or carry along a map), variations of smaller figure-eight rides can be stitched together in a landscape gradually sinking toward Lake Jackson in the west.

The 500 acres between the lake and the sports complex adjacent to Meridian Road carry the biker (or hiker or horseback rider) along open stretches reminiscent of lush tropical savannas. Nearby streams have cut white banks through upland tracts of loblolly pines, and in places the water has backed up, forming ponds that are home to mallards and muskrats alike.

Stands of live oaks, embraced by thick mantles of Spanish moss, shade hummocks where picnic tables have been placed as an invitation to reflect on this area's quiet beauty. If you're lucky, you may observe deer on the move from one of the many clearings. Spots throughout the ride give wide overlooks onto Lake Jackson, fed in part by the wild Ochlockonee River, whose headwaters drain Georgia's southern swamps 50 miles to the northeast.

General location: This trail system is located a few miles north of Tallahassee.

Elevation change: Although the elevation changes as much as 100 feet, it does so fairly gradually in most places.

Season: This trail system is well maintained, holding up well to periods of either drought or rain. Ride it 52 weeks a year.

Services: All services can be found in nearby Tallahassee.

Hazards: Beware of sandy sections. If you approach them unaware—either too fast or too slow—the front wheel can be quickly twisted out of your control, leaving you de-biked and blinking in surprise. You'll see riders on horseback, as well as hikers. Yield them the trail in a courteous manner.

Rescue index: The many miles of trail, while located in a fairly urbanized area, lead into remote areas that could go unexplored for hours. Plan on self-rescue if you ride this trail.

Land status: The city of Tallahassee, along with the Northwest Florida Water Management District, keeps this land open for public use.

Maps: Call and request the Elinor Klapp–Phipps Park map from either the area's bike shops (see "Tallahassee Area Rides") or the Park Office.

Finding the trail: From downtown Tallahassee, head north on Thomasville Highway (FL 61). Almost immediately, take the left turn onto FL 155, Meridian Road, and follow it for approximately 5 miles. Signs for the park will be on the left. Look for the trailhead at the end of the service road leading south through the park.

Source of additional information:

> Elinor Klapp–Phipps Park
> 3540 Thomasville Road
> Tallahassee, Florida 32308
> (850) 891-3975

Notes on the trail: Beginning from the trailhead accessed from Miller Landing Road, each intersection has a number from 1 to 35, with 1 being the first intersection encountered traveling counterclockwise; the 34th intersection is the first one in a clockwise direction. Riding east to west generally means a downhill direction—toward Lake Jackson. Going back west to east, you'll regain the lost elevation in a rolling manner. Some lower ground around Coonbottom Loop and Swamp Forest Loop can be explored via intersections 27 (head south) and 28–31 (take the south trail to 35 where you continue south across a stream).

RIDE 17 · Fern Trail

AT A GLANCE

Length/configuration: 3.3 miles one-way or 6.6 miles out-and-back

Aerobic difficulty: Moderate to high; the ups and downs are abrupt and exaggerated

Technical difficulty: Very challenging; technical maneuvering is necessary to ride the entire length of this single-track (dangerous for riders unprepared for the technical challenge)

Scenery: Nice pine and hardwood forest; lots of birds

Special comments: Watch out for poison ivy!

Seldom will you get a chance to ride through as wide an assortment of technical single-track as Fern Trail. Add to it the fact that this 3.3-mile, one-way out-and-back (6.6 total) sits in the middle of urbania Tallahassee-style, and you've got a trail already worthy of classic reputation. But it gets better.

How many trails do you know that have a grocery store and an Italian restaurant at the trailhead? It makes my mouth water almost as much as riding some of the sections. The first section drops through a wooded area where a green and lush growth of poison ivy borders the single-track. Sets of three notched leaves with a red stem indicate the plant this trail is nicknamed for. I've broken out in a poison ivy rash twice in my cautious life, and one time was after riding this trail.

"Why did God have to make poison ivy?" my son Jared asked me after getting a particularly bad case. Part of the reason will be evident as you ride through the pine and mixed hardwood forest: birds, and plenty of them. The berries from the toxic vine are an important food source for cardinals, jays, and many other of our fine feathered friends.

Fern Trail will be food for your inner-city soul. Although it is considered technically rideable, only the experts and better will be taking the entire length without a few discretionary dismounts. How many depends on your confidence at the Cliff Jump, railroad trestle, and the Park Avenue ditch. I don't believe it gets any better than this for the city-locked, off-road cyclist.

General location: Downtown Tallahassee is the site for Fern Trail, which parallels US 90 (Mahan Drive) on the south for 2 miles.

Elevation change: Some of the elevation changes can be quite dramatic on this trail. For example, passage over a 10-foot deep stream bed is accomplished via a city sewer main.

Season: Periods of high water could make riding in the bottom of the drainage ditch inadvisable at those times. Other than that, this is an all-season trail.

Services: With a grocery store and an Italian restaurant at the trailhead and the rest of Tallahassee a short bike ride away, getting goods and services couldn't get any easier.

Hazards: Many technical maneuvers are required in order to ride the entire length. Failure to execute these moves is likely to result in dire consequences. In addition, traffic is a consideration when you cross Park Avenue and Victory Garden Drive.

Rescue index: You could be easily rescued should there prove a need.

Land status: This trail has been constructed on privately owned land. No signs are posted forbidding riding on this single-track route, however.

Maps: I picked up the Fern Trail map—the model for the map in this book—at About Bikes, at the intersection of Magnolia and Mahan drives. You might be able to acquire a similar map at another bike shop.

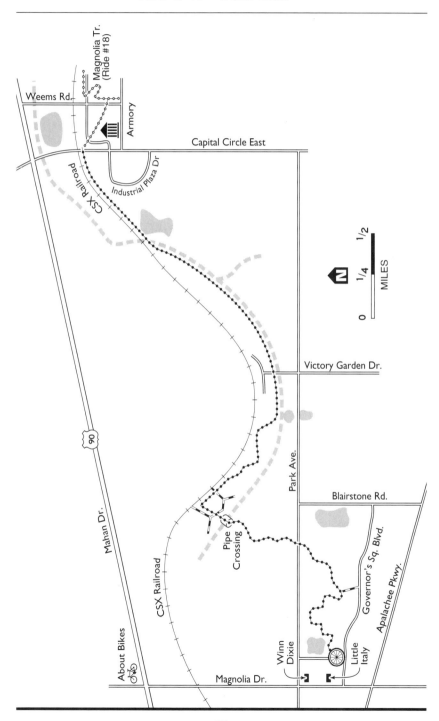

Finding the trail: From the capital, drive north on Monroe Street, taking the right onto US 90 (east). Magnolia Drive intersects with US 90 a little over a mile away. Turn right onto Magnolia Drive and turn left onto Governor's Square Boulevard just past Winn-Dixie. Park in the lot and ride behind the store to locate the hole in the fence serving as the trailhead.

Source of additional information:

About Bikes
411 North Magnolia Drive
Tallahassee, Florida 32308-5082
(850) 942-7506

Notes on the trail: This single-track receives much use; consequently, the route is easy to follow. The first half-mile section comes between Winn-Dixie and Park Avenue. Walk, or ride cautiously, across Park Avenue and continue the general descent for nearly another half-mile until you reach the sewer pipe; you should dismount and walk over it. Climb up the hill, taking the dirt road north for slightly more than a tenth of a mile where a right leads to a mile-long section north of—and above—the ditch. Before crossing the first of 2 bridges, you'll descend to the drainage ditch, cross another street (Victory Garden Drive), and cross the second bridge before you begin a climb to the train trestle. Give yourself a kick in the saddle in order to get over, and a pat on the back if you make it. Do not, however, cross over the tracks and continue with the drainage ditch. Parallel the train tracks until coming to the underpass at Capital Circle. Here you must decide whether to continue to Magnolia Trail inside Tom Brown Park or turn around and grab a pizza at the trailhead. If you've ridden the entire way (not the pipe), you can pick up your Gonzo Riding Patch. Also, don't forget to go home and use plenty of soap and warm water to scrub off any poison ivy juice sticking to your legs. If you remove it within a couple of hours after exposure, your chances of acquiring a rash are significantly reduced.

RIDE 18 · Magnolia Trail

AT A GLANCE

Length/configuration: 6-mile loop

Aerobic difficulty: High; ascents are frequent and steep

Technical difficulty: Moderate to challenging

Scenery: Spanish moss–covered live oaks, kudzu, and thick woods

Special comments: One of the more popular rides in Tallahassee area

I met and rode with two guys at Phipps Park who gave me these last words of advice: "Go to Tom Brown Park and ride the trail there." Although I had only spent a few hours with these bikers, I had developed a trust in their opinions on good places to ride off-road in the Tallahassee area. And, even though I had ridden two other trails that day, I promised the two Gonzos I would, without fail, ride Magnolia Trail, the six-mile loop of technical single-track inside Tom Brown Park.

That evening as I drove into the parking lot near the trailhead, I checked my watch. With only a little over an hour to complete the loop before the already reddening sun slipped beneath the green Florida horizon, I knew I would have to be quick about it: my usual research speed averages in the four-miles-an-hour range. (Okay, okay, I may not be fast, but I'm honest.)

The trailhead seemed deserted that Friday evening. After finding the BMX track, I saw where the narrow mountain bike trail dove into the woods northwest of it. Heading out counterclockwise, I balanced my way along a section where the ground was covered thick with ivy, although it wasn't the poison kind so common along trails in the Deep South; this time it was English ivy, giving a manicured and cultured feel to this part of the ride.

After riding for a while with my pinkies extended, I drew my focus down to a pinpoint in front of me. This trail is not a white-glove affair. Narrow chutes—so typical of the trails found in Florida—wind their way up, down, and along steeply pitched treadways.

Making the pull up from the rail bed below, I came out on a dirt road. Above me, a live oak loomed in front of a sky filled with thunderheads building below the sinking sun. The light sparkled through shreds of Spanish moss hanging from thick boughs, and I was reminded of a wizard, arms spreading a tattered tunic wide.

The image inspired me to pedal faster than I normally travel—up through a kudzu chute, threatening to grow together in places. I hammered past the tendrils as they switched my forearms and legs. I kept my ears alert for the sound of an approaching bike, wondering what tactic I would use to avoid a head-on collision in such close quarters. But the rhythm of climb-and-drop, climb-and-drop put the trail beside me in a blur, and before I was ready, I came back to the trailhead . . . wishing I could pin the sun against the sky and ride around one more time.

General location: Tom Brown Park is located just east of Capital Circle in Tallahassee, Florida, near the Armory.

Elevation change: Although no climbs go on for long, they are frequent and steep. It is this regular elevation change—often in the middle of turns—that gives this trail a special appeal.

Season: I rode this trail in early summer—before the kudzu reached maximum growth; therefore, I could easily make it through the tangle of vine.

Some of Florida's trails remain wild, thick, and tangly.

Knowing, however, the speedy growth kudzu can produce, it is possible that a few days without riders breaking through could cause strands to form a substantial gate. Little chance of that happening, though, as this trail is among the most popular rides in the Tallahassee area.

Services: Chances are good that you would not have to venture off Capital Circle, Tallahassee's perimeter highway, in order to find whatever you may need . . . quickly.

Hazards: Oncoming bikers could present a danger if you were to meet them at a high rate of speed through the kudzu patches. Exposed roots in the middle of sections requiring other maneuvers could throw you off balance.

Rescue index: The urban locale of this route makes rescue a simple affair.

Land status: Tom Brown Park is managed by the city of Tallahassee for public use from sunrise to sunset.

Maps: I picked up the detailed map of Magnolia Trail from About Bikes. An information station inside the park may have these maps available.

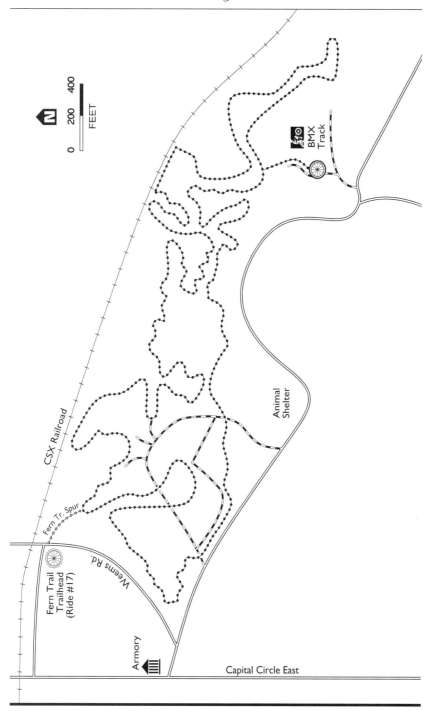

N

0 200 400
FEET

BMX Track

Animal Shelter

CSX Railroad

Fern Tr. Spur

Fern Trail Trailhead (Ride #17)

Weems Rd.

Armory

Capital Circle East

Finding the trail: From Interstate 10, exit onto US 90 (Mahan Drive, exit 31) and head west toward Tallahassee. Take a left (south) onto Capital Circle and look for the sign announcing the entrance to Tom Brown Park on your left—approximately a half-mile down. There are 2 entrances in case you miss the first one; in fact, it is easier to find the trailhead by taking the second (most southern) entrance. To do this, continue straight past the animal shelter, turning left at the next paved road. Stop as soon as you make the turn (traffic allowing) and notice the dirt road to the left. Drive down it until you see the bare banks and berms of the BMX track. The trailhead enters the forest north-northeast of the BMX track.

Source of additional information:

Tom Brown Park
Tallahassee, Florida 32304
(850) 891-3965

Notes on the trail: This route through the forest inside Tom Brown Park is well marked and easy to follow. Blazes indicate sharp turns on the single-track portion, as well as directions across and on service roads criss-crossing among the kudzu field and power line right-of-way. A short, single-track connector in the northwestern part of the loop, near the train tracks, leads to the 3.3-mile (6.6 miles total), out-and-back Fern Trail. Look for it on the right after making the climb from the rail bed approximately 2.5 miles into the loop.

CYCLING THE SUWANNEE RIVER

The dark waters of the Suwannee River roll past tall white banks of sand and limestone. The elevation of north Florida is lost along its shoals and meanders as it drops 120 feet from the Okefenokee Swamp to the Gulf of Mexico, a trip of nearly 300 miles. The most important section of the great Suwannee's run, however, is located just south of its source, along one of the many springs that feed up from limestone caverns.

White Springs, Florida, is not a big place; only two flashing lights are needed to control the light town traffic. But if you ride off-road in Florida, you have heard of the great trails nearby. During the period when the Save Our Rivers program was buying up critical watershed around the state, the Suwannee Bicycle Association (SBA) incorporated its efforts to bring together the leadership of its members with the policy makers of the Suwannee River Water Management District. Result? Fifteen trails and counting.

The museum for Stephen Foster's musical efforts sits on the banks of the river he made famous, just down the road from where the SBA has its office. Of all the parks I stayed in during my Florida research, the one in White Springs proved to be the best bargain. Not only was the camping fee the lowest I encountered, but its location allowed me to use it as a beginning to some of the state's better single-track. With just a short mile or so on US 41 for the connector, I was able to pedal a total of five different trails, most of which included tight trails along the river.

I have long associated the rocking rhythms and pleasures of riding a mountain bike with paddling a canoe. For the likewise-thinking off-road cyclist, there is no better place in Florida than the upper Suwannee River to come for a vacation combining the two means of exploration. But if you don't paddle, don't worry. You'll find more than enough two-wheeled fun to keep you happy all year round.

Sources of additional information:

Suwannee River Water Management District
9225 County Road 49
Live Oak, Florida 32060
(904) 362-1001 or
(800) 226-1066 (Florida only)

Suwannee Bicycle Association
P.O. Box 247
White Springs,Florida 32096
(904) 397-2347

RIDE 19 · Gar Pond

AT A GLANCE

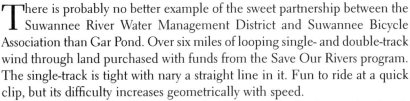

Length/configuration: 6 miles of loops, combination of single- and double-tracks

Aerobic difficulty: Moderate; more turns than hills;
gently rolls in places

Technical difficulty: Moderate; difficulty increases
with speed; single-track near the river is narrow,
windy, and has its share of roots

Scenery: Gar Pond, thick woods, and river bank vegetation and wildlife

Special comments: Smooth track allows for fast riding

There is probably no better example of the sweet partnership between the
Suwannee River Water Management District and Suwannee Bicycle
Association than Gar Pond. Over six miles of looping single- and double-track
wind through land purchased with funds from the Save Our Rivers program.
The single-track is tight with nary a straight line in it. Fun to ride at a quick
clip, but its difficulty increases geometrically with speed.

The wildlife and landscape seemed to blur into the background as I took
advantage of Gar Pond's smooth track. I stopped at the pond and saw, to my
slight surprise, no gars. Or gators. But I'm sure they were both there, watching me as I made my way along the bank. I scared a great blue heron from its
perch on a downed cypress where the single-track turns away from the pond.
But other than that, the only other living thing I saw on this Monday morning ride was a tiny black snake whose tail I accidentally clipped, causing it to
writhe like it was on a hot rock.

General location: Gar Pond is located off US 41, southeast (barely) of
White Springs.

Elevation change: In places the land rolls, making for fun, quick descents.

Season: Some areas become flooded during periods of heavy rain.

Services: White Springs has many of the basics. A wider selection can be
found in Lake City, but you may have to go all the way to Gainesville.

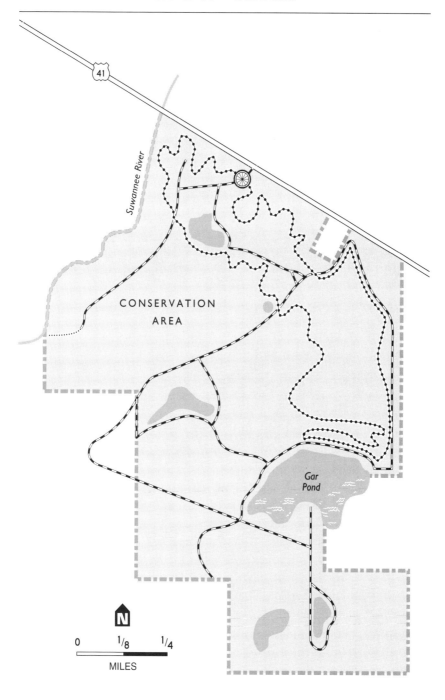

41

Suwannee River

CONSERVATION
AREA

Gar
Pond

N

0   1/8   1/4
MILES

Shafts of sunlight stab the forest floor through a canopy of live oak limbs.

Hazards: Short stumps of saplings can catch a pedal or turn a tire unexpectedly. The trail has an overall smooth track, but the obstacles require caution, especially the first few times you ride the course.

Rescue index: If you need a rescue, this is a good place to receive one quickly, especially on the weekend.

Land status: This land is managed by the Suwannee River Water Management District and open for public use.

Maps: An enlarged map is posted at the information station at the trailhead. You can also request the complete packet of off-road biking sites from the Suwannee Bicycle Association or just get the map for Gar Pond (Suwannee Valley Conservation Area).

Finding the trail: Exit Interstate 75 onto County Road 136, heading east toward White Springs. Turn right on US 41 (at the flashing light) and go approximately 2 miles to cross the river. Look to the right for Miss Lilly's Package Store. The information station is found 20 yards south of the parking lot.

Sources of additional information:

Suwannee River Water Management District
9225 County Road 49
Live Oak, Florida 32060
(904) 362-1001 or
(800) 226-1066 (Florida only)

Suwannee Bicycle Association
P.O. Box 247
White Springs, Florida 32096
(904) 397-2347

Notes on the trail: Begin riding on the double-track heading south. After about a quarter mile, look for the white blazes that signal the beginning of the single-track on the right. The gatorbacks on the trail will keep you alert, as will the tight turns and occasional sections of loose sand. I arrived at the small sink left from the days when the excavation for the bridge embankment took place and wondered if I had come to Gar Pond (I had left my map in the car). But Gar Pond lies to the east, and the single-track hugs its north shore before diving back into the thick understory. As the single-track gets closer to the river, the trail gets more rolling and rooty, with some great spots to work on short descents. It was so inviting that I forgot my promise to myself to go slowly and take notes. The last mile or so comes close to US 41 as well, where the white noise of traffic comes down from above.

RIDE 20 · White Springs and Bridge-to-Bridge Trails

AT A GLANCE

Length/configuration: 8.5-mile out-and-back if all trails are ridden

Aerobic difficulty: Low to moderate; flat and speedy in places, slow-paced and windy in others, and some gentle rolling by the river

Technical difficulty: Moderate; double-track is easy, but single-track requires some technical savvy

Scenery: Thick vegetation and woods, a couple of nice spots for gazing out onto the river

Special comments: This ride offers something for everyone

White Springs Trail follows double-track for a total of four miles out-and-back, but I would guess that it is seldom ridden without adding on the 4.5-mile bridge-to-bridge single-track between the Suwannee River's intersections with US 41 and County Road 136. My ride of this deep forest course started from the double-track coming from the boat ramp. I parked at Gar Pond's trailhead, riding a short section of US 41 (after riding the fast single-track of Gar Pond).

The straight, flat double-track service road (gated) provides a good warm-up before getting to the technical moves required on the single-track. The grassy track has grown over to stitch the sugar sand back together again, creating a firm surface and a fast pace. The move onto the single-track calls more on agility than strength. The thick understory clings to the sides of the trail like a cloak, wrapping riders with frond, leaf, and branch. Gatorbacks rise up in the middle of the trail and force a slower ride.

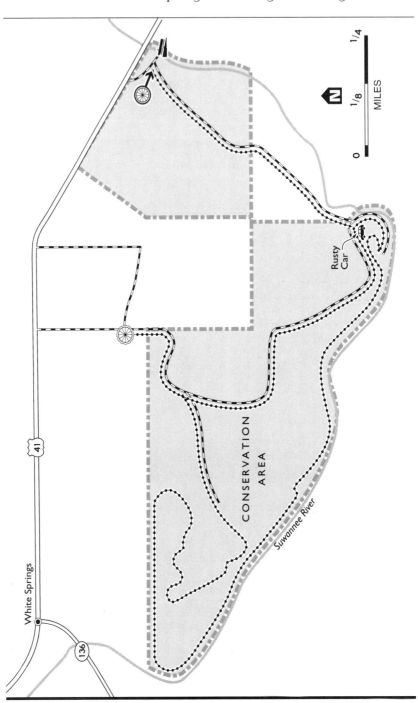

Sights like this will keep you coming back to bike the banks of the Suwannee River.

General location: White Springs is located in White Springs, way down upon the Suwannee River.

Elevation change: You can expect some rolling by the riverside; short and sweet stuff.

Season: This trail can be easily ridden all year long.

Services: White Springs has the basics, but a trip to Gainesville will be needed for the special items.

Hazards: There are tire-stabbers—short, small sapling stumps approximately 3 inches high—in places, and the exposed roots are especially treacherous when wet. Watch for other bikers and hikers and follow the recommended route.

Rescue index: It should be no trouble to effect a rescue on the weekends; the weekdays, however, could make for an extended wait.

Land status: This is land managed by the Suwannee River Water Management District; the trails are maintained by the kind folks of Suwannee Bicycle Association.

Maps: You can request a map of White Springs, or any of the other SBA trails on Suwannee River Water Management District lands, from SBA.

Finding the trail: Exit Interstate 75 onto County Road 136, heading east toward White Springs. There are 2 trailheads in White Springs for White Springs Trail. The first, Adams Memorial Drive, is on the right, 8 blocks south on US 41. Park in the lot for the baseball fields or directly across the street from the parking lot. The other trailhead is located at the US 41 bridge and boat ramp; turn right before crossing the bridge onto the paved service road.

Sources of additional information:

Suwannee River Water Management District
9225 County Road 49
Live Oak, Florida 32060
(904) 362-1001 or (800) 226-1066
(Florida only)

Suwannee Bicycle Association
P.O. Box 247
White Springs, Florida 32096
(904) 397-2347

Notes on the trail: I began this trail at the gated double-track at the US 41 bridge and boat ramp. From there I rode approximately a half mile until I reached an intersection marked by a rusty car, where I turned right. Three quarters of a mile later, I turned left for a quarter-mile section of double-track that becomes the single-track Bridge-to-Bridge Trail. I saw a sign requesting bikers to dismount at one point in The Gorge, where root erosion has damaged a bank. The White Springs double-track returns a short distance before you see the rusty car again on the left. The US 41 bridge is straight ahead.

RIDE 21 · Big Shoals

AT A GLANCE

Length/configuration: 18-mile loop

Aerobic difficulty: Low to moderate; combination of Jeep roads, fire lanes, and single-track make for variety

Technical difficulty: Moderate; erosion, roots, and other natural obstacles can be dangerous for unaware riders

Scenery: Whitewater, limestone, thick woods filled with various wildlife

Special comments: Some of the best riding in Florida, but do be prepared for erosion, roots and other natural obstacles.

The Suwannee Bicycle Association touts Big Shoals as a place where "scores of miles of jeep roads, fire lanes, and single-track can easily keep an off-road bicyclist busy exploring for an entire weekend." At least. The typical 18-mile loop that SBA members have put together represents some of the best riding anywhere in the state. Located on the opposite shore of Little Shoals, over 4,000 acres in the conservation area–state forest combo are home to scads of deer, turkeys, wild pigs, and the endangered gopher tortoise (what one old-timer called "Hoover Chicken").

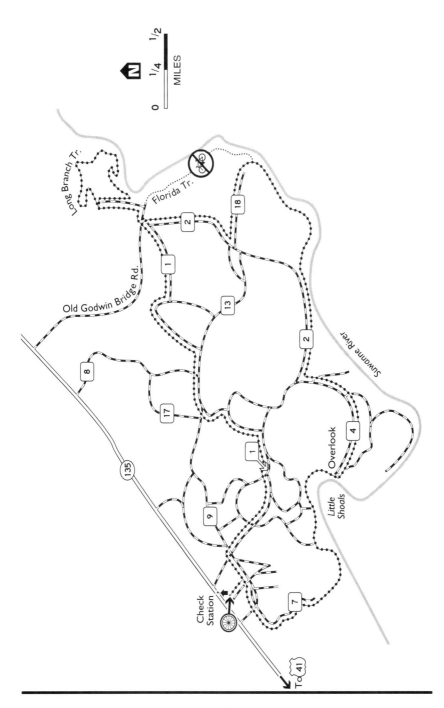

Biking off-road at Big Shoals can seem like pedaling the forest primeval.

It's also home to some of Florida's scant whitewater, Big Shoals, whose roar over exposed limestone ledges announces the natural attraction as you ride your way onto the single-track north and upriver. Some sections have been posted in this area as sensitive, and should be covered gently . . . by foot. If you're lucky, a quiet approach may allow you to see the beaver, whose pond made me ponder this toothsome wonder's intelligence.

General location: Big Shoals Conservation Area is located 2 miles northeast of White Springs.

Elevation change: You will have a chance to try out a smaller ring than you ever thought you'd use in Florida.

Season: Hunting is occasionally allowed here, so call if you're in doubt about the season. Periods of heavy rain will make portions of this trail unsuitable for riding.

Services: White Springs has the basics, but you will have to travel to Gainesville for more specialized services.

Hazards: Hunters, at times, will be out and about. Also, some of the track has roots and slick obstacles that will upend an unwary biker. Vehicles are on some sections as well.

Rescue index: This is a popular destination all the time, but especially on the weekend. Should you need someone's assistance, it shouldn't take more than several hours in most cases. Still, sections are remote enough that you should plan on being self-sufficient for the duration.

Land status: This land is managed jointly by the Suwannee River Water Management District, Florida Division of Forestry, and Florida Department of Environmental Protection Division of Recreation and Parks.

Maps: An enlarged map of the area is posted at the information station near the check station. For maps of Big Shoals and other lands managed by SRWMD (maintained by the SBA), contact the SBA.

Finding the trail: Exit Interstate 75 onto County Road 136 and head north to White Springs. At the flashing light, turn right onto US 41. At the next flashing light, turn left onto County Road 135 (known locally as Woodpecker Route and signed that way after you make the turn). Approximately a mile and a half down on the right, look for the signed entrance to Big Shoals. Park at the check station and head south behind gated Road 7 (to the right after the entrance road dead-ends).

Sources of additional information:

Suwannee River Water Management District
9225 County Road 49
Live Oak, Florida 32060
(904) 362-1001 or (800) 226-1066
(Florida only)

Suwannee Bicycle Association
P.O. Box 247
White Springs, Florida 32096
(904) 397-2347

Notes on the trail: Begin the counterclockwise loop by heading south onto gated Road 7, which turns into a single-track that comes close to the Suwannee's shore across from Little Shoals. Take care in certain sections on the single-track; it is wet and prone to erosion, especially if any skidding occurs. (But you wouldn't skid anyway, would you?) The single-track feeds into Road 4, which leads to Road 2. Take a right at the Road 4–Road 1 intersection and ride behind the gate on another section that requires extra caution before more single-track appears at the blue marker—the color of more challenging trail ahead. As you approach the overlook for Big Shoals, notices request that bikes be walked to minimize erosion (go ahead, real men and women really do walk their bikes). And if you want, you can continue walking out on the yellow-blazed Hiking Trail, or if you've had enough of hoofing it, ride out on Road 18, which intersects with Road 2. Roads 1 and 2 come together near the ranger's residence close to Old Godwin Road. Of course, if you've had enough mileage for one day, you can turn west on Road 1 and head back to the check station. But some time or another, ride the single-track section (Long Branch Trail) north of Old Godwin Road. When you reach Old Godwin Road, turn right and look for the gated road leading to the left. If you've walked out on the Hiking Trail, the road will be on your right before you come to the ranger's house.

RIDE 22 · Little Shoals, Deep Creek Conservation Area

AT A GLANCE

Length/configuration: 3.5-mile loop

Aerobic difficulty: Low; mostly flat terrain, and a short ride

Technical difficulty: Easy; during dry weather double-track is sandy and harder to pedal, but otherwise a cinch

Scenery: Woodsy ride to the river

Special comments: A nice ride after a rigorous day at longer trails nearby, or a good short trip for beginners

The 3.5-mile loop of sandy double-track comes last on the list of White Springs in-town, off-road rides, but it does make the list. It is typically tacked on by Suwannee bikers as the cool-down after riding other nearby trails—Big Shoals, Gar Pond, and Bridge-to-Bridge (aka White Springs). But you can ride it as a short, separate ride to the old ford where the Suwannee oxbows and spend some time fishing and swimming at the former ford.

You may have to fight off the folks who are fishing, though. Great blue herons, egrets, and osprey take their limit, as do river otters and alligators. And, as I rode one evening, I was passed by two grizzled men pulling a boat on a trailer. They explained to me as I caught up to them at the put-in that they were headed out to run a "trot line," baited hooks on lines tied to trees or branches. When I asked what they were hoping to find on the other end of the line, one guy said, "Channel cats. Some of 'em are as long as a man is tall."

General location: Little Shoals is located in White Springs.

Elevation change: On this side of the river, little elevation change occurs, unlike what you'll find upriver at Big Shoals.

Season: This is an all-season ride; however, there can be times of either too much water or too little. When the track dries out, it can be too sandy to cycle.

Services: White Springs has the basics. For more specialized services, you can take your pick: Tallahassee (west), Jacksonville (east), or Gainesville (south).

Hazards: Motorized vehicles have access to this route; some of them might be pulling boats on trailers.

RIDE 22 · Little Shoals, Deep Creek Conservation Area

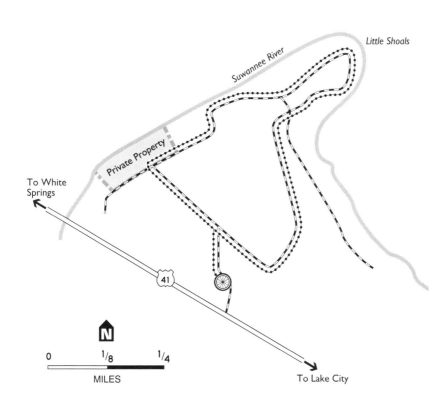

Rescue index: This is a short trail and easily accessible; rescue should not be a problem.

Land status: This land is managed by the Suwannee River Water Management District.

Maps: An enlarged map of Little Shoals is posted at the information station by the entrance. You can request this map and maps to other SRWMD lands allowing bicycling from the Suwannee Bicycle Association.

Finding the trail: Exit Interstate 75 onto County Road 136 toward White

Springs. At the flashing light, turn right onto US 41 south. Cross the river, and before you reach the agricultural inspection station, look to the left for the dirt road crossing the railroad tracks. The information station will be down the short hill.

Sources of additional information:

Suwannee River Water Management District
9225 County Road 49
Live Oak, Florida 32060
(904) 362-1001 or (800) 226-1066
(Florida only)

Suwannee Bicycle Association
P.O. Box 247
White Springs, Florida 32096
(904) 397-2347

Notes on the trail: The short approach from the road allows for a right turn that begins a counterclockwise route to the river. After approximately a mile, the spur leading to the river passes a dirt road coming in from the right. The main loop continues left at this intersection and the next. After reaching private land on the right (about a half mile later) turn left to go back to the trailhead.

RIDE 23 · Stephen Foster State Folk Culture Center

AT A GLANCE

Length/configuration: 3-plus miles of looping double-track

Aerobic difficulty: Not much to get in a huff about here

Technical difficulty: Sandy spots provide the only difficulty

Scenery: Palmetto thickets between limestone sinks

Special comments: Keep an eye out for wildlife

With all the other choices for off-road biking in the White Springs area, the temptation may be to overlook this approximately three-mile, double-track loop. But don't. It gives the off-road cyclist at least three more miles, plus a combination of other loops and fire-road single-track. You will also like taking a two-wheeled tour on asphalt of the rest of the 247-acre state recreation area.

The conservation area's landscape does not dramatically differ from that of the rest of the Suwannee River region, so expect to ride in palmetto thickets growing between hardwood hammocks and limestone sinks. Coyotes cavort

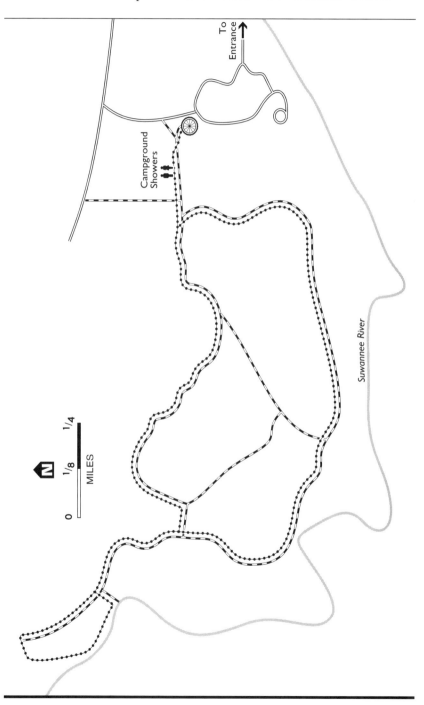

with you in this protected environment, as do gray foxes, gopher tortoises, deer, and turkey. Don't be surprised to hear rustling in the saw palmetto fronds of large, dark-furred, unidentified mammals. (It could've been a bear; I don't know.)

General location: This state folk culture center lies in downtown White Springs.

Elevation change: There is no appreciable elevation change on the double-track. The culture center's paved roads have a slight elevation change.

Season: This is an all-season biking site.

Services: White Springs can provide the basics; the park has camping with accompanying showers and rest rooms.

Hazards: You may meet hikers on these trails; otherwise, expect few hazards.

Rescue index: This small park has a rather large number of visitors. You should not worry about a lengthy rescue here.

Land status: This land is managed by the Florida Department of Environmental Protection, Division of Parks and Recreation.

Maps: The entrance station has plenty of maps; just ask for the map to the Stephen Foster: Swift Creek Conservation Area–Carter Camp Trail when making the request from the Suwannee Bicycle Association.

Finding the trail: Exit Interstate 75 onto County Road 136, heading east toward White Springs. Turn left at US 41 (the flashing light) and go down the hill one block to the entrance to the Stephen Foster Culture Center on the left.

Sources of additional information:

Stephen Foster Folk Culture Center
P.O. Drawer G
White Springs, Florida 32096
(904) 397-4331

Suwannee Bicycle Association
P.O. Box 247
White Springs, Florida 32096
(904) 397-2347

Notes on the trail: Although this trail is fairly easy to follow, there are a few critical junctions. Look for the double-track trailhead behind the Carillon Tower, either just before the camping area on the left or within the camping area. The first significant intersection occurs approximately a quarter mile in, where a left turn takes you through some of the palmetto thicket near the river. You'll pass at least 2 roads heading back toward the main loop, but continue straight until you either come to a dead end or notice a double-track to the left. If you take the short double-track southwest toward the river, look for a single-track fire road to the right and ride it north to where it returns to the double-track. If you dead-end on the double-track, look to the left for the single-track fire road that becomes a double-track that you turn left on to get back to the main trail. Once back on the main trail, take the first and next lefts. Two other roads will come in from the left (you're welcome to explore, but they don't go far) before you need to bear left at an intersection approximately half a mile later. Stay straight to return to the trailhead either in the camping area or behind the Carillon Tower, from which you will probably hear some of Stephen Foster's more famous tunes: "Oh! Susanna," "Camptown Races," "Jeanie with the Light Brown Hair," "My Old Kentucky Home," and, yes, Florida's state song, "Old Folks at Home."

RIDE 24 · The Spirit of the Suwannee

AT A GLANCE

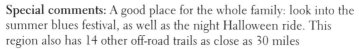

Length/configuration: Several loops totaling 10 miles

Aerobic difficulty: Wide, mostly flat loops make for a relaxing ride

Technical difficulty: Easy

Scenery: Dense forest

Special comments: A good place for the whole family: look into the summer blues festival, as well as the night Halloween ride. This region also has 14 other off-road trails as close as 30 miles

The nearly ten miles of trail open to off-road biking in this park are wide enough for a golf cart and just as easy to ride, making a series of several loops. The dense upland forest on the banks of the upper Suwannee River shelters many deer and birds, in addition to a healthy population of gopher tortoises. You'll probably see them all—including the golf cart—if you decide to stay a few days in the neighborhood.

The day before I arrived to ride the trails, the Spirit of the Suwannee had hosted a blues concert that began at noon and went for nearly 12 hours, concluding with the king, B.B. I didn't find out about it until it was too late, but I've put in my request for next year. I may even come down a week early to take in a couple of days' paddling on Florida's great Suwannee River, sourced from Georgia's famous Okefenokee Swamp.

The park was originally built as a county recreation area under one of the federal government's giveaways intended to encourage development of public lands. The local population (along with the rest of the nation) was suffering from too much TV and disco, and after the gate stayed locked for two years, the Cornetts bought the land and brought a vision that included "getting out in the woods, on the water . . . and listening to some good music." You say you don't like the blues? How about some bluegrass then? Or you can join the campers and locals who've got an axe of their own to grind, sitting around under the "pickin' shed."

RIDE 24 · The Spirit of the Suwannee

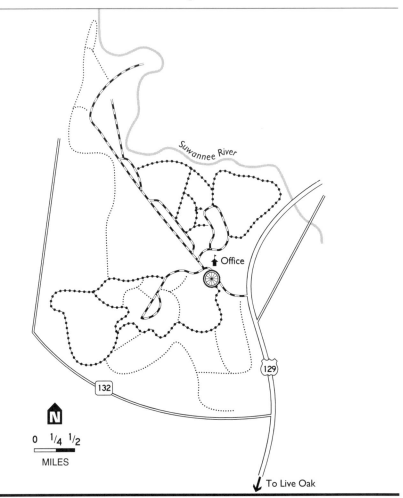

Combine all the park's attractions with the fact that the region has some-where in the neighborhood of 14 other off-road biking trails—all within a half hour's drive—and you have all the reasons you need to tap into the Spirit of the Suwannee.

General location: Spirit of the Suwannee is located north of Live Oak near the Georgia border.

Elevation change: There is some change here, but you probably won't notice unless you head down to the river.

Season: If it's happening anywhere, it's probably happening here at Spirit of the Suwannee. My research took place in what is Florida's off-season for

The trail at Spirit of the Suwannee is a good place for the whole family to spin time together.

camping, the summer. But you couldn't tell inside the park. You may want to keep abreast of the rainfall in this area; several extremely high floods put parts of the park under water. Try to picture that as you look down on this river at the canoe put-in.

Services: Live Oak has more than the basics, even providing some specialties. Either Gainesville or Tallahassee can fill the complete list of needs. But you won't need to leave the park for anything except riding some of the other nearby trails.

Hazards: Others—hikers included, with the possibility of horses on some trails—may be met head-on, but the biggest hazard is running out of time before you run out of things to do.

Rescue index: All you need to do is give a good yell and you're likely to bring someone to your aid within a few minutes.

Land status: This is private property, which charges a (small) day-use fee to bikers.

Maps: The front office (on the right a hundred yards or so after you enter) has a current map of the trails open for cycling.

Finding the trail: North of Live Oak, exit Interstate 75 onto US 129 heading south. Just after crossing the Suwannee River, look for the park's entrance on your right. The trailhead is on the left before you get to the restaurant.

Source of additional information:

The Spirit of the Suwannee
3076 95th Drive
Live Oak, Florida 32060
(904) 364-1683

Notes on the trail: Some of the trails can be temporarily opened or closed due to current conditions, but you can expect a fairly groomed surface making a southerly loop toward Rees Lake, with its ring of cypress trees lining the shore. A wildlife sanctuary lies southwest of the lake, and north of that a "fright trail" was constructed as part of the park's Halloween celebration-on-bike—night-riding only. The park's north trails loop along the Suwannee River's high chalky banks. Plans are not definite, but with biking's popularity in Florida showing no signs of stopping, it is a pretty safe bet to see more trails being cut in to take advantage of some of the park's undeveloped acres.

RIDE 25 · Camp Branch

AT A GLANCE

Length/configuration: 2.5 mile out-and-back (5 miles total)

Aerobic difficulty: Low; only a rise and fall at the trail's start—after that it's flat

Technical difficulty: Easy; mostly flat double-track; a single-track loop around Disappearing Creek is a short, highly technical ride for the more experienced

Scenery: Nice woods, Disappearing Creek, Suwanee River, and a lot of blooming plants in the spring and fall

Special comments: A nice ride for the whole family

This 2.5-mile, out-and-back (five miles total) double-track was described to me as a "boring trail," and that was my first impression, too. But after taking a look at the hill on the other side of the wire gate (which I jumped over on my bike like a log), I knew I had to check out this unassuming course on the north shore of the Suwannee.

After the initial drop into and climb out of the swale behind Camp Branch, I turned the crankarms slowly, enjoying the autumn tint on the leaves of sweet gums. Goldenrod shot out spikes of flowers, and an electric yellow and black butterfly danced nearby, then moved on to the soft purple four-foot-tall stalks of blazing star. I saw blue-blazed single-track going off to the right, overgrown in its harvest garb, and I perked up.

RIDE 25 · Camp Branch

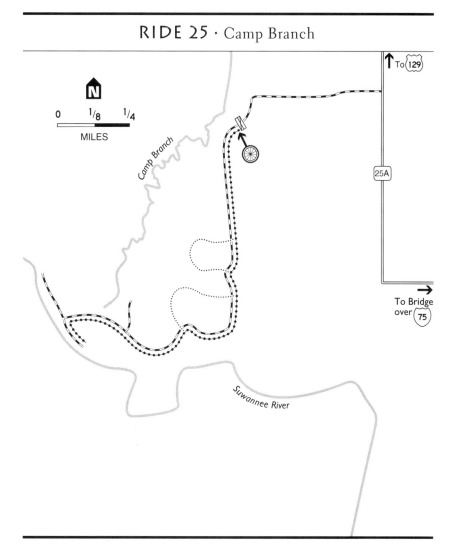

I normally would have explored the single-track right away, but I kept straight on the double-track another eighth of a mile, noticing where the single-track hooked back in. At this point I came up on what I later determined was the ride's mission—two gopher tortoises, one on its back and the other looking upset. I figured this was not an interrupted tortoise tryst, but a genuine endangered species emergency, so I got off and put the one back on its feet again. The way that turtle looked at me as it bobbed off into the palmetto thicket, I wouldn't have been surprised to hear a raspy "thank you" come out of its mouth.

General location: Camp Branch is located among the grouping of approximately 15 trails groomed by the Suwannee Bicycle Association.

Elevation change: Although the opening drop and climb promised a trail where elevation might play a role, the only significant elevation changes I saw afterward were along Disappearing Creek and going down to the river.

Season: This is an all-season trail. Enjoy.

Services: An information station has been placed at the gate; other than that, bring your other supplies. For replenishment, head to White Springs for the basics, and include a stop at the Suwannee Bicycle Association's headquarters for all kinds of information and friendly folks.

Hazards: You will have few, if any, hazards to contend with along this easy trail.

Rescue index: Providing you have a partner, rescue should be easy to effect. The roads are in good shape and close to an interstate.

Land status: This land is managed by the Suwannee River Water Management District and is open to the public.

Maps: SBA has maps of Camp Branch at its office in White Springs. You'll see an enlarged map at the information station at the wire gate.

Finding the trail: Exit either Interstate 10 or Interstate 75 onto US 129. From I-75 head south and turn left onto County Road 132, approximately 2.5 miles away. From I-10 head north approximately 6 miles (crossing the Suwannee River) and turn right onto CR 132. After about 1.5 miles, look for County Road 25A on the right (just past a hardware store) and follow it for roughly 3 miles. You'll pass a truck weigh station on I-75 on your left (on the other side of the fence) just before the road curves to the right. Look for the dirt road on the right just after this curve. It leads past an old rusted gate and goes under the power line. Take this dirt road to the wire gate, park, and ride the double-track behind the gate—down, then up a hill.

Sources of additional information:

Suwannee River Water Management District
9225 County Road 49
Live Oak, Florida 32060
(904) 362-1001 or
(800) 226-1066 (Florida only)

Suwannee Bicycle Association
P.O. Box 247
White Springs, Florida 32096
(904) 397-2347

Notes on the trail: The double-track offers little challenge, either in terrain or direction. It goes straight for a little over a mile, then dog-legs to the right in a meandering course for another mile or so. A short spur to the right leads to a blue-blazed loop around Disappearing Creek. I was told that the blue-blazed sections (single-track of a highly technical nature in places) are for the more adventurous at heart. The double-track continues down to the Suwannee River via either the left or right turn.

RIDE 26 · Allen Mill Pond

AT A GLANCE

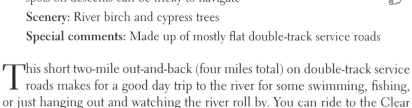

Length/configuration: 2-mile out-and-back (4 miles total)

Aerobic difficulty: Low; a few slight grades

Technical difficulty: Easy to moderate; some sandy spots on descents can be tricky to navigate

Scenery: River birch and cypress trees

Special comments: Made up of mostly flat double-track service roads

This short two-mile out-and-back (four miles total) on double-track service roads makes for a good day trip to the river for some swimming, fishing, or just hanging out and watching the river roll by. You can ride to the Clear Spring source, which gushes out anywhere from 4,500 to 45,000 gallons per minute before it reaches the murky red confluence with the Suwannee River less than a half mile downstream.

The double-track is not a technical workout, although the remnants of an old sand mine have spilled out on a slight grade. The big, soft ruts can catch the front tire (going slightly downhill at this point) and knock it around like a bobcat catching a chipmunk. When you're prepared for it, it's a lot of fun. If it sneaks up on you, watch out. You could be thrown quicker than a cat's swat. Churning through the white stuff is a significant challenge even on level ground, but you will find the upper limit of your legs' explosive strength when you get a hill with a sandy purchase.

I rode this trail in late summer when handlebar-high grasses and flowers were growing in the middle of the trail. Spider webs larger than a bike helmet were strung across the trail at various heights. The low ones wrapped around my face and glasses, creating an immediate urge to reach up and claw them off. Most of the time I would stop first, but there were times when I almost wrecked in my haste to become unwebbed. I know bikers who—at this time of year—carry web sticks in front of them to knock down the clingy strings on the "out," returning full speed on the "back" along a web-free track.

But speed is not necessary here at Allen Pond. The joy of riding this trail comes from other sources. As I made my way under a stretch of tall pines shading the trail, the scream of a sharp-shinned hawk tore the morning air. I stopped and looked up at this acrobat wheeling through the thick maze of

RIDE 26 · Allen Mill Pond

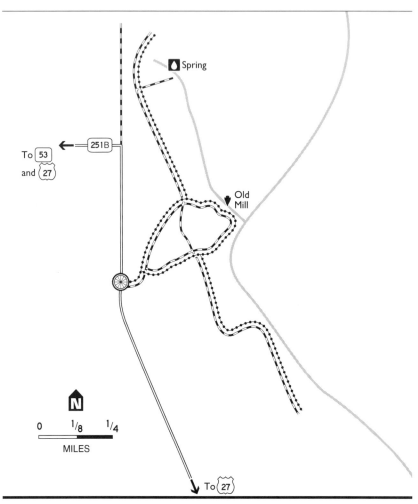

boughs. After the bird disappeared, I rode through a thick scattering of loblolly cones, bobbing and leaning in my own aerial dance.

General location: Allen Mill Pond Trail is located just southwest of White Springs, but just northeast of San Pedro Bay.

Elevation change: The descent to the river and spring marks the only remarkable change in elevation.

Season: This is an all-season trail.

Services: The basics can be found in Dowling Park, a curious community concept. The next largest and closest cities are Live Oak (to the northeast)

River birch and cypress shade the banks of the Suwannee River near Allen Mill.

and Perry (to the west). Either Gainesville or Tallahassee can provide all necessities.

Hazards: After having contracted 2 doses of poison ivy in 2 consecutive weeks, I was especially anxious to avoid the shin-high growth I saw in the double-track down to the river. You may encounter vehicles on certain sections; usually their presence can be determined by excessively sandy ruts.

Rescue index: You are never far from help.

Land status: This land is managed by the Suwannee River Water Management District.

Maps: You can request maps of Allen Mill Pond from the Suwannee Bicycle Association.

Finding the trail: Exit Interstate 75 onto County Road 136 heading west toward Live Oak and continuing to Dowling Park. Turn right onto CR 250 and cross the river. The first paved road to the left is CR 251, where you turn and drive approximately 6 miles to the left turn onto CR 251B. After about

2 miles, a hard right turn marks the intersection nearest the Allen Mill Pond entrance road to the left, approximately one-half mile after the right turn.

Sources of additional information:

Suwannee River Water Management District
9225 County Road 49
Live Oak, Florida 32060
(904) 362-1001 or (800) 226-1066
(Florida only)

Suwannee Bicycle Association
P.O. Box 247
White Springs, Florida 32096
(904) 397-2347

Notes on the trail: After starting out toward the river, look for a gated double-track turning right. It's less than a half mile to the river and back to the turn down to the old mill site. The road has tall banks, and some of the undergrowth is poison to touch. After reaching the river, head across the small meadow (northeast) toward the old mill site. The next road to the right leads up to the springhead and back for a total distance of less than a mile.

RIDE 27 · Holton Creek

AT A GLANCE

Length/configuration: Series of Forest Service loops ranging from an 18-mile loop to one that is less than a mile

Aerobic difficulty: Low; terrain is mostly flat with some gently rolling hills

Technical difficulty: Easy

Scenery: Holton Creek's magical rise from underground, Florida's Champion Cypress trees, and numerous water-filled basins (complete with wetland wildlife)

Special comments: The longer rides here are best

A system of sandy, but basically level, Forest Service roads connect in a variety of loops, ranging from an 18-miler down to one less than a mile long. But I recommend the longer rides in this Land of a Thousand Sinks. In this mysterious land, entire rivers disappear before your eyes. One such river, the Alapaha, flows out of Georgia on top but goes subterranean soon thereafter, only to pool up at Holton Creek and other rises.

It is worth the ride to Holton Creek, if for no other reason than to contemplate one of these rises. It tweaks the imagination to watch this dark water appear—totally surrounded by tall limestone banks except for one opening, where it moves slowly downstream to the Suwannee River a mile away.

Subterranean currents—like the dark waters of Holton Creek—break free from the many limestone channels running underneath Florida.

Holton Creek's flow is only slighter faster than a full gallop by a gopher tortoise, a creature you'll likely see during the summer months going about its endangered business. Other reptiles—basker turtles among them—are encountered by the basketful in the summer. Some can reach the size of dinner plates, but they sound much larger as they plop into the water.

The size of Holton Creek Wildlife Management Area may seem small at 2,529 acres, but it contains one of Florida's Champion Cypress trees, viewed from a side loop off (Forest Service) Road 8. Sinks are common in this area along the Suwannee River, and an especially diverse collection border the ride on Road 16. Some are small, shallow basins with no water; others reach sizes large enough to support a community of birds, bugs, and frogs.

General location: This trail system of Forest Service roads can be found northeast of Suwannee River State Park in Hamilton County.

Elevation change: The roads traverse wide, gently rolling hills.

Season: The roads sometimes become too sandy to ride during the dry spells. But if you believe the motto, "If you aren't hiking, you aren't biking,"

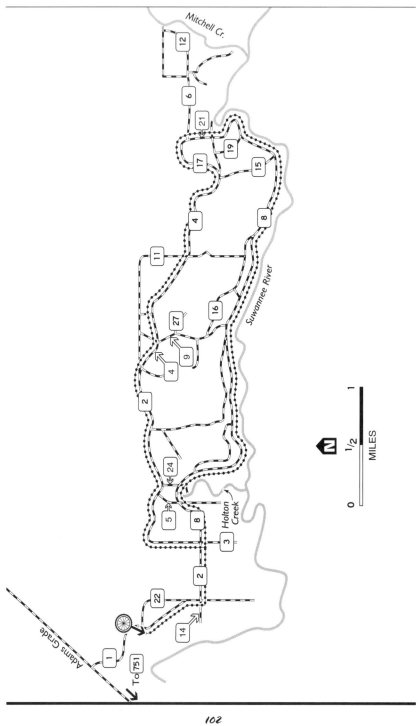

then you'll be riding this route all year long.

Services: Live Oak, Florida — about 1.5 miles to the south — can provide general needs. Tallahassee is the closest place where a mountain biker needing equipment repair can get those specialized services.

Hazards: Sandy trail surfaces and trigger-happy hunters (remember, this is a wildlife management area and subject to seasonal hunts) need to be considered at times. Horseback riders also use the service roads, which are wide enough for easy clearance . . . after a proper and considerate warning (in a friendly voice).

Rescue index: The roads are flat and easy to get to. But despite being only a short time away from both Interstate 10 and US 90, this is fairly remote country and a rescue could take a while to effect.

Land status: This public land is managed by Florida's Suwannee River Water Management District.

Maps: I was able to pick up a map of the Holton Creek Wildlife Management Area at the information station at the entrance. In addition to using the map in this book, you can call (904) 362-1001 and ask for one to be sent.

Finding the trail: Exit Interstate 75 at FL 6 and drive west approximately 4 miles to County Road 751; turn left and then left again at the sign for Holton Creek WMA, just before reaching the bridge and the agricultural check station. About 1 mile down the road, turn right at the sign for the entrance. The information station is located at the trailhead.

Sources of additional information:

Suwannee Bicycle Association
P.O. Box 247
White Springs, Florida 32096
(904) 397-2347

Suwannee River State Park
20185 County Road 132
Live Oak, Florida 32060
(904) 362-2746

Suwannee River Water Management District
9225 County Road 49
Live Oak, Florida 32060
(904) 362-1001 or
(800) 226-1066 (Florida only)

Notes on the trail: Forest Service Road 2 takes the long way to Holton Creek Rise from the entrance, staying on the north boundary of the WMA. A southern jaunt on FS 11 takes you to the next road paralleling the river, FS 4, which you could have taken back at the fork with FS 2. In order to get to FS 6 and Mitchell Creek, turn left (north) on FS 17 or FS 21. Otherwise, continue the loop on FS 8, which begins on the Suwannee River at the end of FS 4. Take the right fork to FS 16 for a look at the Land of a Thousand Sinks. Reconnect to FS 8 by taking FS 9 south after FS 16 dead-ends into it. FS 8 takes you back, and you continue straight at the intersection with FS 2 and FS 3. It just sounds complicated. If you can keep your basic east-west orientation, you will find it difficult to get lost because you can't travel far north-to-south in this small, well-marked road system. The map fits nicely into one of Tom Myers' Bar-Maps (CycoActive Products, 117 East Louisa Street, Seattle, Washington 98102), which allows easy access and quick referral.

RIDE 28 · Twin Rivers Wildlife Management Area

AT A GLANCE

Length/configuration: 7-mile loop

Aerobic difficulty: Low; gently rolling hills

Technical difficulty: Easy; only one sandy spot at the bottom of a steepish hill requires dismount for novice riders

Scenery: The Suwannee River, red maples and river birch, limestone banks, dense forests broken up by pine sapling clearings, and high canopies that allow for long views

Special comments: Perfect for a family day trip

This seven-mile loop on wildlife management area service roads—with a two-mile section of single-track along the Suwannee River—will have you humming a few bars to the Stephen Foster classic "Old Folks at Home." And you can take the old folks along on this easy ride on the rolling hills near the confluence of the Withlacoochee and Suwannee rivers. The flat service roads enter dense and shady forests only to break out into clearings surrounded by pine saplings. By the time the trail reaches the interstate, the mood is set. A tall forest forms a solid canopy of green shade, but the understory allows long views.

An area of natural, sunken depressions line the trail, scattered among the massive trunks like craters from meteorites. Some are deep enough to tease the imagination into wondering what could be hiding there. Plenty of evidence suggests turkeys and wild hogs root about in the rich river soil. A solitary buck sporting a velvet rack was standing in the palmetto fronds when I approached. I stopped and watched as he stamped his hooves, then suddenly leaped off, long white tail held high. Seeing that will definitely change the way you ride.

The route along the river could hardly get any prettier. The sound of the Suwannee gurgling over the shoals combines with the numerous songbirds high in the crowns of river birch and red maples. The trail rises gently on the Suwannee's shores, and you can see the big, dark water swirling against the high, limestone banks. Without too much encouragement, you can imagine

This ancient river birch along the Suwannee River sports a girdle of "resurrection fern."

the shape of a paddle-wheel steamboat making its way through the channel and almost hear the strums of an old banjo.

General location: Twin Rivers, a Madison County Conservation Area, is located between Interstate 10 and US 90, just west of the Suwannee River.

Elevation change: The trail's flat and gently rolling terrain is interrupted only once. Just before the trail turns away from the river nearest US 90, a steeper drop and climb—with sand at the bottom—demands more than novice skills to ensure a safe, bike-bound passage.

Season: Since this is a wildlife management area and subject to seasonal hunts, you should choose another trail when hunters are present.

Services: Madison, Florida, 15 miles to the northwest on US 90, provides a source of general goods and services, but for specialty items, a trip back to Tallahassee—about 70 miles west—is necessary.

Hazards: Hunters in season, but otherwise no significant or unusual hazards; however, remember that natural conditions may be dangerous; for example, high water, poison ivy, wasps, or stampedes of surprised feral pigs.

Rescue index: This would be a fairly easy place to effect a rescue; the roads are wide, level, and well maintained, not to mention being between two of the busiest highways in northern Florida.

RIDE 28 · Twin Rivers Wildlife Management Area

Land status: This public land is managed by the Suwannee River Water Management District.

Maps: I picked up my maps from the Suwannee River State Park, approximately 1 mile east of the trailhead, on US 90 in Ellaville, Florida.

Finding the trail: Exit Interstate 10 at the sign for Suwannee River State Park and turn west on US 90 toward Ellaville and the park. Begin looking for the left turn into the WMA check station, where the power line cuts across the road, approximately 1 mile beyond the river. The trail starts out south on the service road underneath the power line.

Sources of additional information:

Suwannee Bicycle Association
P.O. Box 247
White Springs, Florida 32096
(904) 397-2347

Suwannee River State Park
20185 County Road 132
Live Oak, Florida 32060
(904) 362-2746

Suwannee River Water Management District
9225 County Road 49
Live Oak, Florida 32060
(904) 362-1001 or
(800) 226-1066 (Florida only)

Notes on the trail: Begin the ride by heading through the gate for the service road following the power line. Look for the return leg of the loop coming in on the left approximately one-half mile later; the first leg continues straight. About a mile farther, after passing a service road on the left, look for the fork in the road and take the right one. This road dead-ends into another road turning left. Go another half mile or so before turning right at the next intersection. At this point, you'll be approaching the traffic noise from Interstate 10. The road dead-ends again just on the other side of the fence that separates you from the interstate highway; take a left and ride along this fence for nearly a mile, crossing the power line approximately halfway through. A service road goes off to the left just before getting to the river, but the trail changes shape and character at this intersection if you continue straight.

Single-track—the Florida Trail, marked by orange blazes—hugs the western shore of the Suwannee River for the next 2 miles, with power lines crossing at 4 different places. Just after the fourth power line intersection, prepare for the steepest descent and climb of the trail. It is possible to ride both down and up this wide, sandy ditch, but scout it before making your first run on it. After making the opposite bank, ruins from an old stall signal the left turn—away from the Florida Trail—onto the wide, grassy service road. You'll go under the power lines one more time before you see a service road coming in on the right, very near US 90 where the road turns left. Shortly after that turn, the road forks again; take the left one for a longer ride in the woods and for another ride along the shores of the Suwannee. The right fork leads directly back to the trailhead, approximately 1 mile away.

JACKSONVILLE AND
GAINESVILLE AREA RIDES

It was over 50 years after Ponce de Leon first sighted land off Florida's east coast before the continent's first permanent settlement was established in St. Augustine in 1565. Those early days were harsh struggles to survive the seasonally fierce onslaught of tropical weather (Jacksonville has the dubious distinction of being the lightning capital of America) and the even fiercer battles with the Timucan, the natives who laid claim to these white beaches.

Eventually, the white men learned to make the fertile inland soil grow crops. The Indians were forced off their lands, and the struggle for control shifted among the armies of the Old World. Amelia Island reflects this as the only site in America governed by eight different countries in the last 400 years. All this has worked to create a cultural eccentricity best seen in present-day St. Augustine.

Even the St. Johns River reflects this eccentricity. Beginning in the south over 200 miles away, this river flows almost straight north—past Cape Canaveral and Daytona Beach—into Ocala National Forest. By the time it leaves Putnam County, a few miles shy of the Georgia border, the St. Johns resembles a huge inland bay rather than a flowing river. The park employee who was kind enough to help me register at one of the area campgrounds saw that I was from Georgia and asked, "Do you know why the St. Johns River flows north?" When I shook my head, he delivered the line I'm sure he'd practiced many times: "Because Georgia sucks."

Away from the pounding of the surf and the large populations of the northeast coast, Gainesville attracts a less defensive crowd. The prairies and rivers of this central region were among the first of Florida's geographic features to emerge from the sea. Springs bubble up along the lower slopes of an area called the Scrub, which inspired Marjorie Kinnan Rawlings to write her stories of the whites who first settled this area. The rolling hills have been cleared for herds of cattle, horses, and even bison. The interest mining companies had for the limestone underneath the green pastures can be seen in some places—like Ocala and Bellview—where the off-road rider can experience the closest thing to a mountain adventure anywhere in the state.

The closer you get to the Gulf Coast in the northern region, the closer you are to the setting of primitive Florida. By the time you reach Manatee Springs State Park, just north of where the Suwannee River enters the Gulf of Mexico, swamps with names like Pumpkin and Tates Hell paint all things green, wet, and flat. But as I swam in the cool waters of Manatee Springs one late September afternoon, cypress hugging the banks and 80,000 gallons of water rushing past my legs, I swore it could not get any better than this.

Sources of additional information:

GONE RIDING!
10915 S.W. 58th Avenue
Ocala, Florida 34476
(352) 873-9279

Champion Cycling
1025 Arlington Road
Jacksonville, Florida 32211
(904) 724-4922

Spin Cycle
424 West University Avenue
Gainesville, Florida 32601
(352) 373-3355
fax (352) 338-7889

RIDE 29 · Hanna Park

AT A GLANCE

Length/configuration: 20 miles if all loops are ridden

Aerobic difficulty: Low to high

Technical difficulty: Easy to challenging; numerous trails, both single- and double-track, marked as "beginner," "intermediate," and "expert"

Scenery: Part of one trail goes beachside

Special comments: Hard to pedal during a dry spell

The nearly 20 miles of looping single- and double-track inside this city park offer trails for every class of off-road biker: beginner, intermediate, and expert. In addition to hosting sanctioned races on a seasonal schedule, the track sees many local bikers on a daily basis. I was able to hook up with a couple of local guys and a racin' fiend from Orlando. The trails are expertly maintained by the Jacksonville Mountain Bike Organization (JMBO).

Hanna Park's single-track will explain the sign at lower left.

I rode the trail the first time more quickly than I normally try to, and I was having fun handling the extra speed. If that strangler vine hadn't reached out and grabbed my handlebars, I would've made a good impression. I still took advantage of the packed track (sometimes it can be sandy and very difficult to pedal) and used the canted turns to my advantage, traveling as quickly as I could without putting my camera pack at too much risk.

This trail wins the award for "Most Difficult Close to the Sea." The ride travels near the Atlantic for approximately a mile of beach riding, and the expanse of blue contrasts to the compact canopy of green. Names of sections like "Raspberry Court" (my favorite), "Grunt," and "Dead Dog" do little to break the spell of adventure that the rest of the trail creates.

General location: Hanna Park is located on the beach, just a few miles east of Jacksonville.

Elevation change: A few short sections have significant elevation change. Some sections (like "Misery") never seem to level or straighten out.

Season: Although I had no difficulty riding here in late September after a rainy spell, I was told that this trail can be extremely difficult to pedal when it dries out, due to loose sand.

Services: The park has all the services normally expected of a top-level park, camping included. Jacksonville proper is across the river, and most of what you will need can be found outside the park gates on Highway A1A.

RIDE 29 · Hanna Park

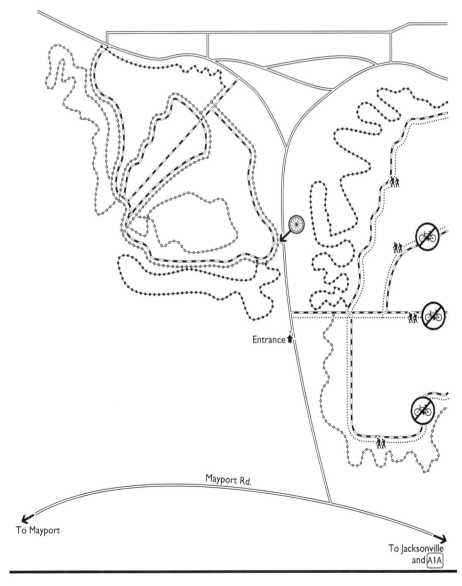

ATLANTIC OCEAN

NOTE: ○○○○○○ BEGINNER TRAIL
○○○○○○ INTERMEDIATE TRAIL
●●●●●●● EXPERT TRAIL

Entrance

Mayport Rd.

To Mayport

To Jacksonville
and A1A

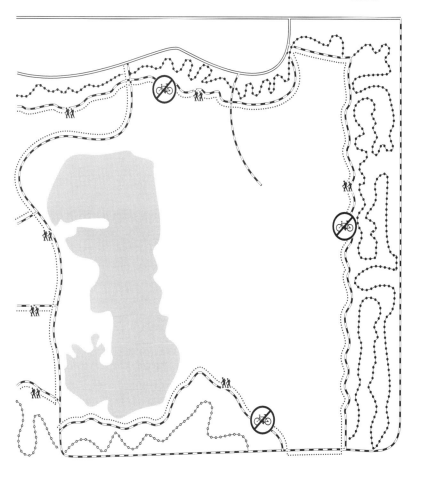

Hazards: You can easily go faster than you should on this trail, especially given the possibility of meeting other riders head-on. Roots and ruts will also test your strength and agility.

Rescue index: A loud voice or whistle should attract more attention than you could hope for.

Land status: This land is managed by the Jacksonville municipal government.

Maps: Maps of the complete hiking and biking trails can be picked up at the entrance.

Finding the trail: Exit onto Atlantic Boulevard from whichever interstate you happen to be coming in on. General destination: A1A heading north to Mayport. When County Road 101 splits to the right and A1A turns left to Mayport, continue straight on 101 for a short distance and turn right at the sign. After paying the entrance fee, look for the "Bikers Only" parking on the left about a quarter mile away.

Source of additional information:

Kathryn A. Hanna Park
500 Wonderwood Drive
Jacksonville, Florida 32233
(904) 249-4700

Notes on the trail: My native guides began the expert course by crossing the pavement and hitting the single-track off the parking lot southeast of the entrance station. The easterly direction is masked by the convolutions of the trail, which switches back west a few times before stretching out south nearest the beach's paved and divided road. Beginner double-track is used to connect the expert trail in the southern portion of the park. After finishing this section, a break on the road allows a higher gear, or you can take to the beach and cycle in the loose sand or the tighter strand. The northern loops have single-track suited for beginning, intermediate, and expert bikers. And if once around isn't enough, you've paid for all day. Take another lap and hit "Log Jam" one more time. It's more than worth it.

RIDE 30 · Cary State Forest

AT A GLANCE

Length/configuration: 18 miles of loops

Aerobic difficulty: Low; flat terrain

Technical difficulty: Easy; wide double-track

Scenery: Forest of longleaf and slash pine allowing for long views

To Georgia

North Boundary Rd.

Deer Track Tr.

Hog Trap Rd.

Big Oaks Rd.

Moccasin Slough Rd.

Turkey Bait Tr.

Main Entrance

Pavilion Dr.

Fire Tower Rd.

Fox Squirrel Rd.

Pond Rd.

No Catch Rd.

Bryceville
Fire Dept.

Motes Rd.

Chicken Farm Rd.

Red Root Rd

Gator Splash
Trail

119

301

To 75
and Baldwin

Power Line Rd.

N

0   1/4   1/2

MILES

Special comments: Wild creatures can be spotted here, including deer, turkey, raccoons, gators, and the endangered fox squirrel

Granted, Cary State Forest will never host a national off-road mountain bike competition. What with its flat, wide double-track, it lacks much of the challenge found at racing venues (no matter how sandy or wet it gets). But the 18 miles of loops among pure stands of longleaf and slash pine allow a long day of riding and exploring 3,400 acres of one of Florida's 36 state forests.

Cary's added dimension as an outdoor classroom for Duval County's students (fourth- and sixth-graders study forest ecology as part of their curriculum) makes it a good place to observe the effects of forestry on the environment. It is also a good place to observe many wild creatures.

General location: Cary State Forest is located approximately 25 miles west of Jacksonville.

Elevation change: There is no appreciable elevation change.

Season: Hunting season is two weekends in October, November, December, and January. Call for exact dates, since most of the forest roads are closed during hunting season. It can get awfully wet here, especially if the Okefenokee Swamp floods.

Services: There are 3 primitive campsites, and camping is allowed inside the forest, where a bathhouse with showers is also available. Very basic services can be located at Bryceville, while Baldwin (7 miles south on US 301) has gas stations and lodging. Callahan is 15 miles north on US 301 and offers lodging, grocery stores, and gas stations. Otherwise, Jacksonville is the best bet for finding what you need.

Hazards: Hunters, hikers, and horses can all be encountered here at certain times of the year. Besides the other natural conditions of a typical Florida landscape, no hazards exist.

Rescue index: You can be a surprisingly long way from help should you need it at No Catch Road, approximately 5 miles from US 301.

Land status: This is 1 of 36 state forests managed by the Florida Division of Forestry.

Maps: No maps were available at the information station when I showed up; however, I was able to get my copy by phoning Bill Therrell, Cary forest ranger. I asked for "Cary State Forest—Nature's Classroom."

Finding the trail: Exit north off the Interstate 10 ramp at Baldwin and head north on US 301. After approximately 6 miles, drive through the small community of Bryceville, and you'll see the fire department on the right. The next road to the right is the main entrance. You can pull off and find some shade to park under anywhere along the service roads and begin your ride; that is, if it's not posted.

Source of additional information:

Cary State Forest
Route 2, Box 60
Bryceville, FL 32009
(904) 266-5021 or 266-5020

Notes on the trail: This is a good place to let your mind and sight wander. The roads are straight, wide, and flat. Despite this, they have the stately atmosphere of a fairly old forest. The planted pines, with their saw palmetto understory, allow long views. Most of the mileage you ride occurs west of the power line road, and with names like Hog Trap Road, Fox Squirrel Road, and Cypress Pond Road, you'll want to bike them all.

RIDE 31 · Guana River State Park

AT A GLANCE

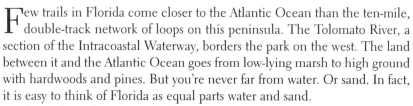

Length/configuration: 10 miles of loops

Aerobic difficulty: Low; flat terrain

Technical difficulty: Easy; wide double-track

Scenery: Varied; you'll ride through, and next to, everything from low marshland to high forest to oceanside sand dunes

Special comments: Great ride for beginners. Trail is less than half a mile away from the Atlantic Ocean and is bordered by the Tolomato River

Few trails in Florida come closer to the Atlantic Ocean than the ten-mile, double-track network of loops on this peninsula. The Tolomato River, a section of the Intracoastal Waterway, borders the park on the west. The land between it and the Atlantic Ocean goes from low-lying marsh to high ground with hardwoods and pines. But you're never far from water. Or sand. In fact, it is easy to think of Florida as equal parts water and sand.

The wide paths are marked by color codes and can be easily followed except on the north end, where the trails leave the park and enter the wildlife management area. Otherwise, you can expect to see high dunes and a large midden—mounds of shells whose clams and oysters fed the first humans in this area. As you ride near the beach, be alert to signs showing the nesting area of the threatened migratory sea bird, the Least Tern.

Guana River State Park is a good place to bring the beginning biker, especially in the cooler months. Its wide, firm track encourages a pace bent more on discovery than speed. So what do you say if someone asks if you wanna go ride Guana? I'm g'wana do it.

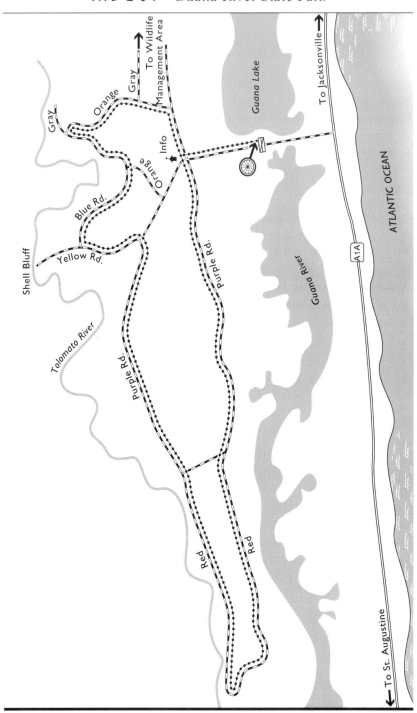

Guana River joins the Tolomato River less than three miles from the dam in the foreground. The Atlantic Ocean lies less than half a mile away (as the pelican flies).

General location: Guana River State Park is located off A1A, south of Jacksonville and north of St. Augustine.

Elevation change: There is little elevation change, but more than you would expect, especially at the midden.

Season: Except for periods of heavy rain, these trails can be ridden with alacrity. No hunting is allowed inside the park.

Services: St. Augustine is a short drive south, and Jacksonville is a little farther north; either can resupply you. Except for a rest room and water, the improvements are rather sparse at this self-pay park.

Hazards: Hikers, bikers, and horseback riders are on these trails; watch out for them. However, hunting is allowed inside the wildlife management area that adjoins the park. Other dangerous natural conditions may be present.

Rescue index: Although Guana River State Park is situated on the populous east coast, a rescue here could take longer than desired. Ride prepared to self-rescue.

Land status: The park is managed by the Florida Department of Environmental Protection, Division of Recreation and Parks.

Maps: Maps of part of the park can be picked up at the self-pay station (where you can expect to pay at least $2). Trail maps are located at the information station across the dam.

Finding the trail: After leaving the hubbub of Jacksonville behind, head south on A1A. Or, if you're coming from the mainland's oldest city, St. Augustine, head north on A1A. The trip there is a particular treat. Large, canopied dunes line the eastern side, with an expanse of flat, marshy landscape just inland. As I headed south on A1A, 4 brown pelicans flew southward in formation a quarter mile ahead of me. It took a few moments to realize I was not overtaking them quickly. Several minutes passed before I got alongside and determined that they were flap-flap-gliding at 40 mph.

Source of additional information:

> Guana River State Park
> 2690 South Ponte Vedra Boulevard
> Ponte Vedra Beach, Florida 32082
> (904) 825-5071

Notes on the trail: Ride past the gate on the near side of the dam. On the way to the information station, you'll pass a trail to the left (purple) and another trail to the right (orange). Both loop back into the central (yellow) trail. An added loop is attached at the end of the purple trail. For off-road riding inside the wildlife management area, turn onto the orange trail and ride the gray trails. Shell Bluff, where an ancient midden attests to the Indians' appetite for shellfish, is at the end of the yellow trail.

RIDE 32 · Spruce Creek Preserve

AT A GLANCE

Length/configuration: 10 miles of loops

Aerobic difficulty: Low to high, depending on which trails you opt for

Technical difficulty: Easy to very challenging; sandy double-track for beginners and windy narrow single-track with steep climbs and descents for the more experienced

Scenery: Close-up, slightly elevated view of Spruce Creek; dense forest

Special comments: Most technical riding in Florida

A tight and twisting network of over ten miles of single-track and double-track provides enough loops to keep you riding most of the morning. The less experienced biker can enjoy the challenge of the sandy double-track that bisects this jointly owned and managed Volusia County property. The single-track sections contain some of the most technical off-road riding in Florida.

RIDE 32 · Spruce Creek Preserve

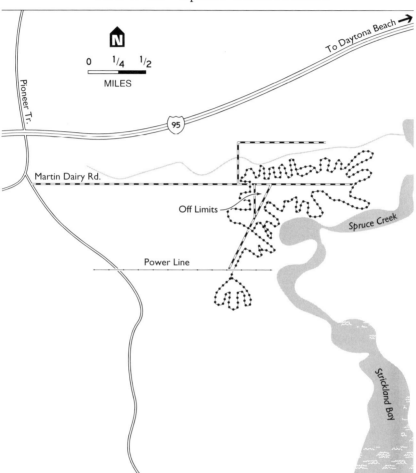

Although this site is among the most heavily used in the area, drawing bikers here from all over the state on a regular basis, its future as an off-road course is uncertain. The terrain is atypically steep and prone to quick, massive erosion. An area in the middle of the preserve has been declared off-limits to all, and it's too bad. The elevation changes along the sharper contours of an inland dune, which is shaded by a thick canopy of hardwoods and saw palmetto. It is a small but hilly section where some of the original single-track was placed. But now it is strictly off-limits . . . some bikers ignore this and continue to ride. And there's the rub.

After speaking with an environmental assessor at Volusia County (I was trying to get an official map of the trails; there is none), I learned that there are some areas of concern as far as the trails' environmental stability goes, and bikers—though currently tolerated—are not encouraged or discouraged from using the trail network, which was built by some of the area's earliest bikers.

The single-track on the high ground seldom stays straight for more than a bike length or two, or at least it seems that way. The technical downhills and climbs around the small branch feeding Spruce Creek are among the most difficult to ride anywhere. I stayed off the most extreme sections, but what I rode was still more than I could handle without coming off a time or ten.

General location: Spruce Creek is located a little south of Daytona Beach, not too far from Interstate 95.

Elevation change: Only a handful of Floridian off-road trails have elevation changes equal to or greater than those at Spruce Creek.

Season: This trail can be ridden when wet, but it should be avoided unless dry.

Services: Daytona Beach is a few miles north on I-95. There is limited parking and no water or rest rooms nearby. It is simply a trail system of magnificent proportions.

Hazards: The hazards on this trail remind me of those much farther north: steep dropoffs; large roots (gatorbacks) exposed in the middle of turns, climbs, and drops; speeding, unsmiling bikers coming head-on. Horses are also allowed to use this trail system.

Rescue index: Despite the remote feeling you get in the tight single-track, you are quite close to help and the trailhead in most places. The destination's popularity, especially on the weekend, should assure a quick discovery by someone.

Land status: This land is officially under the management of the Volusia County Parks and Recreation Department; however, I heard discussion concerning the possible transfer of title to the Nature Conservancy, which would dim the future of the preserve as an off-road biking site.

Maps: This one was a tough assignment. No official maps have been painstakingly plotted by a global positioning system, nor anything close to that. Being the intrepid biking guide that I am, I gave my best shot at indicating the numerous intersections at Spruce Creek by using a topo map and detailed notes. If in doubt, orient yourself by riding the double-track sections first, noting the various single-tracks diving into the understory.

Finding the trail: Exit I-95 at FL 44 (Deland) and head toward the ocean. Turn left at the large sign approximately half a mile down indicating the Sugar Mill subdivision. Continue straight 1.3 miles; turn left at a flashing red light (at the intersection with Pioneer Trail). After almost 2 miles, look on the right for Turnbull Bay Road; turn onto it. The first dirt road on the left is Martin Dairy Road; take it for 2 miles until it turns to the left. Park in

You'll find a good spot to rest on the southern bluff overlooking Spruce Creek's wide oxbow.

one of the spaces off the road. The trail heads north on either double-track or single-track.

Source of additional information:

County of Volusia
Parks and Recreation Department
123 West Indiana Avenue
Deland, Florida 32720-4618
(904) 322-5133

Notes on the trail: No blazes adorn this trail, nor are any needed. The double-track basically bisects 2 halves of a single-track loop cutting across it. Beginning in a counterclockwise direction, take the single-track along the small creek. It comes close to rejoining the main double-track in a couple of places before it finally does. By taking the double-track northwest, you'll find another single-track half-loop that turns off to the left. This shorter section (perhaps the shortest of the half-loops) rejoins the double-track across 2 single-track sections: one (the left) goes toward Spruce Creek and the other (the right) goes toward the trailhead. I went left on the double-track at this point, however, and turned left onto another single-track section that winds its way to the point where Spruce Creek makes a large oxbow. Double-track leads for a short distance before single-track turns off to the left. You should notice at this intersection that the single-track on the right is the section leading back to Spruce Creek. But the single-track heading east stays to the left of the double-track, coming eventually to an intersection at the power lines, but not before passing the off-limits section on the right. At the power lines, look for the ruts under the massive stanchion. They lead to another single-track section that eventually winds its way back into the power line road. Recross the very sandy section under the power line stanchions, aiming about two o'clock in the direction of Spruce Creek. Now here's the tricky part. One double-track leads downhill and dead-ends soon. Others either lead into a dense understory or loop back around. Only one takes you back to the double-track that leads to the trailhead. My notes for the maps are a bit fuzzy on which road it is, but is not difficult to eliminate the wrong ones. Hopefully, this trail will still be open for you to enjoy . . . and to amend my map.

RIDE 33 · Hardrock Ocala MTB Park

AT A GLANCE

Length/configuration: 8-mile loop

Aerobic difficulty: High; intended as a racer's course

Technical difficulty: Very challenging; obstacle-laden, narrow, windy single-track with steep hills and extremely fast determined riders

Scenery: Probably won't have time to notice any given the speed this trail expects

Special comments: For racers only; riders are required to pay an entrance fee and sign a release form

Hard-nosed mountain bike riders looking for a challenging course need go no farther than the former limestone quarry in Ocala. The eight-mile, single-track loop takes the off-road biker through a gauntlet of obstacles better suited for the motorcycles that occasionally churn up the steep hills. It is not entirely unsuited for the novice rider, but if this site is selected for an intro to Florida bike trail riding, it will be difficult for beginners to recover from the daunting experience.

It is better to gain some experience on some of Florida's tamer single-tracks before launching off down one of the many steep descents. Despite its former life as a quarry, the trees reach high above the course to give ample shade in most places. Chances are, however, that the only wildlife you will spy will be on the back of a mountain bike.

My only experience with Hardrock came on Labor Day as some 200-plus

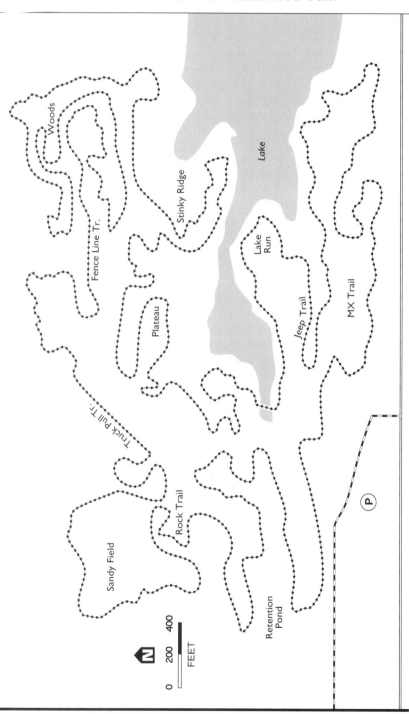

Woods

Fence Line Tr.

Stinky Ridge

Lake

Lake Run

Jeep Trail

MX Trail

Plateau

Truck Pull Tr.

Rock Trail

Sandy Field

Retention Pond

P

N

0   200   400
FEET

Hardrock's former life as a limestone quarry created descents that defy Florida's flatland status.

racers came to sharpen their skills for the upcoming season at the Labor Day Bash. I could tell the intensity of the course by the number of walking wounded who took the bash literally—new initiates, no doubt, to the travails of Hardrock's trails.

General location: This course is located just north of Ocala, Florida, where the whinny of thoroughbreds can be heard off in the distance; or is it the sound of some half-crazed cyclist whooshing down Truck Pull Trail?

Elevation change: There is more than enough significant elevation change to challenge most bikers. The limestone pits accentuate an already rolling landscape. This is only one of a handful of trails in the entire state where I had to hike-and-bike . . . several times.

Season: When it's too dry, the sandy stretches strain thighs and test balance; when it gets wet like the afternoon I rode, the rocks and roots slicken to the point of treachery.

Services: Ocala is a large city where many services can be acquired. Hardrock itself occasionally provides a camping spot (modern rest rooms and wash areas for the steel steeds in your family) for weekend biking festivals.

Hazards: Although the rocks and roots can cause a cyclist's crack-up and deserve the utmost respect—especially when they occur on some of the devilishly steep descents—the major obstacle comes in the form of hell-bent bikers searching the edge of their own abilities, thereby running over the more tortoise-like riders. But you're forewarned that this is a racer's course; you pay an entrance fee and sign a waiver releasing the management of all liability in the event that you have an injury-causing upset.

Rescue index: You are likely to receive fairly prompt attention on this busy course, especially if it occurs during a race.

Land status: Admission is charged at the gate.

Maps: Hardrock is a well-marked trail with clear signs showing the direction to take at intersections where there may be confusion.

Finding the trail: Exit Interstate 75 at Exit 71 (FL 326). Take FL 326 east approximately a half mile until the first light where a right turn heads south on C-25A. The entrance lies approximately three quarters of a mile on the left behind a large chain-link fence.

Source of additional information: None

Notes on the trail: Some trails in this guide have been included for the racer, not the rubbernecker and naturalist. Hardrock is one such trail. You will be hard-pressed to find a tougher course anywhere to test your mountain biking mettle. There are some serious hills where you can lose speed quickly. The first part of the course sets out across a field where the group of racers can begin to string out according to ability. By the time the pack gets through the hills at the end of the field, an individual's climbing ability will be thoroughly tested. But hills are only a small part of the overall challenges found at Hardrock. Tight, twisting single-track requires agility and concentration in order to stay upright, not a small feat when the sound of your own breathing roars in your ears like a locomotive. But if you develop the right cadence on these sections, you can hear that tiny voice inside you chanting, "I think I can, I think I can, I know I can."

RIDE 34 · Bellview-Santos Trailhead

AT A GLANCE

Length/configuration: 15 miles of loops

Aerobic difficulty: Low to high, depending which trail section you're up for

Technical difficulty: Easy to challenging; trail sections are marked for different levels; beginner trails are wide and gently rolling, while intermediate and expert sections have dramatic climbs and descents

Scenery: Hardwood and pine forest

Special comments: One of Florida's more popular off-road areas

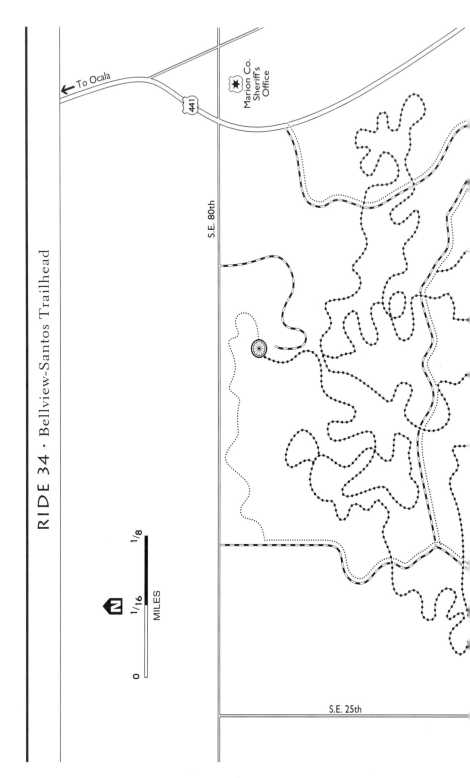

RIDE 34 · Bellview-Santos Trailhead

To Ocala

441

Marion Co.
Sheriff's
Office

S.E. 80th

S.E. 25th

N

0   1/16   1/8
MILES

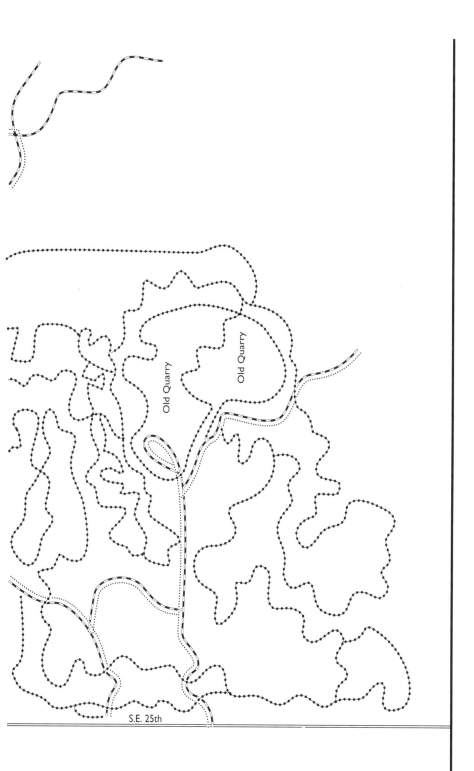

Old Quarry

Old Quarry

S.E. 25th

Few bikers can ride Florida's steepest climbs without the help of a weenie gear.

Bordered by the asphalt of a major highway and subdivision roads, this former limestone quarry has taken shape as one of Florida's more popular off-road destinations. A combination of single- and double-track makes a series of loops swirling over 15 miles (and expanding on a regular basis) through a forest of hardwoods and pines. Different trail sections are blazed with yellow (easiest), blue (intermediate), and red (whoa, now!).

This trail system on 300 acres is part of the Florida Greenways project, an ambitious undertaking to develop a cross-Florida network of off-road biking opportunities akin to the hiker's Florida Trail. The Bellview information station at the trailhead wore its inaugural coat of (Florida) green lettering when I visited in September 1996. As I unloaded my bike on a late Sunday afternoon, I watched two younger riders practice trial moves next to their truck. A family of four—with mom towing the baby trailer—prepared to take on the yellow trails. A middle-aged man arrived in a Delta 88 with the half-tied trunk of his car snapping up and down on his new mountain bike like a gator eating a poodle. And pretty soon, a wayward author hit the track with them to taste a trail as sweet as guava jelly.

And if the members of organizations like Ocala Mountain Bike Association (who helped build the Bellview trails) and the folks who showed up in Brooksville for the first ever Florida Off-Road Bicycle Trail Organizational Meeting have their way, Florida will possess a statewide set of single-track built on the order of what lies behind the Santos Trailhead in Bellview. I can hardly wait!

General location: Look for this trailhead 1 block off US 441, about 10 miles south of Ocala.

Elevation change: Consistent with what you would expect from an unrepaired quarry setting, you will experience as dramatic an elevation change as anywhere in Florida. The intermediate trails have sections that will test your best moves as you attempt to ride straight through.

Season: Few days in the year are inappropriate for enjoying Bellview.

Services: Ocala lies just a few miles north on US 441, and most services can be found there or nearby. Plans call for placing rest rooms and water at the trailhead.

Hazards: The easiest trails are wide but occasionally sandy. Sand always has the potential for an upsetting experience; in addition, the other trails have rocks and gatorbacks that make the consequence of a tumble greater. Also, trail direction had not yet been determined; therefore, the possibility of oncoming bike traffic exists.

Rescue index: 300 acres is not that large, but you will be surprised at how remote it can seem. In practice, you should not be far from a quick recovery once you're discovered, which (based on the park's popularity) should not be long.

Land status: This is a parcel of the Florida Greenway management plan.

Maps: A map is posted behind Plexiglas at the information station, which does you little good when you're out in the middle of all the trail's twists and intersections. The frequent blazes help make that first trip around relatively simple, however. The map used for this guide was acquired at the Florida Greenway office on County Road 314.

Finding the trail: Leave Ocala headed south on US 441. Approximately 10 miles later, begin looking for the northbound and southbound lanes to split around a median forest. A green-roofed sheriff's office faces the southbound traffic and marks the intersection where you turn to the west (right) onto S.E. 80th Street. Approximately a quarter mile on the left lies the road leading to the parking area.

Sources of additional information:

Mike's Cycle Center
6675 S.E. 10th Street
Bellview, Florida 34420
(352) 245-3355

Ocala Mountain Bike Club
Ocala Motorcross Park
6849 N.W. Gainesville Road
Ocala, Florida 32675

Southwest Florida Water Management District
2379 Broad Street (US 41 South)
Brooksville, Florida 34609-6899
(352) 796-1211 or
(800) 423-1476 (Florida only)

Notes on the trail: This network has nearly as many trail names as it does miles of trails. For a beginner's ride, take off on Yellow Trail until you come to Trish's Trail on the right at the third intersection. It comes back into the Yellow Trail, which ends at the Pits. By picking up some of the easier trails— Ant Hill Trail, Pine Tree Trail, and Dr. Ruth's Run—a complete loop can be made. The intermediate and expert trails include courses on Sink Hole, Marshmallow, and Cow Bone Trails, but you can easily add Canopy, Speedway, Bunny, Termite, Snake, and Rattlesnake Trails before attempting to fathom the depths of John Brown Trail or scale the ridge on Magic Mountain. Plus, if you haven't had enough by the time you return to the trailhead, you can head back out on Cow Bone to throw some sand in Back Pit.

RIDE 35 · Half Moon Lake, Ocala National Forest

AT A GLANCE

Length/configuration: A total of 5–30 miles can be ridden in this area on various out-and-backs

Aerobic difficulty: Low; mostly flat double-track roads

Technical difficulty: Easy

Scenery: Gently rolling hills and forest

Special comments: Read *The Yearling* before riding here to get a feel for the area

Many bikers I know like to combine camping and boating with cycling Forest Service back roads. For those who think like them, an out-and-back ride of anywhere from 5 to 30 miles (total) can be ridden on roads with long, gradual hills between Half Moon Lake and Doe Lake to the south. Tack those exploratory rides onto the numerous oak hammocks on the drier knolls and you can easily wind up with a good 50-miler venturing into the Big Scrub Country of the Ocala National Forest.

Much of the land is managed toward producing board feet of pine lumber, and large tracts once cleared of trees can be seen in various stages of regrowth. Osprey build nests in the tops of tall, dead pines close to good hunting grounds, such as Half Moon Lake appears to be. The lake is also the happy hunting waters of one rather large gator that has guarded the boat ramp for approximately the last ten years.

I arrived at Half Moon not really expecting to find much in the way of exciting off-roads to explore; the camping is free and I was on a tight budget—plus it was the only place I could find at midnight. But the next morning, as I was sipping the last of my coffee, I heard the sound of four fat tires swishing

RIDE 35 · Half Moon Lake, Ocala National Forest

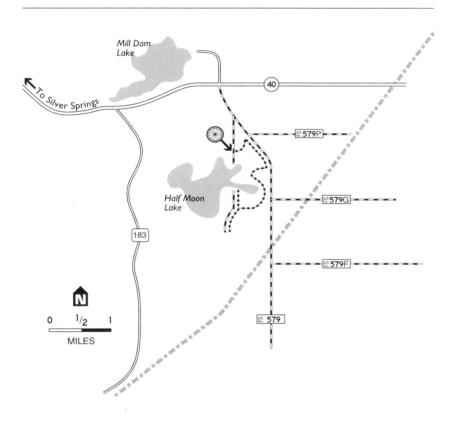

through the sand on the road. Although they couldn't see me and my camp, I could see the two bikers were wearing smiles bright as the sun streaking through the trees.

"Aha!" I said to myself, "Once more, fate has sent me cycling serendipity."

General location: This biking opportunity is found just off FL 40, approximately 25 miles east of Ocala, Florida, in Ocala National Forest.

Elevation change: The elevation changes gradually, for the most part.

Season: Hunting is a popular activity in the fall. Call to make sure hunting is not in progress at the time you ride any but the main forest service roads, and even those you should traverse with caution.

Services: Silver Springs can provide many services, but Ocala is just a few minutes farther and much more likely to provide all your needs.

Hazards: The main roads are open to vehicular traffic and lack the afternoon shade that feels so good in the summer. Hunting happens seasonally in this forest.

Rescue index: It's a big forest with lots of side roads to explore. You can get quite a ways off the beaten path. After getting rescued, you would have a relatively short trip to medical or mechanical attention.

Land status: This is part of the Ocala National Forest.

Maps: The Ocala National Forest map is very good. It is with this map and my notes that I put together the route shown.

Finding the trail: Head east out of Ocala on FL 40, and after approximately 25 miles you will see a sign that indicates a left turn onto the paved entrance to Mill Dam Recreation Area and a right turn onto a dirt road to Half Moon Lake. The camping area is found on the next dirt road to the right, toward the boat ramp. The main trail for the out-and-back is Forest Service Road 579; explore the side roads.

Source of additional information:

Lake George District Ranger
Ocala National Forest
17147 East State Highway 40
Silver Springs, Florida 34488
(352) 625-2520

Notes on the trail: As this is not a designated bike trail, don't look for any blazes or other marking devices other than the double-track you're riding. Also, since this is a heavily timbered area, what is here today can be blocked and lost tomorrow. Likewise, you should know that some of the older logging roads have been kept open for seasonal use by hunters. These make for good exploration into the less disturbed areas of the Ocala National Forest. Watch for their sudden appearance. If you have trouble finding a good route at first, leave the boat ramp at Half Moon Lake. At the top of the grade, look for a slightly overgrown double-track entrance into the forest to your right. You can follow this until it reaches the edge of a vast section of cleared timber. Follow the edge north until another double-track appears on the left in less than half a mile. Take this double-track back to FS 579 and turn right. Not far on your right, you will notice a fairly open double-track leading into an oak hammock, or canopy. In less than a mile, you will come to a great camping spot in the middle of several large live oaks. The trail continues on from there in two directions, and since I turned around at this point, I don't know where they lead—probably an out-and-back. What I do know is that this is just one of a large number of similar side roads open for riding in this section of the Ocala National Forest.

RIDE 36 · Alexander Springs Loop

AT A GLANCE

Length/configuration: 11-mile loop

Aerobic difficulty: Low to moderate; certain sections have frequent moderate climbs

Technical difficulty: Moderate; tight chutes and deadfalls on the single-track sections invite the more experienced rider

Scenery: Live oaks, pine forest, and saw palmetto thickets

Special comments: Watch out for hunters during hunting season!

This 11-mile loop of single-track, beginning at the entrance to Alexander Springs Recreation Area, comprises the northern half of what is officially known as Paisley Woods Bicycle Trail, with the other trailhead found at the Clearwater Lake Recreation Area. I decided to treat these two trailheads as individual rides primarily because it became evident from talking to people and riding the trail that the two halves are often ridden separately.

I met a couple visiting from the Tampa area who were told—by a park employee at the Alexander Springs Recreation Area entrance—that the trail only begins at Clearwater Lake. But it's just as well. These two had been biking off-road for just a few weeks, and the numerous tight squeezes and carries over deadfalls on this loop—Alexander Springs—would be less enjoyable to an inexperienced rider.

As expected, this forest differs little from the longleaf–wire grass landscape seen from the southern terminus. There do seem to be fewer areas of mature stands of live oak, a particular favorite of mine. But what works against the oaks serves the open understory of a pine forest, where turkey love to run. I spied a big tom (whose head came up at least to my handlebars) sprint into the saw palmetto thicket like it was on rails. A roadrunner's got nothing on a turkey when it comes to quick two-legged travel.

General location: This loop is located in the Ocala National Forest, north of Orlando and west of Daytona Beach.

Elevation change: The grades on this northern loop of Paisley Woods Bicycle Trail are more numerous and more steep.

Season: I can imagine sections of this trail being sugar-sandy to the extreme in the drier months. Also, Florida's off-road bikers are serious about staying out of the woods when it's hunting season; if you insist on biking in the woods when firearms are present, dress like a pumpkin.

RIDE 36 · Alexander Springs Loop
RIDE 37 · Clearwater Lake Loop

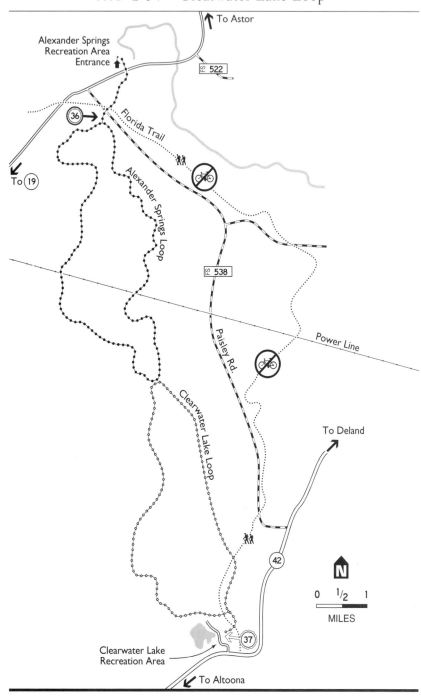

To Astor

Alexander Springs
Recreation Area
Entrance

FS 522

Florida Trail

36

To 19

Alexander Springs Loop

FS 538

Paisley Rd.

Power Line

Clearwater Lake Loop

To Deland

42

N

0   1/2   1

MILES

37

Clearwater Lake
Recreation Area

To Altoona

Thanks to the hard work of Florida's Freewheelers, this trail intersection is well marked.

Services: Basics can be acquired in the small towns of Altoona and Umatilla, but for specialized needs, head to Leesburg or Orlando.

Hazards: Hunters and sand, both seasonal threats, can present dangers not worth risking for the sake of riding. There is also one tricky section where the single-track splits off a double-track portion of trail; you may miss the turn if you concentrate too hard on the downhill that happens at this juncture.

Rescue index: You can get pretty far off the beaten path here. Combine the remoteness with the lack of use this loop gets, and the likelihood for a quick rescue decreases.

Land status: This land is in Ocala National Forest.

Maps: One of the best investments a biker coming to central Florida can make is the purchase of the official map to the 430,000 acres of public land in Ocala National Forest. Maps and brochures can be purchased at Pittman Visitor Center on Highway 19 north of Altoona. The center is open 7 days a week, 9 a.m.–5 p.m.

Finding the trail: On FL 19, approximately 5 miles north of Altoona, turn east onto County Road 445. A little over half a mile west of the entrance to Alexander Springs Recreation Area, look for Forest Service Road 538-1, which will be turning to the southeast (right if you're headed east on CR 445). A parking area under the small pines is near the information station at the trailhead.

Source of additional information:

Seminole District Ranger
Ocala National Forest
40929 State Highway 19
Umatilla, Florida 32784
(352) 669-3153

Notes on the trail: Recent storms had tossed many a branch, bough, and trunk across the single-track in this northern loop. The grass grew across the trail in several places, and I would not have been surprised to ride up on a black bear gathering berries off the palmetto and ripping into the cabbage palm. The first section also lacks the shade found elsewhere on this trail. Just before intersecting with Clearwater Lake Loop, the trail follows some old double-track. A motorcycle had been through (illegally) recently and left behind some soft, deep sandy areas that gave a good workout. On the back side of the northern loop (4.9 miles), the deadfalls are fewer, but the sandy double-track crops up again—this time at a critical turn back onto single-track. After crossing the power line road for the second time in a counter-clockwise direction, make note of the second significant (by Florida standards) downhill. Just before you're midway down, the single-track cuts off to the left. Pay attention to the frequent yellow diamonds marking the trail. If you haven't seen one recently, you probably need to backtrack and make sure you haven't missed a turn. The ride ends with a significant uphill made more difficult by the profusion of loose sugar-sand slipping under the back tire.

RIDE 37 · Clearwater Lake Loop

AT A GLANCE

Length/configuration: 10-mile loop

Aerobic difficulty: Low to moderate; some stretches of sand call for serious lung power

Technical difficulty: Moderate single-track

Scenery: Open woods, Spanish moss–covered live oaks, cabbage palm, and saw palmetto thickets

Special comments: A great spot for a summertime ride—canopied trees provide steady shade

A ten-mile loop of single-track through the Ocala National Forest leads the biker into a remote and reclaimed central Florida bear habitat. A mix of live oaks and longleaf pines grows over the typical wire grass communities native to much of the Sunshine State. The resulting shade that covers most of this moderately challenging trail makes for an ideal summertime ride, especially in the early morning or late afternoon.

The gnarled and twisted canopy of oaks contrasts with the tall, straight, green-needled crowns of pines. The single-track occasionally loses its firm surface—especially in curves—where sugar-sand is banked and furrowed. It's a great surface for four-legged reptiles that skitter just out of tire's way. One biker told me he is convinced the numerous little lizards scamper only as fast as they need to go to avoid becoming trail-kill. Whatever their intelligence, they display behavior that makes for amusing, multicolored trail camaraderie and diversion.

The open woodland is punctuated with the ubiquitous cabbage palm and saw palmetto. Looking like spiked explosions of green in places, the fronds grow tall enough to touch the drapery of Spanish moss hanging from boughs of live oak. Where fire has been used to manage the forest, the shade becomes more dappled, and the views expand to display the evidence of the slow roll of water and tides that formed this sandscape eons ago.

General location: This section of the Ocala National Forest is found north of Orlando and west of Daytona Beach.

Elevation change: You won't remember this trail for its demanding elevation changes, but there are stretches—when compounded with outcrops of loose sugar-sand—that make for periods of arduous pumping.

Season: This would be an all-season trail if it weren't for the hunting in these woods in the fall and spring. This is, however, a good trail to ride in the teeth of a Florida summer. The day I rode produced a heat index of over 100 degrees, but I felt cool for the most part . . . until I stopped riding.

Services: The serviceless trailhead is surrounded by Paisley, Altoona, and Umatilla, which can provide the basics. For anything out of the ordinary, plan on going at least as far as Deland (to the east) or Eustis and Leesburg (to the south).

Hazards: Despite the abundance of water to the north and east of the trailhead, this loop has no naturally occurring creeks or streams, so pack plenty of water (I carried 2 bottles after downing a full bottle before setting out, and I drained them both before making it back). Hunters will be out during hunting seasons; call ahead to make sure the woods are clear of flying rounds.

Rescue index: Quite a few Forest Service roads cut across the single-track, making rescue technically an easy task; however, this is one of the more remote sections in Ocala National Forest. On the day I rode this trail—a weekday in summer—I was the only one who had been on this trail in a while. Plan for self-sufficiency and talk a buddy into going along.

Land status: This is part of Ocala National Forest, a wonderful place to bike.

What some of Florida's trails lack in elevation is more than made up for with tight curves and sand.

Maps: Go ahead and purchase the official map of Ocala National Forest; it will pay for itself several times over. It can be purchased at the Pittman Visitor Center located on Highway 19 north of Altoona. The center is open 7 days a week, 9 a.m.–5 p.m.

Finding the trail: Take FL 42 east from its intersection with FL 19 in Altoona. Approximately 10 miles down the road on the left a sign indicates the entrance to Clearwater Lake Recreation Area. Look for the parking area on the right before you enter the recreation area behind the gate. The trail begins to the left of the information station and is blazed with yellow diamonds tacked onto trees.

Source of additional information:

Seminole District Ranger
Ocala National Forest
40929 State Highway 19
Umatilla, Florida 32784
(352) 669-3153

Notes on the trail: A short (half-mile) spur leads to where the loop splits. Although no signs indicate the trail direction that should be taken, I followed the trail counterclockwise. I crossed several unimproved double-track service roads before reaching the well-marked intersection of Alexander Springs Loop with Clearwater Lake Loop. In a few places the single-track forks indistinctly, and I got off the trail accidentally several times. But what this trail lacks in heavy use, it more than makes up for in regular and frequent diamond blazes. Take note of the double (in many cases) half-diamonds (one on top of the other) pointing in the direction of the turn in the trail. Should you want to make a 22-mile loop out of the affair, you can continue toward Alexander Springs, but for many the 10-mile loop is sufficient.

RIDE 38 · O'Leno State Park

AT A GLANCE

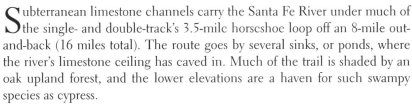

Length/configuration: 3.5-mile horseshoe loop off an 8-mile out-and-back (16 miles total)

Aerobic difficulty: Only some slight grades

Technical difficulty: Moderate; single-track sections are tight, twisty, and full of roots in some places

Scenery: The route passes by several ponds and much of the trail is shaded by an oak forest

Special comments: If you decide to cool off in the Santa Fe River, watch for gators

Subterranean limestone channels carry the Santa Fe River under much of the single- and double-track's 3.5-mile horseshoe loop off an 8-mile out-and-back (16 miles total). The route goes by several sinks, or ponds, where the river's limestone ceiling has caved in. Much of the trail is shaded by an oak upland forest, and the lower elevations are a haven for such swampy species as cypress.

Your ride on the double-track at O'Leno will no doubt bring several sightings of deer, and you can tell where turkeys scratch in the leaf litter. The single-track sections are tight, with twists and curves to rival the best off-road track in Florida. And for technical tests of balance, the bottoms between Riverrise and Bellemy Road (one of Florida's oldest examples of roadwork) have a long section of thick roots rising above the soil. Ken at Gainesville's Spin Cycle remembers riding this part under several inches of dark brown water that hid the roots, adding an extra degree of difficulty to an already slow, tedious challenge.

This same dark water of the Santa Fe River also hid the five-foot gator that must've liked what he saw when I took a couple of dips into the park's

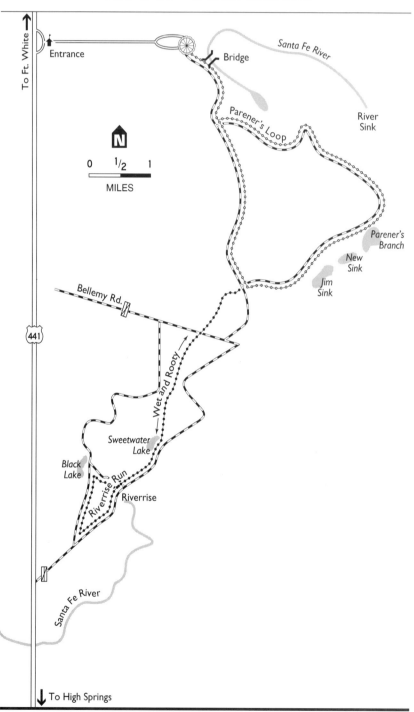

On some of Florida's more remote trails, pedaling with a partner is a wise precaution.

swimming area above the suspension bridge. It was a hot day and I needed to cool off. I saw the signs warning that an alligator might be sharing the river with me, but I saw no gatorbacks in the swift current. That is, not until I was almost ready to put my toes in for a third time, and I saw the snout and eyes moving down and across stream, pointed absolutely in my direction.

The gator paused upstream in the current as if to say, "Well? Don't you want to go back in just one more time?" After I said out loud, "Ain't no way, Mr. Gator-man!" the beast swam the rapid and disappeared in the direction in which I had seen an Irish setter playing among the riffles.

General location: O'Leno State Park is located north of Gainesville, between Exits 79 and 80 of Interstate 75.

Elevation change: Some slight grades generate at least the illusion of elevation change.

Season: This is an all-season route—that is, if you can stand the sand in the drier months.

Services: The state park has camping, showers, and rest rooms. For the more specialized services, you will have to reach Gainesville, about a half hour's drive south of the trailhead. The smaller community of High Springs lies 6 minutes south on US 441 and may have what you need.

Hazards: The bumpy section in the bottom by Sweetwater Lake deserves caution. You may meet horses on shared sections of the trail. I found the double-track from Sweetwater Lake to Riverrise only after some difficulty.

Rescue index: This popular trail has fairly high use; should you break down or need other assistance, it should be fairly easy to acquire. You are asked to register at the entrance if you plan on riding the bike trails.

Land status: This land is managed by the state of Florida for public use.

Maps: The map—O'Leno State Park Bike Trail—can be picked up at the entrance to the state park.

Finding the trail: Exit I-75 at the High Springs ramp (Exit 79) or the next exit north (80) and head either north (from Exit 79) or south (from Exit 80) on US 441. The entrance is nearly equidistant between the two points east on US 441.

Source of additional information:

O'Leno State Park
Route 2, Box 1010
High Springs, Florida 32643
(904) 454-1853

Notes on the trail: Begin the single-track south of the suspension bridge at the swimming area. Take a left on Parener's Branch Loop but stay off the single-track that goes to the river sink of the Santa Fe; it's part of the foot-travel-only trail system. At the next intersection, you can ride straight, left, or right. Unless you want a wet and sandy ride to the Riverrise (left) or a return to the trailhead (right, thereby completing a 3.5-mile loop), continue straight to Sweetwater Lake. But before you reach the lake, you'll attempt a ride through the challenging gate across Bellemy Road. The signs leading to Riverrise are mounted on posts, but a word of caution here. Stop at each intersection and familiarize yourself with the way you need to return—if you don't continue the clockwise loop from Riverrise to Black Lake. Look for the sharp right turn (west) toward Black Lake and away from the gated road leading in from US 441. At Black Lake, look for the right turn leading back and dead-ending into the trail connecting Sweetwater Lake (left turn) and Riverrise (right turn). After another time through the gate at Bellemy Road, take a left at the intersection with the single-track and the service road (Wire Road). Continue straight until you reach the trailhead.

RIDE 39 · Gainesville-Hawthorne State Trail

AT A GLANCE

Length/configuration: 34-mile out-and-back (17 miles each way)

Aerobic difficulty: Low; only a few slight grades

Technical difficulty: Easy to moderate; paved, but still some tight downhill curves to navigate

Scenery: Sink holes, ponds, and springs during the first part of the trip

Special comments: Good for beginners and for those who enjoy distance riding

For those who enjoy an off-road adventure without the challenge of tight single-track, the 17-mile, out-and-back (34 miles total), asphalt trail following the former railroad right-of-way could be the ticket. Situated on the north of Paynes Prairie Preserve for the western third of its length, the trail abandons the normal notion of a rail-trail by the hills and curves for the first three miles.

Sink holes, ponds, and springs mark the first six miles or so of trail, and where there's water in Florida, you'll find wildlife congregating around it.

The more natural setting falls by the wayside after you leave behind Paynes Prairie Preserve, but you can still see where the birds of the air and fishes of the waters stand ready to replace us after our race is done.

General location: Gainesville-Hawthorne State Trail is located between Gainesville and Hawthorne.

Elevation change: Locomotives sought the level grades, which is what you'll find here, except within Paynes Prairie, where the trail was rerouted to include numerous hills and curves.

Season: This is an all-season trail.

Services: Gainesville has all the services you would expect in a university city . . . and then some.

Hazards: Although paved, the trail does have some tight downhill curves that should not be taken lightly. Gainesville Fire-Rescue and Ambulance services are quite familiar with these spots.

Rescue index: Rescue is easy on this trail.

Land status: This trail is managed by the Florida Department of Environmental Protection, Division of Recreation and Parks.

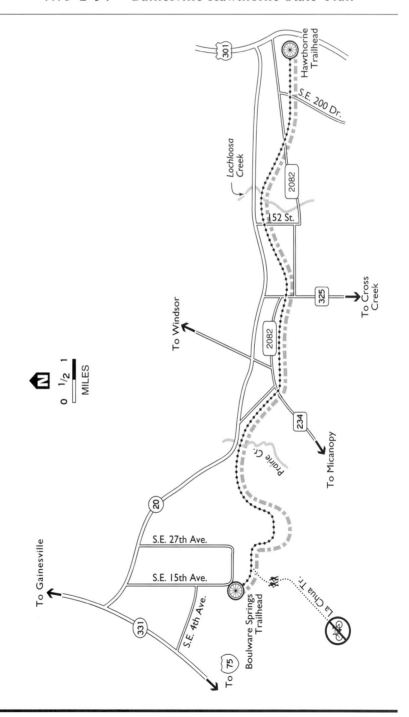

Maps: Maps of Paynes Prairie State Preserve show the length of the entire Gainesville-Hawthorne State Trail and can be picked up at the main office in Micanopy, or on the Internet at **www.afn.org/~pprairie.**

Finding the trail: The Gainesville trailhead can be found by turning south onto County Road 331 from University Avenue. Look for the Boulware Springs Park sign at 3300 S.E. 17th Street. The Hawthorne trailheads—there are 2—can be found off S.E. 200 Drive (slightly west of Hawthorne) and off 300 S.W. 2nd Avenue (in downtown Hawthorne).

Source of additional information:

Paynes Prairie State Preserve
100 Savannah Boulevard
Micanopy, Florida 32667-9702
(352) 466-3397 (Gainesville-Hawthorne Ranger)

Notes on the trail: There are no turns (a few curves, however) on this former railroad bed. Take care crossing roads that intersect with the trail, and ride as far as you want in a day. Many people choose Gainesville as their starting point. Take note of the La Chua Trail on your right (starting from Gainesville and heading east); it is for foot travel only.

RIDE 40 · Chacala Trail, Paynes Prairie State Preserve

AT A GLANCE

Length/configuration: 8-mile loop

Aerobic difficulty: Low; flat and grassy terrain

Technical difficulty: Easy

Scenery: Winds through hardwood forest and saw palmetto thickets arriving at the edge of mile-long Chacala Pond

Special comments: Often ridden in conjunction with Cone's Dike

The eight-mile loop of flat and grassy double-track, which reaches Chacala Pond in the southern section of the preserve, twists its way through a mature hardwood forest in some parts; in others, thickets of saw palmetto stand close and tall enough in places to give the ride a tunnel effect.

A thunderstorm had dumped several inches of rain the evening before, and the trail showed where the lower spots are. At times, I rode through standing water several inches deep, but the grassy, firm bottom allowed the front tire to push water out in a wake like the prow of a ship. I came to a deadfall blocking the trail at the same place a swollen slough had jumped its

RIDE 40 · Chacala Trail, Paynes Prairie State Preserve
RIDE 41 · Cone's Dike

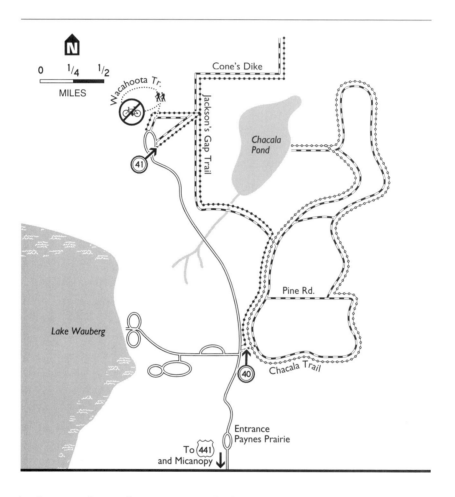

banks to use the treadway as a stream bed. I managed to keep my feet dry only because I was wearing ankle-high boots.

I reached the picnic table at the eastern shore of Chacala Pond, which at a half mile wide and a mile long is larger than a pond by my north Georgian way of thinking. But in Florida, a body of water this size is a pond. So I guess the eight-foot gator I saw swimming in the pond was just a lizard. And those 70-foot trees? Just saplings.

General location: Paynes Prairie State Preserve is located south of Gainesville off US 441 (Exit 73 on I-75).

Elevation change: It starts out around 100 feet above sea level and pretty much stays there.

Season: Except for periods of high water, this trail is open to ride all year long.

Services: Gainesville is a university city; all needs can be met there—a scant 15 minutes away . . . if the traffic's bad. You may want to stay at the preserve's camping area, one of the nicest in Florida.

Hazards: Some natural conditions can be dangerous, and there are some unnatural conditions as well. Although you probably won't see them in this part of the preserve, wild bison and even wilder horses roam inside the preserve. Also, be careful of horseback riders sharing the trail.

Rescue index: The preserve's proximity to Gainesville makes a rescue relatively easy; however, the remote (at least it seems that way) route of the trail could prevent help from arriving quickly.

Land status: This land is managed by the Florida Department of Environmental Protection, Division of Recreation and Parks.

Maps: The entrance has a free map of the trail; I used it to make notes for the map here.

Finding the trail: Leave Interstate 75 on Exit 73 at Micanopy and head north on US 441. The entrance to Paynes Prairie State Preserve is on the right 1 mile north of Micanopy. The trailhead and parking are on the right where the paved road turns left toward the camping area.

Source of additional information:

Paynes Prairie State Preserve
100 Savannah Boulevard
Micanopy, Florida 32667-9702
(352) 466-3397

Notes on the trail: Each intersection is plainly marked with posts and arrows pointing either to Jackson's Gap, Pine Road, or Chacala Pond. Going clockwise, turn right at the first fork shortly after getting on the trail. Approximately a mile and a half later, Pine Road continues straight (a half-mile connector to the other side of the Chacala Pond Loop Trail) and a right turn takes you on a windy route to Chacala Pond. After approximately another mile, a short connector turns left to the far side of Chacala Pond Trail; continue straight to get to the pond the roundabout way. One more right turn takes you to the pond on the half-mile spur to its eastern shore. Take a left at the next intersection for a return to the trailhead. After passing Pine Road's entrance from the left, the going could get a little wet. You may have to pedal through part of a run or a creek that flows through the middle of the trailway.

RIDE 41 · Cone's Dike

AT A GLANCE

Length/configuration: 6-mile out-and-back

Aerobic difficulty: Low; flat double-track terrain

Technical difficulty: Easy

Scenery: Moisture-laden grasslands provide frequent wildlife sightings; beautiful view of the prairie from the dike where you might spot wild horses and bison

Special comments: Most enjoyable when traveled at a leisurely pace

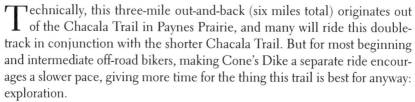

Technically, this three-mile out-and-back (six miles total) originates out of the Chacala Trail in Paynes Prairie, and many will ride this double-track in conjunction with the shorter Chacala Trail. But for most beginning and intermediate off-road bikers, making Cone's Dike a separate ride encourages a slower pace, giving more time for the thing this trail is best for anyway: exploration.

The wet prairie has long been the home of a large assortment of wildlife. Taking a more deliberate pace through this grassland understory makes it possible to catch a family of raccoons out on an early morning forage. When they're surprised, they gallop through the dry palmetto fronds, knocking them together like castanets.

Up on the dike, you can gaze across the prairie where wild bison and horses roam on 6,000 acres set aside for them and other animals. Watching a wild stallion thunder across the plain can change not only the way you ride a bike, but where you ride your bike. If I hear you neighing, I'll understand.

General location: Cone's Dike is located in Paynes Prairie State Preserve, just south of Gainesville.

Elevation change: There is little elevation change to consider here.

Season: Heavy rains can flood sections of the trail, although the dike itself remains dry in all but the most extreme flooding.

Services: Paynes Prairie has all the modern conveniences of any top-notch campground and recreation area. For supplies or services, nearby Gainesville should satisfy all your needs.

Hazards: Hikers also use this trail. Be especially careful around the wild horses and bison.

Rescue index: This trail is regularly traveled, especially on the weekends, but several hours could elapse before you're discovered on a weekday.

Land status: This land is managed by the Florida Department of Environmental Protection, Division of Recreation and Parks.

Maps: You can get a map of Paynes Prairie State Preserve from the main office, either when you arrive or by mail.

Finding the trail: Travel south out of Gainesville on US 441 for approximately 10 miles. Just prior to entering Micanopy, look to the left for the entrance to PPSP. You can begin at Chacala Trail (directly across the road on the right from where you turn into the camping area), or go on a shorter ride by beginning at Jackson's Gap Trail, at the end of the paved preserve road that continues north (straight).

Source of additional information:

Paynes Prairie State Preserve
100 Savannah Boulevard
Micanopy, Florida 32667-9702
(352) 466-3397 (Gainesville-Hawthorne Ranger)

Notes on the trail: From the Chacala trailhead, head north to Jackson's Gap on a counterclockwise route. Continue straight past the 2 trails coming in from the right; those head to Chacala Pond and should be saved for another day. The next trail comes from the left and leads to Wacahoota Trail (foot travel only) and Jackson's Gap Trail parking. If you begin your ride out to the dike from Jackson's Gap, expect a total length of just over 2.5 miles for the out-and-back. Using Jackson's Gap Trail as a 2-mile (4 miles total) out-and-back connector to Chacala Trail makes a total of 12 miles (Chacala Trail is an 8-mile loop).

RIDE 42 · Manatee Springs State Park

AT A GLANCE

Length/configuration: 8.5 miles of loops

Aerobic difficulty: Low; flat terrain

Technical difficulty: Easy

Scenery: Dense forest and active Manatee Springs (great for a post-ride swim)

Special comments: Bring bug spray and wear tick preventive clothing

The perfect complement to the day's ride on over 8.5 miles of looping double-track is to plunge into the cool waters of Manatee Springs and swim in the clear currents of over 80,000 pulsing gallons of water per minute.

RIDE 42 · Manatee Springs State Park

But the north-end trail system, surrounded on the east by the Suwannee River, delves into a dense forest where wild pigs, deer, turkey, and evidence of an ancient way of life can be seen.

The large trees in this state park provide food and shelter for many varieties of plant and animal life. In no other Florida setting (other than Lion Country Safari) have I had as many close encounters with fleet-hooved ruminants. Plus, I startled a drift of black feral swine . . . twice. Armadillos, grubbing for worms or whatever else can be gleaned under the cabbage palms, can be heard rattling off into the leaves and dry branches. But the most interesting sighting was a chikee, a traditional dwelling of the Indians, sort of a Florida version of a tepee.

This authentic hunting chikee found inside Manatee Springs State Park was built by the Indian who used it. Piles of hog bones in the foreground attest his success.

This authentic replica stands situated off a side road in the middle of the network of double-track trail. Its roof is thatched with fronds from the sabal palm. The poles are cypress, and the cross members are juniper. As I stood beside an old fire and a pile of pig and turtle bones, I could almost hear the old stories crackle in the night as the hunters sat on the hewn log benches. Before I left, I walked under the roof and inspected the structure. As I raised my head inside, I detected the distinct aroma of the juniper used for portions of the building. This explained why there were probably few bugs that bothered a sleeper in the top loft area. Although I was tempted to try it out and catch a snooze, it was growing dark and I had miles to go before I slept.

General location: Manatee Springs State Park is located approximately 1 hour west of Gainesville, near the small town of Chiefland.

Elevation change: In a few places, 5 or 6 feet may have been lost over the course of a hundred yards or so, but it is basically flat.

Season: No hunting is allowed inside the park, and the wide, well-cared-for trails can be ridden as long as they aren't under (too much) water.

Services: Your basic necessities can be met in Chiefland a few miles away from the park, but Gainesville is the closest city where all your needs can be met.

Hazards: I was advised by Ken at Gainesville's Spin Cycle—and again by postings in the park office—that you will encounter ticks. Take full precautionary measures to repel the tiny bloodsuckers.

Rescue index: The park's 2,000-plus acres are not expansive, but the atmosphere created is quite remote and primitive; however, a shrill whistle should attract the attention of one of the park's employees at the entrance, no more than a mile or two away.

Land status: This land has been managed—since 1955—by the Florida Department of Environmental Protection.

Maps: The park office offers a free map of the North End Trail System. In addition, you'll find some large wooden maps with "You are here x" signage at some intersections. Maps can also be found on the Internet at **www. dep.state.fl.us/parks/District_2/Manatee Springs.**

Finding the trail: Leave Chiefland on County Road 320 heading west. It dead-ends into the park after approximately 5 miles. Two separate trailheads are located on the right between the entrance and Hickory Camp.

Sources of additional information:

Manatee Springs State Park
11650 N.W. 115th Street
Chiefland, Florida 32626
(352) 493-6072

Spin Cycle
424 West University Avenue
Gainesville, Florida 32601
(352) 373-3355

Notes on the trail: Each intersection has a small sign indicating the names of the roads involved. Combine this convenience with the fact that a great map can be picked up at the entrance and you have a nearly fail-safe way of staying on the route you want. The portion running along the fence line—with its higher grass and proximity to the road—was the least enjoyable, except near Graveyard and Shacklefoot Ponds. This is one of those rides that encourages a slow, quiet pace. Expect to see some unsuspecting wildlife. And don't forget about that swim waiting for you back at the springs.

CENTRAL FLORIDA RIDES—
ORLANDO AND BEYOND

Although it's easy to associate central Florida and Orlando with the Disney theme park, the real magic lies outside its gates. However, as a young man going through boot camp at the Naval Training Center, I failed to understand this. All I remember of Orlando and central Florida from those days were the Black Flags that flew when the heat (and the humidity) grew so great that we were no longer required to participate in extensive physical training. So what do I do? Twenty years later I showed up when the Black Flags flew every day, riding my bike off-road 15–20 miles a day. And you know what? I loved it.

It's true that I had moments when I wanted to be out on one of the many area lakes. I would've liked dipping my paddle in the water and flinging some ten-pound test line to tease a top-water strike from Florida's state freshwater fish, the bass. It would've been nice to shed my sweaty clothes and swim with the gators more often. But those regrets are few and far between. So many excellent off-road sites were nearby, begging to be ridden, that it's tough to be disappointed about anything.

Although I didn't realize it at the time, I was just one of over 26 million annual visitors to the region. As I made my way to the Tosohatchee State Reserve and the Ocala National Forest's nearly 400,000 acres, I found places where it seemed hardly anyone had gone before me. Thousands of lakes and ponds dot the landscape of (what else?) Lake County. The citrus groves that so many associate with Florida flush green on the hilltops of Orange County and spread southward along the ridges of Highlands County.

Water skiing, hiking, camping, shopping, gator farms, and amusement parks—you name it, and central Florida has it in spades, a full house of outdoor recreation that includes 18 off-road rides within an hour's drive of downtown Orlando. So the next time your family starts talking up a trip to go see Mickey and Goofy, pin some mouse ears on your helmet and say, "I'm ready!"

Sources of additional information:

Florida Freewheelers, Inc.
P.O. Box 547201
Orlando, Florida 32854-7201
(407) 788-BIKE

Bike Works
9100 East Colonial Drive
Orlando, Florida 32817-4107
(407) 275-3976

Bike Works
2445 South Hiawassee Road
Orlando, Florida 32835
(407) 297-1550

Bike Works
2177 East Semoran Boulevard
Orlando, Florida 32703
(407) 880-0141

Bike Works
12473 South Orange Blossom Trail
Orlando, Florida 32837-6508
(407) 438-8484

RIDE 43 · Tosohatchee State Reserve

AT A GLANCE

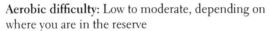

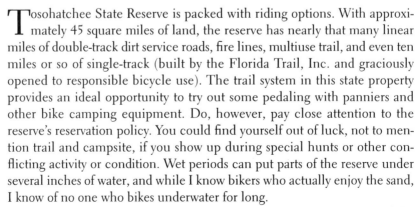

Length/configuration: Close to 50 miles of linear service roads, fire lanes, multi-use trail, and single- and double-track trails

Aerobic difficulty: Low to moderate, depending on where you are in the reserve

Technical difficulty: Easy to moderate

Scenery: Swamps, creeks, marshes, and sloughs house numerous species of wetland wildlife

Special comments: If you make this an overnighter, be sure to call more than two weeks prior to your arrival

Tosohatchee State Reserve is packed with riding options. With approximately 45 square miles of land, the reserve has nearly that many linear miles of double-track dirt service roads, fire lines, multiuse trail, and even ten miles or so of single-track (built by the Florida Trail, Inc. and graciously opened to responsible bicycle use). The trail system in this state property provides an ideal opportunity to try out some pedaling with panniers and other bike camping equipment. Do, however, pay close attention to the reserve's reservation policy. You could find yourself out of luck, not to mention trail and campsite, if you show up during special hunts or other conflicting activity or condition. Wet periods can put parts of the reserve under several inches of water, and while I know bikers who actually enjoy the sand, I know of no one who bikes underwater for long.

Your meticulous plans will be rewarded as you get to enjoy one of the

RIDE 43 · Tosohatchee State Reserve

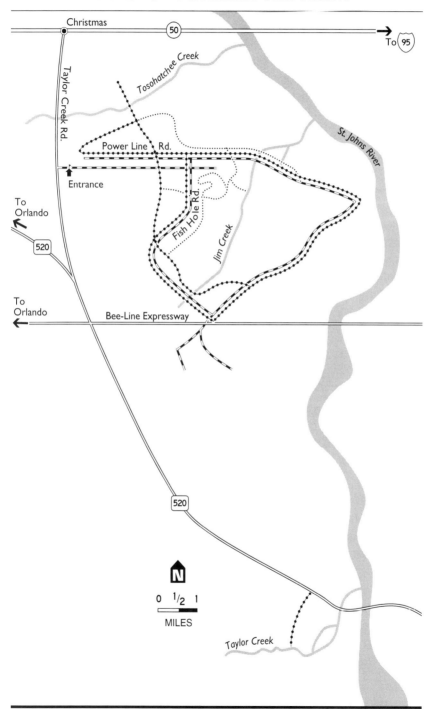

premier wilderness rides in Florida. You'll see swamps, creeks, marshes, and sloughs on your way to the St. Johns River, but the nicest part about the water is the abundance of wildlife you see hopping, slithering, stalking, pouncing, running, leaping, gliding, and crawling near and in it. The reserve offers a smorgasbord of experiences for the off-road biker willing to adapt to the land's strict rules. Ongoing hydrological restoration of wetlands has required re-routing of trails, and we expect further re-routing to be necessary.

General location: The Tosohatchee State Reserve is located about 20 miles east of Orlando, with its eastern border the St. Johns River and its northern border nearly to Christmas.

Elevation change: Starting at 30 feet above sea level, the trail slopes gradually into the sea via the St. Johns River.

Season: Periods of high water are not the times to ride Tosohatchee; hunts are sometimes held. Call ahead for hunt dates and terrain conditions.

Services: Orlando lies a half-hour's drive to the west, with the east coast and its abundance about 15 miles to the east. Camping and making it a biking overnighter (or 2) is a good idea here. Make sure to reserve your place at least 2 weeks before expected arrival. This land and its conditions change rapidly to a degree not favorable for outdoor activities, and so the reserve is closed to public use.

Hazards: Tosohatchee is a big place with all the attendant hazards found naturally in a Florida floodplain and forest wetland. Be alert to the presence of horses and their riders. Biting insects are always present; a bee sting kit is highly recommended.

Rescue index: Make plans for self-rescue here, although if you leave an itinerary with Charlie Matthews, the longtime ranger here, he will follow up on any rendezvous you miss.

Land status: This land is managed by the Florida Department of Environmental Protection, Division of Recreation and Parks.

Maps: An information station is located near the self-pay station. Maps are available on the info sheet called "Recreational Trails, Tosohatchee State Reserve."

Finding the trail: Head east out of Orlando on FL 50 until you reach the small community of Christmas, approximately 25 miles from downtown. Turn right onto Taylor Creek Road. The reserve's entrance sign is approximately 3 miles farther on the left. An honor system of payment requires at least $2 per auto.

Source of additional information:

Tosohatchee State Reserve
3365 Taylor Creek Road
Christmas, Florida 32709

(407) 568-5893
fax (407) 568-1704

Notes on the trail: An approximate 15-mile loop of the main double-track at Tosohatchee—Power Line Road, Long Bluff Road, and Fish Hole Road—generally defines the area where single-track, marked with orange diamonds and rust orange blazes, is open for bicycles. You will come across some single-track, however, which is blazed white; this is reserved for foot traffic only.

RIDE 44 · Wekiwa Springs State Park

AT A GLANCE

Length/configuration: 8 miles of loops

Aerobic difficulty: Low; mostly flat terrain

Technical difficulty: Easy; some twisting on the trail keeps it interesting

Scenery: Lots of wildlife and saw palmetto thickets

Special comments: Small day-use fee required.

By riding the park's over eight miles of double-track loops (a figure eight) primarily intended for horseback riding, the Florida off-road biker can experience a setting rife with wildlife. Some of the area's cyclists knock the park as a viable destination, and if I had talked to these people before I mounted my steel steed, I might have missed one of the most exciting rides in my long (however humble) career.

I found the trailhead across the road from the park's Sand Lake. The sun had dropped below the treetops and was casting long shadows. Almost immediately, I startled a covey of quail that rose in a storm of short beating wings. The air hung heavy with a September sogginess that soon drenched me despite the course's flat terrain. I almost became hypnotized by the long, straight stretch leading into a hall of saw palmetto.

Although the late afternoon gave the ride a half-light beauty, I was ready to cut my trip short at the intersection with a shortcut leading back to the trailhead. "Road 9," I thought, "how original." But my cynicism soon disappeared as the grass-covered track twisted and turned like a pine snake climbing a tree. As I got the camera out to snap a scene I thought was particularly inviting, I heard a crash to my left.

"That sounded pretty big," I said aloud, somehow hoping to assert my dominance over whatever was continuing to raise a commotion. When I turned—camera at the ready—to face the noise, I saw a blur of black rise above the saw palmetto as another frond was broken off. I quickly ran down

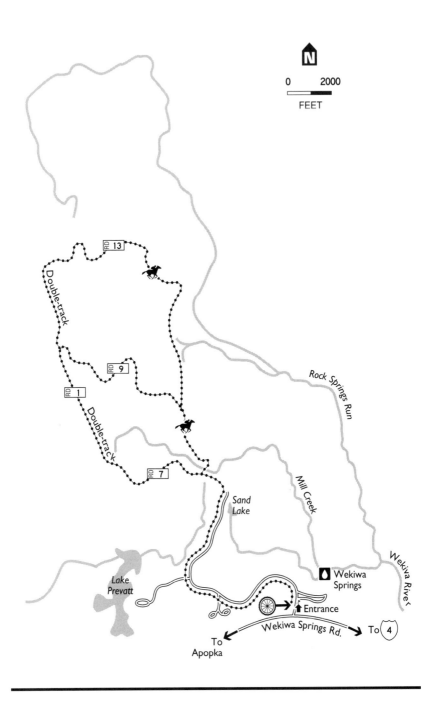

Although this rider escaped, Wekiwa Springs State Park is bear country.

the list of what could be big and black and impervious to the punishment those fronds could deliver to unprotected skin. I recalled the numerous bear crossing signs I had seen not far from the park's entrance. I saw another flash of fur accompanied by another crash.

"It seems to be getting closer," I said, again aloud. I was just about ready to say, "Maybe I can get off a shot for the book," when I heard another— smaller—banging around much closer to me in the palmetto thicket. I said, this time silently, "Uh oh, mama has a cub." I quickly put the camera up and pedaled off, half-expecting to come across a surprised bear blocking the double-track, which now looked as narrow as my front tire.

Later, as I was talking with Bruce Connery of the Florida Park Patrol (an enforcement agency for Florida's parks which now sends out officers—like Bruce—on ATBs), I discovered how lucky I was to have come even that close to a bear, despite Wekiwa Springs being prime habitat. Although you probably won't come away from a bike ride in this park with a bear sighting under your lid, you will find plenty here to satisfy the naturalist in you, and if you're like me, you'll be coming back regularly . . . just in case.

General location: This popular park is located approximately 15 miles northwest of Orlando.

Elevation change: There won't be much here to challenge those hill-climbing quads, but some grades give the suggestion of rolling terrain.

Season: No hunting is allowed, making this a good area to ride when the public woods are handlebar-deep in hunters.

Services: Orlando is less than 30 minutes away, and its suburbs stretch to points close to the park. The camping inside the park is highly recommended.

Hazards: One of the criticisms leveled at this park is that it allows horses to tear up the trails. Although this can be an inconvenience, when I rode here no horses had been on the trail for quite some time. The track was smooth and inviting for the most part.

Rescue index: The wide trails you'll be riding on can accommodate a quick rescue, should you need it.

Land status: This public land is managed by the Florida state park system.

Maps: The entrance (where you'll be asked to pay a day-use fee of at least $4—unless you ride in on your bike, saving at least $3—which is waived if you register as a camper) has a very good map of the trail system you'll be riding, in addition to the foot-travel-only hiking trails where you may want to stretch your legs. But don't ride your bike on them.

Finding the trail: Exit Interstate 4 onto FL 434 and head west approximately 1 mile. A sign for Wekiwa Springs State Park indicates a right turn onto Wekiwa Springs Road. Approximately 4 miles on the right, another sign announces the right turn into the park. You can either park near the entrance or at the trailhead for Sand Lake at the end of the paved park road. The trail begins at the dirt road on the left just before you reach the Sand Lake parking area.

Source of additional information:

Wekiwa Springs State Park
1800 Wekiwa Circle
Apopka, Florida 32712-2599
(407) 884-2008

Notes on the trail: A short spur begins the ride that splits at Road 7 (to the left) and Road 13 (to the right). After reaching the springhead on Road 7 (traveling in a clockwise direction), the number changes to Road 1, a straight stretch. Road 9 turns right, and Road 1 later turns into Road 13 after crossing the hiking trail at approximately the midpoint.

RIDE 45 · Seminole State Forest

AT A GLANCE

Length/configuration: 30 miles total out-and-back

Aerobic difficulty: Terrain here is flat, although sometimes a bit sandy

Technical difficulty: Easy

Scenery: Pretty oak and pine uplands, palmetto prairies, and Blackwater Creek

Special comments: 15 more miles of woods, roads, and trails are in the construction stages

Bikers in the rest of the state will soon consider moving to the Orlando area if the number of possible off-road biking sites is any indication. The nearly 15 miles of closed service roads (for most of the year anyway) can be doubled for a total of 30 miles out-and-back inside the 12,000 acres of this state forest, which is prime black bear country. Although the sand gets a bit loose during the drier times of the year (giving a good workout despite the lack of steep grades), and horse traffic can chew up the surface as well, this area gives another option for a long day of cycling discovery.

The Florida state government appears to be buying into the fact that good bikers make good neighbors . . . literally. Although the park is in the final construction stages, trails are being blazed in the newly purchased parcels of land in the Wekiva River Basin, called the Northern Portion of the Seminole State Forest. Based on the draft received from Robert Duty, Forest Area Supervisor in Leesburg, Florida, approximately 15 more miles of looping woods, roads, and bike trails will not only connect to the Southern Portion of the Seminole Forest, but to the Lower Wekiva River Preserve as well.

The Seminole has a landscape similar to the rest of the river basin, with a mixture of oak and pine uplands rising imperceptibly above the palmetto prairies along Blackwater Creek and Sulphur Run. While the roads can be frustratingly sandy, my conversation with the forest supervisor indicates an eager willingness to work with area bikers to establish and maintain a bike-only trail system.

General location: This is one more of a large number of central Florida area bike sites, found within a 30-minute drive north of Orlando.

Elevation change: There's just not much elevation to change in the Wekiva River Basin.

Season: There's occasional hunting. Call for dates. Also, the drier periods will make for tough riding in the loose sugar-sand, as will the presence of hoof tracks from horses.

Much of Florida's interior is made up of pines and prairie.

Services: Several small communities and towns nearby meet the basic needs of bikers, while Orlando, which will meet all needs, lies a short drive south.

Hazards: Hunting season and horseback riders can combine with floodwaters to make the situation impractical and dangerous for bikers at times.

Rescue index: Although it would take a relatively short time to effect a rescue, the roads are in a primitive setting that should prompt riders to head out self-sufficiently and with a partner.

Land status: This land is managed by the Florida Department of Agriculture and Consumer Services, Division of Forestry.

Maps: Maps of the existing primary roads in the Seminole State Forest–Southern Portion can be acquired at the information station at the trailhead. I received a draft of the planned trails for the Northern Portion, and I used this to indicate the possible placement of the trail system.

Finding the trail: Exit Interstate 4 onto FL 46 headed west. Cross the Wekiva River (approximately 5 miles west on FL 46) and take the next dirt road on the right, where you will see a portion of the Florida Trail with its orange blazes on the right. The normally gated entrance to the service roads lies straight ahead a hundred yards.

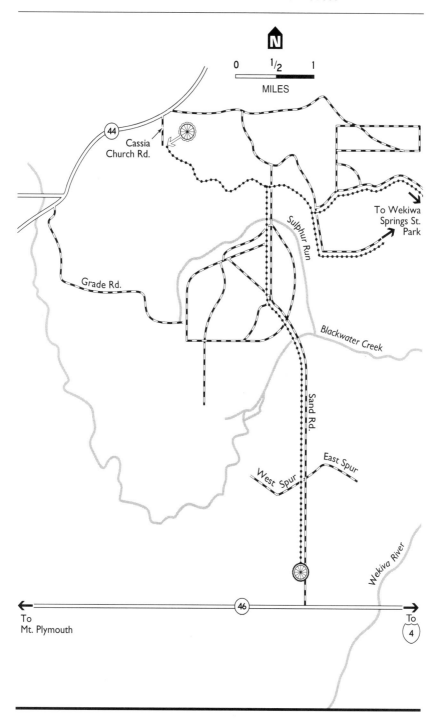

N

0   1/2   1

MILES

44

Cassia
Church Rd.

To Wekiwa
Springs St.
Park

Sulphur Run

Grade Rd.

Blackwater Creek

Sand Rd.

East Spur

West Spur

Wekiva River

46

To
Mt. Plymouth

To
4

Source of additional information:

Seminole State Forest
Division of Forestry
Lake Forestry Station
9610 County Road 44
Leesburg, Florida 34788
(352) 360-6675 or 360-6677

Notes on the trail: For the existing Southern Portion, head out straight on Sand Road (aptly named, so don't expect an easy go of it). An intersection occurs in approximately 2 miles, where the West and/or East Spur can each be taken out-and-back for a total of 2 miles. Sand Road crosses Blackwater Creek after another 2 miles, intersecting first with Pine Road. Taking a right on Pine will lead to the planned connection to the Northern Portion across Sulphur Run; taking a left at the Pine Road intersection will provide the possibility of at least 3 loops, provided by taking either or all of the next 3 dirt roads to the right. You can also go straight on Sand Road, the return leg of loops made by taking any of the 2 roads crossing it before it turns right at Sulphur Run. Also, by taking a right on Pine Road, the draft calls for a connection with the Lower Wekiva River Preserve (described in this guide). I predict that within the next 5 years, this area will not only remain a prime country for black bears, but off-road cyclists will have some of the best hammering habitat in the state.

RIDE 46 · Rock Springs Run State Reserve

AT A GLANCE

Length/configuration: 12-mile loop

Aerobic difficulty: Low; terrain is mostly flat

Technical difficulty: Moderate; some of the single-track is tight and technical (thanks to the Florida Freewheelers bicycle club)

Scenery: Woods, and Rock Springs Run which is a great spot for a quick swim

Special comments: Be sure to bring water on warmer days—the double-track that connects sections of the single-track provides little shade

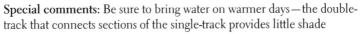

This 12-mile loop east of the confluence of Rock Springs Run with the Wekiva River owes its beginnings to the Florida Freewheelers bicycle club. And, as you might guess with a custom-designed trail, some of the single-track gets a bit technical. Sections of the loop are completed by double-track allowing vehicles and horses. The 8,750 acres stand as one of the finest

RIDE 46 · Rock Springs Run State Reserve

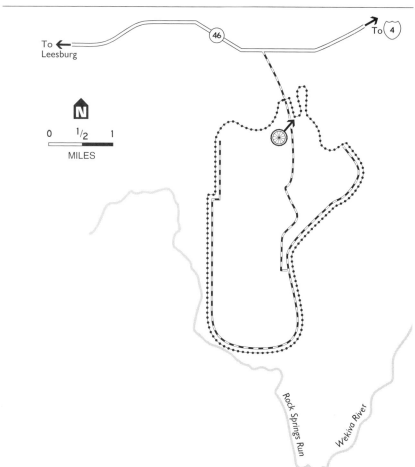

acquisitions by Florida using funds from the CARL (Conservation and Recreation Lands) Program. This parcel—along with Wekiwa Springs State Park, Lower Wekiva River State Preserve, Wekiva Buffers Conservation Area, and Seminole State Forest (in addition to planned land purchases)—allows an unbroken run of its own, straight to the Ocala National Forest to the north.

This expanse of wilderness partly explains the relatively high number of black bears in the region. The land management practices followed in the Wekiva River basin (prescribed burns and eradication of non-native flora, for example) just happen to be what the burly omnivore needs for a happy home. It's also a great habitat for off-road riders looking to pedal through some of Florida's wilder woods.

The ride swings by Rock Springs Run on the southern section of double-track. If you're hot enough, a dip is recommended therapy at this point. And don't ask, "Are there alligators in there?" This is Florida, and wherever there's freshwater, you can assume a gator is not too far away. While it pays to be alert for their approach, you can comfort yourself with the knowledge that they have almost no reputation for unprovoked attacks on humans.

General location: Rock Springs Run State Reserve is located across the river from Wekiwa Springs State Park, approximately 15 miles north of downtown Orlando.

Elevation change: There is little significant change.

Season: Occasionally there is hunting inside the reserve. Other events like flooding and burns may make a trip here ill advised. Call ahead if possible.

Services: Many small communities can be found close to the trailhead, and Orlando lies a short distance to the south.

Hazards: The single-track can get tight in places, and gatorbacks can knock you off, as can small, unseen stumps.

Rescue index: Vehicles can drive to the heart of this reserve, and the single-track never gets very far away from one of the service roads.

Land status: Managed as part of Wekiva Basin Geo Park, part of the Florida state park system.

Maps: A self-pay station at the entrance offered a map. This map, which I used for this guide, does not show the newer single-track blazed by the Florida Freewheelers.

Finding the trail: Exit Interstate 4 onto FL 46 headed west. Approximately 2 miles after crossing the Wekiva River and just after passing the tall bear fencing, you'll see the entrance to Rock Springs Run on the left. Look for the round blue blazes marking the single-track approximately 1 mile (on the left) and three quarters of a mile (on the right).

Source of additional information:

Wekiva Basin Geo Park
1800 Wekiva Circle
Apopka, Florida 32712-2599
(407) 884-2008
Toll-free (in Florida) information on hunting seasons: (800) 342-9620

Notes on the trail: Make sure you bring along plenty of water for this one, especially if it's a summer ride. Although there are some shady areas along the single-track, the double-track's lack of shade can make your head grow hotter and mouth drier. Call the Florida Freewheelers for planned group rides and trail updates.

RIDE 47 · Lower Wekiva River State Preserve

AT A GLANCE

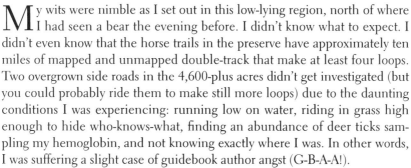

Length/configuration: 10 looping miles of horse trails

Aerobic difficulty: Low; mostly flat terrain

Technical difficulty: Easy

Scenery: Pine woods, saw palmetto thickets, and tall grasses

Special comments: This trail has been torn up a bit by horses and in some places may require a dismount

My wits were nimble as I set out in this low-lying region, north of where I had seen a bear the evening before. I didn't know what to expect. I didn't even know that the horse trails in the preserve have approximately ten miles of mapped and unmapped double-track that make at least four loops. Two overgrown side roads in the 4,600-plus acres didn't get investigated (but you could probably ride them to make still more loops) due to the daunting conditions I was experiencing: running low on water, riding in grass high enough to hide who-knows-what, finding an abundance of deer ticks sampling my hemoglobin, and not knowing exactly where I was. In other words, I was suffering a slight case of guidebook author angst (G-B-A-A!).

Some of the trail showed heavy use by horses, making me yield and walk my bike over the pock marks and loose sugar-sand—the wise choice. In places where the surface still retained some integrity, I could ride fairly easily.

The wind was blowing strongly the day I rode the preserve. Saw palmetto tall enough to block the wind off my legs rattled its dry fronds together in the breeze. Wide prairies of palmetto sat encircled by a thin line of pines. I squinted up at a black vulture wheeling above me in the gusts as I pondered an unfamiliar intersection. "If I had your eyes," I shouted to it, "I'd know which way to go." But instead I followed my nose.

General location: Lower Wekiva River State Preserve is found approximately 25 miles north of downtown Orlando.

Elevation change: Most of the elevation change occurs only in the sandy ruts.

Season: Periods of high water can close sections of the trail, as can prescribed burns. Call for information to be sure.

Services: Orlando is only a short ride to the south.

Hazards: Be sure to carry along plenty of water as there is none along the way or at the trailhead.

RIDE 47 · Lower Wekiva River State Preserve

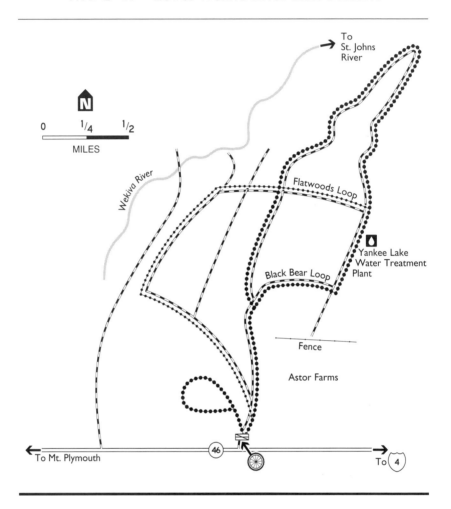

Rescue index: A major highway, FL 46, lies 50 yards from the entrance, and Interstate 4 is only a few miles down it.

Land status: This state preserve is managed by Wekiva Basin Geo Park, a division of the Florida state park system.

Maps: I received the incomplete map from the preserve's office inside Wekiwa Springs State Park. Ask for information on "Horseback Riding in the Lower Wekiva River State Preserve" showing the Flatwoods and Black Bear loops. A brochure showing the preserve's boundaries can be picked up at the information station at the trailhead. Sand Hill Trail, a 1-mile loop near the entrance, has its own map and pamphlet.

Finding the trail: Exit Interstate 4 onto FL 46 and head west. Almost 5 miles down the road, look for the entrance on the right—opposite the intersection where Markham Road joins FL 46. If you cross the Wekiva River, you've gone too far.

Source of additional information:

Wekiva Basin Geo Park (Wekiwa Springs State Park)
1800 Wekiva Circle
Apopka, Florida 32712-2599
(407) 884-2008

Notes on the trail: I took off from the main service road leading to the ranger's residence and office and wound up at an intersection at the park's boundaries across from Katie's, a canoe launch and camping area with a small store. I turned right along the fence line until it dead-ended close to the river. As I returned along the fence, I took the first left onto a wide double-track not shown on the official map (but shown in this guide). I went straight at an intersection about half a mile later that was only marked by an upsidedown U, meaning it was part of the official horse trail. At the next intersection, I saw a sign pointing left (north) for the Flatwoods Loop, but I went straight. The next intersection has Flatwoods Loop coming in on the left (I guessed), and Black Bear Loop goes left past the Yankee Lake Water Treatment Plant on the other side of the fence. Turn right at the intersection where another inverted U on a post points the way, sort of. Other side roads make intersections that are unmarked on the map, but you'll know you're getting close to the trailhead when you take a left onto the extremely sandy section of double-track. A week later, I returned for some info update, and the trail system was under 6 inches of water due to the rain the day before.

RIDE 48 · Prairie Lakes State Reserve

AT A GLANCE

Length/configuration: Over 10 miles out-and-back dirt

Aerobic difficulty: Low; gently rolling terrain

Technical difficulty: Easy; shell-covered roads leave only a few soft, hard-to-navigate, sandy spots

Scenery: Woodsy and lots of wildlife

Special comments: Day-use fee required

It can be argued that what Florida lacks in variety of off-road biking terrain, it more than makes up for in availability and number. Over ten miles (total) of out-and-back dirt roads run through this plain, surrounded by Kissimmee, Jackson, and Marian lakes. Many of the Prairie Lakes roads lack the shade and intimacy of some of our other Florida rides, making it an ideal early morning or late afternoon trip.

I rode these double-rut (for the most part) roads on the grass-covered middle to avoid the sugar-sand that had been worked loose in spots. But it was pretty difficult to watch where I was going. The straight lines of these roads encouraged wildlife watching, and I found the air full of it. I caused a bald eagle to take wing into a cypress dome on the horizon. A rabbit bounded ahead of me, grateful, I suppose, that I was nowhere near as fast as an eagle. A great blue heron became startled after I rounded one of the few curves over Parker Slough, and it flew, legs back, toward Lake Jackson. A dove darted out of the brush, wings whistling in the calm air. By the time I saw the hawk flap into the sunset and the sandhill cranes patrolling the pasture, I was not all that surprised to discover that this reserve is also home to a program for raising endangered whooping cranes.

As the sun dropped below the treeline, a familiar drone filled the air—mosquitoes searching for a sip of warm blood; even that of a crusty biker would do, I discovered. I picked up the pace and left the parasites behind . . . and smacking into my glasses and getting caught in my beard. Before I returned to the trailhead, I had turned my dusky trip into a pedal out of the dark—maybe the best time to ride on those days when the teeth of a September heat wave sink into your back.

General location: Prairie Lakes lies between Lake Kissimmee on the west and Canoe Creek Road on the east, immediately northeast of Lake Jackson.

Elevation change: The elevation ranges from 65 feet or so above sea level to 53 feet above sea level on the surface of Lake Jackson.

Season: As you might guess, the rainy periods do not treat this low-lying ground well for bikers.

Services: Lots of pasture and many farms line the roads north to St. Cloud, 25 miles away. A small store/restaurant with country hours is located in Kenansville, a small community at the intersection of County Road 523 and US 441.

Hazards: Other than the normally occurring natural conditions that can prove difficult, this is a low-key trail as far as hazards go.

Rescue index: This is not a convenient place at all for rescue; it's remote.

Land status: This land is managed by the Florida Fish and Wildlife Conservation Commission.

Maps: All entrances have brochures and maps. I got my map of Prairie Lakes State Reserve from the Florida Fish and Wildlife Conservation Commission

RIDE 48 · Prairie Lakes State Reserve

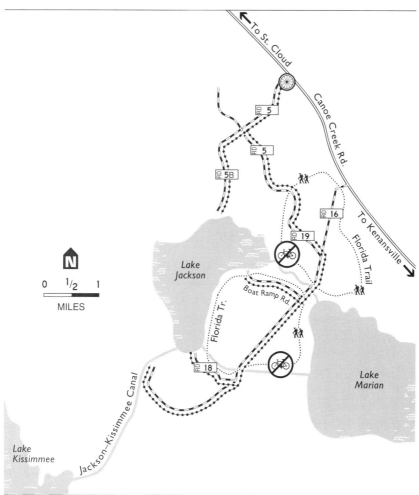

office in Ocala (see Source on page 174). There is a day-use fee of $3 per person or $6 per vehicle upon entrance.

Finding the trail: From downtown St. Cloud, pick up US 192/441 and turn south onto Vermont Avenue (in the eastern third of downtown), which soon turns into Canoe Creek Road, aka County Road 523. Approximately 25 miles down CR 523, look for the entrance to Three Lakes Wildlife Management Area. The highway you cross about a third of the way down is Florida's Turnpike. I parked by the check station, in the grass, and stepped over a black snake with bold yellow stripes running the length of its body.

Source of additional information:

Florida Fish and Wildlife Conservation Commission
1239 S.W. 10th Street
Ocala, Florida 34474
(352) 732-1225

Notes on the trail: The roads within this reserve are unpaved but well marked at intersections, which makes for easy navigating. The road at the trailhead, Road 5, leads straight to Lake Jackson, or you can turn left at its junction with Road 19, which follows a creek for a mile or so before crossing Prairie Slough and coming to shelled Road 16. Although I would have liked the ride less in the middle of a hot summer day, I'll remember Prairie Lakes and its evening shade of suspense with no regret, except for having to leave.

RIDE 49 · Little-Big Econ State Forest

AT A GLANCE

Length/configuration: 2-mile loop

Aerobic difficulty: Low

Technical difficulty: Moderate; the sections of single-track are narrow and windy and the double-track has loose sand in spots

Scenery: Thick pine woods, saw palmetto thickets, and Econlockhatchee River

Special comments: The river is a nice place to fish and canoe

As I told Mike Martin, representative of the Little-Big Econ State Forest, after I had finished riding the approximate two-mile loop of both single- and double-track in this 5,051-acre forest surrounding the Econlockhatchee River, "It was over too quick!" I also told him that despite the heavy rain that morning, the trail—especially the sandier spots—held up fine, with only a little standing water on the section closest to the river.

The state forest will eventually encompass over 15,000 acres, thereby connecting a 100-mile wildlife corridor from FL 46 to the Florida Turnpike. We can only hope this means more bike trail will be developed. The black water of the Econlockhatchee River is also a quiet place to fish and canoe, and if you get a permit for primitive camping you can stay for a long weekend of exploring with the panniers on, or maybe even put in a little trail trimming with the Florida Freewheelers.

General location: The Little-Big Econ State Forest is located about a 20-minute drive northeast of Orlando.

RIDE 49 · Little-Big Econ State Forest

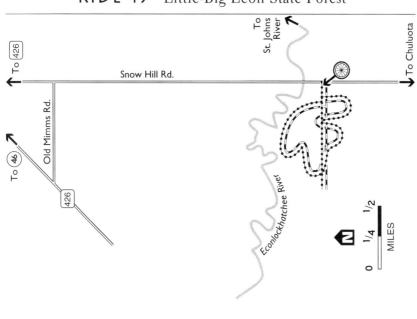

Elevation change: The elevation as you turn onto Snow Hill Road from the south is approximately 56 feet above sea level, and it descends to about 10 feet above sea level at the river.

Season: This is a year-round trail with no hunting allowed. The sections of service road that get the highest use have some longer stretches of loose sugar-sand when it's drier.

Services: You can get just about anything you need in nearby Orlando. The smaller communities, like Chuluota and Oviedo, can provide many of the basic needs.

Hazards: I had to roll over some gatorbacks slowly. And some sand.

Rescue index: Snow Hill Road is a fairly busy secondary highway. FL 46 lies close to the north. Plus, 5,000 acres is not all that big.

Land status: This land is managed by the Florida Division of Forestry.

Maps: The information station at the trailhead has a large map posted behind Plexiglass. An updated map has been prepared and is available in kiosks.

Finding the trail: Exit Interstate 4 north of Orlando at the Sanford/FL 46 ramp. Follow FL 46 east (Geneva Avenue) through Sanford, turning right (south) onto County Road 426, with Snow Hill Road forking to the left less than a mile down 426. Cross the river and look for a wooden fence on your right. The bike trail begins behind the fence and is blazed with a bike symbol.

Biking in the Little-Big Econ State Forest provides moments that are head and shoulders above the rest.

Source of additional information:

Little-Big Econ State Forest
1350 Snowhill Road
Geneva, Florida 32732
(407) 971-3500

Notes on the trail: The trail begins on double-track that serves as the main east-west connector for both sides of the single-track runs. While the trail is easily followed thanks to the superb markings on posts (showing bike symbols and arrows), allow yourself time to check out the Forest Service roads. See if you can find the suspension bridge. This is one of those areas where you hope more single-track gets built. The single-track already in place is tight and twisty, a nice touch in a palmetto thicket 6 feet tall.

RIDE 50 · Bull Creek Wildlife Management Area

AT A GLANCE

Length/configuration: 15 miles of loop; several figure-eight combinations are possible

Aerobic difficulty: Low

Technical difficulty: Easy

Scenery: Cypress domes, sawgrass marsh, and Bull Creek with its abundance of wetland wildlife

Special comments: Ideal place for studying native plants; this land contains several different kinds of ecological habitats

What would you say if I told you there was a wildlife management area where you could ride off-road through a cross-section of several Florida habitats for over 15 miles in a figure-eight combination of loops? Did you say "Bull Creek?" If you did, you already know about the nearly 24,000 acres the U.S. Army Corps of Engineers acquired for the Upper St. Johns River Basin Flood Control Project.

As you might guess, parts of this property will be seasonally wet and/or flooded. This is a good area for studying various native Florida landscapes, because an interpretive ride (with brochure) shows different ecotones, or transition zones. You will see a classic example of the hypericum sink, signaled in the spring and summer by its nearly constant blooming of the yellow St. Johnswort.

Along with the ferns and shrubs of the understory, cypress domes create a mountainous effect as they pop up on the flat line of sawgrass marsh. Bull Creek is a great place to see a large variety of flying, wading, and diving birds and the predators above them in the food chain. Sandhill cranes may be seen nesting in the open wetlands or looking to pick up an amphibian or arthropod meal. With an especially keen sight, you may see a black racer or a hissing hognose snake sliding toward a meal in the maidencane, or sliding down the gut of a great blue heron.

General location: Bull Creek Wildlife Management Area is located 6 miles off US 192, almost 4 miles east of Holopaw, Florida.

Elevation change: Much of the land rises to a little over 65 feet above sea level; however, Jane Green Swamp—5 miles east—hovers at only 20 feet above sea level. The Atlantic Ocean itself lies just 25 miles (as the crow flies) east of the trailhead.

Season: Hunting is allowed at certain times of year, and flooding needs no permission. Call ahead for conditions before you make the long trip off US 192 to the trailhead.

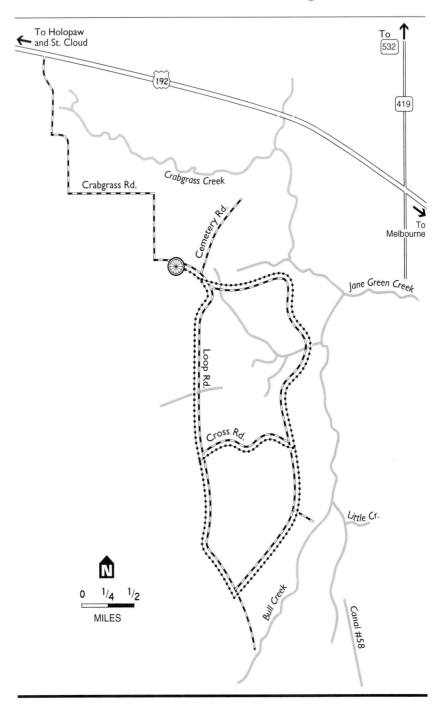

To Holopaw
and St. Cloud

To
532

419

192

Crabgrass Creek

Crabgrass Rd.

Cemetery Rd.

To
Melbourne

Jane Green Creek

Loop Rd.

Cross Rd.

Little Cr.

N

0   1/4   1/2
MILES

Bull Creek

Canal #58

Services: Your best bet for anything out of the ordinary would be to hit the east coast at Melbourne on US 192. Holopaw has the basics.

Hazards: It could be too wet or too dry, with hunters and horseback riders to boot. Vehicles also drive these roads. It is so far off the main roads, though, that I suspect most weekdays would be relatively traffic free.

Rescue index: Except for weekends, when the use increases, prepare for a ride in solitude and a setting as remote as you can get this close to Florida's east coast.

Land status: This land is managed by the Florida Fish and Wildlife Conservation Commission.

Maps: The St. Johns River Water Management District has published the "Recreation Guide to District Lands," available on request.

Finding the trail: Head east out of St. Cloud or west out of Melbourne on US 192. Approximately 3.5 miles east of Holopaw, look for the sign announcing the southern turn to Bull Creek Wildlife Management Area. It's a long 6-mile drive on what can be a washboard road to the trailhead.

Source of additional information:

St. Johns River Water Management District
Division of Public Information
P.O. Box 1429
Palatka, Florida 32178-1429
(904) 329-4500 or (800) 451-7106 (Florida only)

Notes on the trail: Approximately 1 mile on the left after the trailhead, Cemetery Road leads to a private graveyard. Continue on Loop Road until you come to Cross Road, where you can turn right to make a shorter 8-mile loop or continue straight at this point, passing a road on the left to Bull Creek. The next road to the left (actually a dead end heading either north or south) goes to Billy Lake, where a primitive camping area (primarily intended for hikers) can be used by permit. The right turn at this intersection leads back to the trailhead via Loop Road.

RIDE 51 · Environmental Center at Soldier Creek

AT A GLANCE

Length/configuration: Over 5 miles of loops

Aerobic difficulty: Moderate; some abrupt, unexpected hills

Technical difficulty: Moderate; single-track with plenty of roots and mud to contend with

Cabbage palm fronds shade this rider's trip along Soldier Creek.

Scenery: Hardwood forests, cypress trees, Lake Jessup, creeks, and swampland

Special comments: The center's museum houses both stuffed and live wild animals

The five miles plus of looping single-track on this Seminole County property (an agreement with the school board for their environmental studies center) may not be long, but it gives the off-road rider a site to challenge balance and strength. Local bikers speak admiringly of this trail, where they are cordially invited to ride. "Just watch out for people walking on the trail," said a teacher setting up a display inside the center's natural history museum. "We have children from our school coming here to see a part of the outdoors they don't spend much time in."

Alert for the sight of a tiny person chasing a butterfly, I took off through the woods, starting at approximately 28 feet above sea level in what is officially called Spring Hammock Preserve. As I was prepared to notice, the hardwoods (like oaks and gums) in the drier uplands were replaced by trees such as cypress

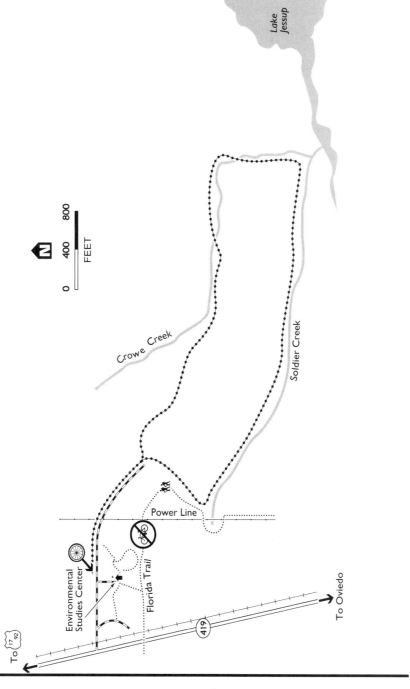

Lake Jessup

Crowe Creek

Soldier Creek

N

0 400 800

FEET

Power Line

Environmental Studies Center

Florida Trail

To 17 92

419

To Oviedo

found in wetter soil. I heard the unmistakable midday call of the towhee, a bird common in thickly forested areas. By the time I got to Lake Jessup at only four feet above sea level, I had passed over the confluence of Crowe Creek with Soldier Creek and boardwalked my way through a freshwater swamp.

Back at the center's museum, I spent some time looking at the many animals (most stuffed, but others alive) found in the woods outside. A bobcat lolls in the crook of a tree opposite a black bear, six feet tall on its hind legs. Two turtles rested on an island in the middle of their aquarium. Next to them, a foot-long gator hissed at me as I walked past. Pure Florida, with some biking on the side. What could be better?

General location: This preserve is located north of Orlando, close to US 17/92.

Elevation change: 28 feet to 4 feet above sea level, some of it quicker than others.

Season: Periods of high water can make for a muddy, boggy ride, better postponed until it's drier.

Services: Orlando lies to the south . . . barely. Its metropolitan sprawl has brought all goods and services nearly to the trailhead.

Hazards: Roots and mud are the bulk of the technical challenges, which are plenty.

Rescue index: A rescue can be quickly effected at this location.

Land status: This public land is managed by Seminole County.

Maps: I was able to pick up a map inside the museum; however, it is not normally open. Call or write ahead for the Seminole County Nature Center at Soldier Creek Park map.

Finding the trail: Exit Interstate 4 headed east. In Sanford, turn right onto US 17/92. Approximately 4 miles after 17/92 splits with the Eastern Beltway, FL 419 begins on the left. Look for the entrance on the left less than a mile after you turn onto 419.

Source of additional information:

Jim Duby
Seminole County Manager
1101 East 1st Street
Sanford, Florida 32771-1460
(407) 665-1130

Notes on the trail: Osprey Trail technically begins as soon as you turn off FL 419, but the gated section of trail (Magnolia Trail) begins past the power line. Approximately halfway through the larger outer loop, a boardwalk and a catwalk provide the option of a shorter loop leading to Soldier Creek. But the longer ride takes you past Question Pond and down Crowe Creek. A trail is planned that will connect the northern end of the swamp to Magnolia Trail. Limpkin Trail follows Soldier Creek back to Magnolia Trail and the power line trailhead.

RIDE 52 · Hal Scott Preserve

AT A GLANCE

Length/configuration: 15 miles of loops attached to an out-and-back (several combinations possible)

Aerobic difficulty: Low to moderate; some rolling terrain

Technical difficulty: Easy

Scenery: Econlockhatchee River, old homesteads

Special comments: Best to ride on cooler days

It took Florida a while to figure out that the wealth of the land is securely tied to its water, resulting in the creation of water authorities to oversee the management of wetlands and the procurement of comparable parcels of land whenever public projects—such as the nearby Bee-Line Expressway—pave over wilderness. The nearly 15 miles (total) of loops attached to an out-and-back in the upper Econlockhatchee River, where the Hal Scott Preserve was established, resulted from one such "asphalt compensation."

It seems fitting that some of the reclaimed primitive roadways in the Hal Scott Preserve first got their beginning in 1871 when Sanford was connected via Curry's Ford and Fort Christmas to Lake Washington near the Indian River to the east. Hal Scott himself was an environmental consultant for the Orlando–Orange County Expressway Authority. The preserve's 3,700 acres will forever be a site where outdoor activities can go undisturbed by the inevitable (and obvious) encroachment of development.

The day I arrived at the trailhead—on a tight schedule—the thunderheads boiled in a black promise of torrential downpour. I walked a short distance onto the trail—with its overgrown, late-summer forelocks of grass—and made a reluctant decision to present this trail unridden by me, but discussed with others who have enjoyed its miles.

General location: The Hal Scott Preserve is located approximately 20 minutes east of Orlando via the Bee-Line Expressway.

Elevation change: This is some of the highest ground around at approximately 90 feet above sea level; it descends to less than 20 feet at the river.

Season: This is one more hunter-free site to enjoy during those late fall and winter days when the woods smell like gunpowder. You may want to try this trail on a not-so-hot day after the grass has died back.

Services: Orlando is not far away, and small communities within a 10-minute drive can provide the basics. The trailhead had neither water nor rest rooms.

Hazards: There are no hunters, but horses and their unpredictable hooves are occasionally seen on this trail.

Rescue index: It's not a big place, so whatever help you need can be acquired fairly quickly. A subdivision lies to the east of the trailhead.

Land status: This land is managed by the St. Johns River Water Management District.

Maps: The St. Johns River Water Management District has a publication called "Recreation Guide to District Lands," which can be acquired upon request. It includes Hal Scott Preserve along with 31 other sites—a good addition to your recreation library.

Finding the trail: Leave Orlando headed east on FL 50. County Road 520 forks to the right (south), and after about a mile you'll see a sign for the Wedgefield subdivision on the right; turn right. After a little over a mile, Maxim Parkway dead-ends into Bancroft; turn left. Take the quick right onto Meredith. After approximately 1 mile, it dead-ends into Dallas. Turn left and go a little less than 2 miles (after driving under the power lines), where you'll see a wooden fence around the parking area on the right.

Sources of additional information:

St. Johns River Water
Management District
Division of Public Service
and Information
P.O. Box 1429
Palatka, Florida 32178-1429
(904) 329-4500 or
(800) 451-7106 (Florida only)

Orange County Parks and
Recreation
4801 West Colonial Drive
Orlando, Florida 32808-7756
(407) 836-6200

Notes on the trail: The main trail starts out heading west. A trail comes in shortly from the right and loops back into the north side of the main trail running east-west, but not before it first crosses the Econlockhatchee River and then Cowpen Branch. Another loop heads south off the main trail and reconnects after a little over a mile. An old homestead lies on the north side of the trail after the river, and a south spur leads to another old home place. A second trail heads south (after crossing the river) and leads to Green Branch and a pretzeled loop of trails before making the return north to the main trail.

RIDE 52 · Hal Scott Preserve

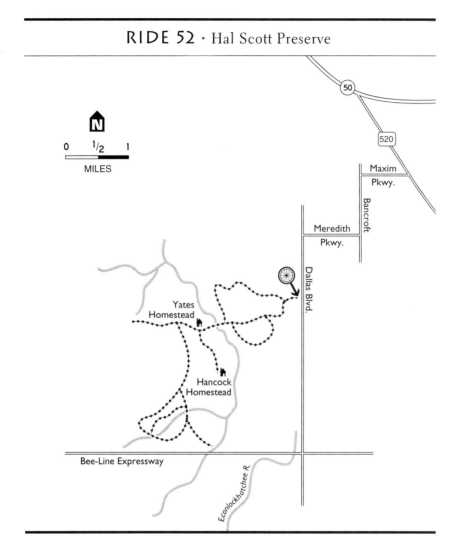

SOUTHEAST FLORIDA RIDES

I had already made my way to West Palm Beach when I walked into a bike shop and learned that some locals, at least, don't consider themselves a part of south Florida. Back at my aunt's condo, I pulled the atlas out again and determined that for my purposes, I was in south Florida. I guess the guy I was talking to felt that the 140 miles of keys bending into the waters off Cape Florida (called the Conch Republic) were "south." With apologies to those who feel otherwise, south Florida begins in this guide on an imaginary line drawn from Tampa in the west to Melbourne in the east.

Much of the land available for off-road biking in this area lies close to the coast. Lake Okeechobee's 730 square miles and expanse of the Everglades necessarily limit the places where much riding can be done. It pretty much has been that way ever since the days when the Spanish explorers first sighted land in the early sixteenth century. Henry Flagler, however, funded the building of a railroad that changed this region into a vacation land unsurpassed by almost anyplace in the world.

Flagler's plan was to lay the track to the hotels he built. The genius of his idea was made apparent with the rapid growth of what can be described as a giant city stretching from Miami in the south to West Palm Beach in the north; it's not all that wide, but it surely is long. Add to this the almost uninterrupted development on the Keys, and urban sprawl becomes defined with south Florida's picture.

Although this dense development has had conflicts with providing trails where the biker can get off-road, local governments—most notably Broward County—have begun providing single-track, built in cooperation with local bike clubs. Of course, the Everglades remain the region's most spectacular

Australian pines—
a pretty but invasive
flora—provide a back-
drop on some rides in
southeast Florida.

geographic feature, and the federal government has made some attempts to open up sections of this wilderness to biking.

South Florida on the Atlantic, in spite of incredible pressures, still manages to keep some of its natural beauty. Golf courses (more courses than anywhere else in America) and tennis courts (over 7,700 facilities) take their share of what's left. Condos creep into the land, butting against the green horizon of sugar cane growing in the black muck of former sawgrass. But today, with bicycling being Florida's second most popular outdoor recreation, it is not uncommon for the sawgrass to part as the wide tires of a mountain bike make their way through.

Sources of additional information:

ClubMud
West Broward Bicycle Center
13612 State Road 84
Davie, Florida 33325
(954) 424-9394

West Palm Beach Bicycle Club
P.O. Box 16764
West Palm Beach, Florida 33416
(561) 842-7414

RIDE 53 · Jonathan Dickinson State Park

AT A GLANCE

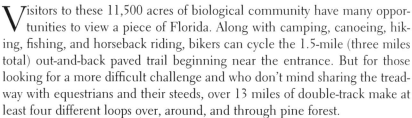

Length/configuration: 1.5 mile out-and-back (3 miles total) of paved bike trail; 4 loops of horse trail that total 13 miles

Aerobic difficulty: Low; mostly flat terrain

Technical difficulty: Easy; some sand in places

Scenery: Loxahatchee River which is known for its variety of wildlife

Special comments: Camping, canoeing, hiking, fishing, and horseback riding are available nearby

Visitors to these 11,500 acres of biological community have many opportunities to view a piece of Florida. Along with camping, canoeing, hiking, fishing, and horseback riding, bikers can cycle the 1.5-mile (three miles total) out-and-back paved trail beginning near the entrance. But for those looking for a more difficult challenge and who don't mind sharing the treadway with equestrians and their steeds, over 13 miles of double-track make at least four different loops over, around, and through pine forest.

The park's namesake came here unintentionally in 1696 when Dickinson, his family, and others survived a shipwreck off the coast. Much of what we know about life in early Florida comes from the journal Dickinson kept during those difficult times along the Loxahatchee River. As you ride under the cypress trees, you can also recall the "Wild Man of the Loxahatchee," Trapper Nelson, who lived off the surrounding land. His death in 1968 was followed by the state's acquisition of his former property, where an interpretive site has been established. The method of transportation here is the Loxahatchee Queen II, a 44-passenger boat.

But the "real fun in the Real Florida" comes from riding a bike off-road. The landscape inside the park is home to a variety of wildlife: mammal, plant, fowl, and reptile. You can expect to see much of this life on the banks of the Loxahatchee River, a National Wild and Scenic River since 1985 that possesses "remarkable ecological and recreational values . . . unique in the United States."

General location: Jonathan Dickinson State Park is located on Florida's Atlantic coast, approximately 30 minutes north of West Palm Beach.

Elevation change: Although no biking is allowed on the dunes, these natural barriers to the sea set the stage for a ride that sees little change in elevation.

Season: No hunting is allowed in the park, so this is a good alternative to those trails closed in hunting seasons. The sandy nature of the trails makes it

RIDE 53 · Jonathan Dickinson State Park

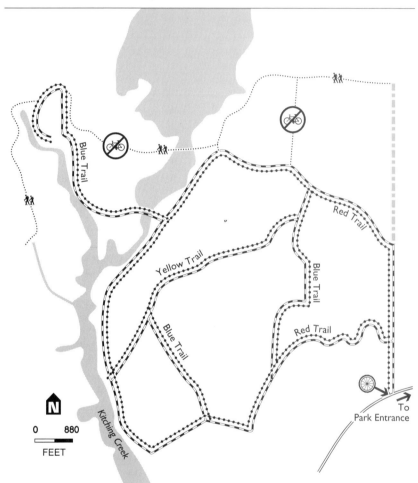

a better place to ride during wetter times. However, after heavy rains the trails may be submerged, so call ahead.

Services: Camping is encouraged in the park, where you can find the normal facilities. Outside the park along US 1, a wide range of services can be acquired. Should you need the exotic or unusual, no fear: you are on Florida's east coast, sometimes referred to as the nation's living monument to the exotic and unusual.

Hazards: Horses on these trails should be handled with an early, friendly greeting. Stepping aside while the beasts pass is required.

Rescue index: You should not have trouble getting help or assistance inside the park. It covers over 11,000 acres, though, so be prepared to take initial steps toward self-rescue.

Land status: This land is operated by the Florida state government.

Maps: The entrance has copies of the horse trails and "Information and Regulations Concerning Camping with Horses."

Finding the trail: Exit Interstate 95 at either 59 or 60, heading east toward the coast and US 1. From Exit 59 go north on US 1, and from 60 head south. The entrance to the park will be on the west side of US 1, north of Jupiter. The trailhead is inside the park on the right at the Eaglesview Area.

Source of additional information:

Jonathan Dickinson State Park
16450 S.E. Federal Highway
Hobe Sound, Florida 33455
(561) 546-2771

Notes on the trail: Begin riding north along the Power Line Road, and after approximately a quarter mile look to the left for the marked red trail, which makes a horseshoe loop to the power line. You'll be headed toward Kitching Creek unless you take the blue or yellow trails back to the northern leg of the red trail. By taking the outer loop and staying on the red trail, you'll cover approximately 4.25 miles.

RIDE 54 · DuPuis Reserve

AT A GLANCE

Length/configuration: A 5.5-mile out-and-back (11 miles total) trail, plus a 14-mile out-and-back (28 miles total) on service roads

Aerobic difficulty: Very low because it's very flat

Technical difficulty: Easy; flat double-track

Scenery: Lake Okeechobee, Cypress domes, saw grass prairie, pasture, and citrus trees

Special comments: Bikers are only allowed on named and numbered roads

This state forest's 20,000-plus acres used to be the domain of the DuPuis (pronounced "do PWEE") family, but it now serves as a state reserve where a 5.5-mile, out-and-back (11 miles total) trail plus a 14-mile out-and-

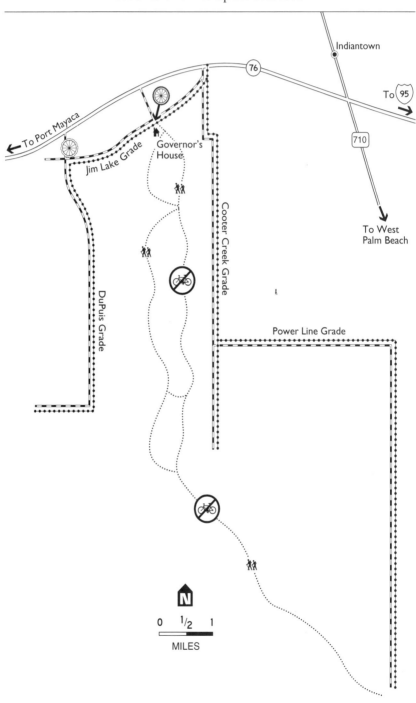

back (28 miles total) on double-track service roads provide the setting for a memorable ride near the great Lake Okeechobee. In addition to those two out-and-backs, you can ride a two-mile connector between DuPuis Grade and Power Line Grade, and a short 1.5-mile continuation (an out-and-back of three miles total) called Cooter Creek Grade. *Note:* Bicycles are only allowed on main grades—named and numbered roads.

Although Okeechobee now stays inside the bowl created by the levee surrounding it, this land contains plenty of wetlands. Native forests and flatwoods make up the bulk of the acreage, but the diversity of this landscape is revealed by its cypress domes, sawgrass prairie, and pasture; there's even 60-some-odd acres in citrus trees. Likewise, a wide range of animals make their home inside the reserve—wiggling, flapping, and galloping to their hearts' content.

The only thing lacking for the off-road rider in this reserve is a system of single-track like the selection of four hiking loops built and maintained by the Florida Trail. Perhaps in the near future, as biking in these state reserves and preserves becomes more common and accepted, DuPuis Reserve will be included as a site for some single-track cycling.

General location: DuPuis Reserve is located near the east shore of Lake Okeechobee, where the St. Lucie Canal begins.

Elevation change: There is slim to none in the way of elevation change here; that is, unless you get off and climb some of the trees near the DuPuis family home, which serves as reserve headquarters.

Season: Portions of this trail system can be flooded at any time, but especially during the wetter summer months. Since this is a reserve and not a preserve, some hunting is allowed on the grounds on certain dates. You can call and request a list of the times for those hunts, or just call ahead whenever you're planning a trip there.

Services: The services inside the reserve are limited to water, phone, and rest rooms. Other than that, you will have to try your luck at the tiny towns of Canal Point and Pahokee. A much larger (if not complete) choice of services lies to the east near West Palm Beach and Stuart.

Hazards: The horses that use this reserve are restricted to their own trail system, so you should not encounter any. Hunters, also, should be no problem, as they are the sole users on those days when hunts are going on; bikers are not allowed on those days.

Rescue index: Should you have to depend solely on others to bring aid, you could have quite a wait. Be prepared for self-rescue.

Land status: This land is owned by the state of Florida.

Maps: A map of DuPuis Reserve showing the double-track service roads and horseback trails, along with the single-track biking/hiking trails, is found at the information station inside the park.

Finding the trail: Exit Interstate 95 onto either FL 76 or County Road 708 and head west. CR 708 dead-ends into SR 76, where you turn left and head west 5 miles to DuPuis. The main entrance is gated.

Sources of additional information:

South Florida Water Management
District
P.O. Box 24680
3301 Gun Club Road
West Palm Beach, Florida 33416-
4680
(800) 432-2045 (Florida only)

South Florida Water Management
District
23500 S.W. Kanner Highway
Canal Point, Florida 33438
(561) 924-5310

Notes on the trail: The main entrance serves as the trailhead where DuPuis Grade and Jim Lake Grade intersect. DuPuis Grade goes south 5.5 miles, and Jim Lake Grade connects to the Power Line Grade, which makes up the bulk of the nearly 50 miles of total riding on the double-track service roads. Power Line Grade heads south and turns east at the 5-mile mark. Cooter Creek Grade is the 1.5-mile out-and-back that continues straight. The power line marks the double-track under it, and if you don't mind the hum of high voltage transformers overhead, in addition to the sometimes wet or sandy conditions, you have a great place to ride.

RIDE 55 · Lake Trail, Palm Beach (Trail of Conspicuous Consumption)

AT A GLANCE

Length/configuration: 4.5-mile out-and-back (9 miles total)

Aerobic difficulty: Low; mostly flat

Technical difficulty: Easy; paved and used also by walkers, joggers, and skaters

Scenery: Trail winds along the banks of Lake Worth

Special comments: Several unusual sights decorate the trail (including a tree with a fluted trunk)

In only a few places in the world, the nickname of this trail would be an understatement, and Palm Beach, Florida, is one of them. The approximately 4.5-mile out-and-back (nine miles total) along the ritzy intracoastal waterway near Lake Worth attracts all sorts to ride its golf-cart width of asphalt: from people rich enough to hire their own full-time yacht crews to grizzled bike guide authors and their friends.

RIDE 55 · Lake Trail, Palm Beach
(Trail of Conspicuous Consumption)

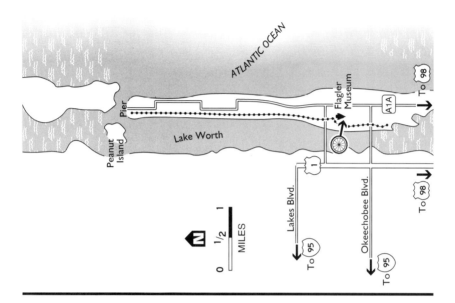

One of those friends, Mike, had mentioned this trail to me as one he and our friend Brian had ridden in the days of innocence when young boys could still climb trees in the backyard of Flagler Museum. You know, Flagler, the railroad guy who spanned the Keys, making mere opulence seem middle-class in the process.

The trail still makes those same turns near the museum shaded by button-wood, Christmas palm, and other native species. One of those, the gumbo limbo, is also called the "tourist tree" for its red, peeling bark. Lake Trail is a popular site not only for bikers, but for walkers, joggers, and in-line skaters.

General location: Lake Trail is located in Palm Beach.

Elevation change: There is an occasional, slight change in elevation, but only what you would expect on land so close to the ocean.

Season: This is an all-season trail.

Services: You name it, you can get it and quick—for a price.

Hazards: Take care in passing other users and be alert to others passing you.

Rescue index: This could be the easiest rescue ever.

Land status: The trail lies on land owned by the Palm Beach city government.

Maps: There are no maps, nor is there much need for any. Refer to the one in this guide.

The fluted trunk of this tree in the backyard of the Flagler Museum is but one of many unusual sights along Lake Trail.

Finding the trail: Exit Interstate 95 at Okeechobee Boulevard and head east across the bridge. Turn left onto A1A (Coconut Avenue) and go past Flagler Museum. You can park, in the off-season and low-use times, in the Royal Poinciana Plaza. Other public parking can be acquired with just a bit of scouting. My next choice would be the parking lot for Flagler Museum. Ride toward the intracoastal waterway until coming to the asphalt path.

Source of additional information:

West Palm Beach Bicycle Club
P.O. Box 16764
West Palm Beach, Florida 33416
(561) 842-7414

Notes on the trail: The trail has one detour near the bridge on Okeechobee Boulevard. Other than that, it goes straight along Lake Worth's banks until coming to the pier across the way from Peanut Island Park. For the last half mile or so, the ride goes along the back streets. Just keep heading north and the road ends at the pier. If you feel lost, don't hesitate to stop and ask directions from the people using this trail; they are generally friendly.

RIDE 56 · Quiet Waters Park

AT A GLANCE

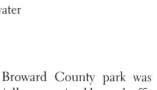

Length/configuration: 5.5-mile loop

Aerobic difficulty: Moderate; some short, steep, abrupt hills

Technical difficulty: Moderate to challenging; single-track sections can be narrow and have roots, rocks, and some big hills (one 10-foot drop)

Scenery: Boat rental area, cable-skiing area, water amusement park

Special comments: Small park-entrance fee

The single-track loop inside this popular Broward County park was designed and built months before it was officially recognized by park officials in September 1996. As a result, the pirate rides on this technical loop of 5.5 miles created a reputation too good for area bikers to resist.

I was warned by the management that the trail's difficulty had already caused its share of crack-ups—breaking bones and laying open shins. After talking with Dan Edgar at the West Broward Cycle Center, who informed me in detail of the trail's status, I learned that due to a bureaucratic slowdown, the trail's construction had not been completed, which explained the large number of highly technical maneuvers required to ride this trail safely.

Now that the trail is officially recognized and maintained, however, the surface has been brought up to the standards recommended by the International Mountain Bike Association. Although the waters inside this small park may be quiet, you won't be when you finish riding this single-track. And while you're at it, pick up the phone and give the fun folks at ClubMud (and Quiet Waters Park) a call to thank them for persisting in the face of a bureaucratic stonewall.

General location: Quiet Waters Park is located in Broward County, Pompano Beach, Florida.

Elevation change: There is no extended change in elevation, but be prepared for some climbs that exceed 10 feet over a short span. Cheat chutes exist for those who prefer to ride more typical Floridian terrain.

Season: This appears to be an all-season trail, although the wetter months will put sections of this trail under water or make them extremely soggy.

The single-track inside Quiet Waters Park provides both challenges and beauty.

Services: Quiet Waters Park has many of the modern conveniences you would expect from a facility offering day activities like tent camping, fishing, picnicking, and a children's water park. Pompano Beach—just outside the gate—offers whatever else you might need.

Hazards: While many of the hazards I experienced on my preofficial ride have been taken care of, you can still expect to be challenged by exposed roots and rocks and some steeper sections requiring nerves of cro-moly.

Rescue index: You should not have to make any extended plans for an elaborate rescue here at Quiet Waters; however, if you bust your collarbone coming off the 10-foot drop, every minute will seem like a painful eternity.

Land status: This land is managed by the Broward County government.

Maps: The front office has a map showing all the major attractions inside Quiet Waters Park.

Finding the trail: Exit Interstate 95 onto Hillsboro Boulevard headed west. Turn left onto Power Line Road and look for the park's entrance on your

RIDE 56 · Quiet Waters Park

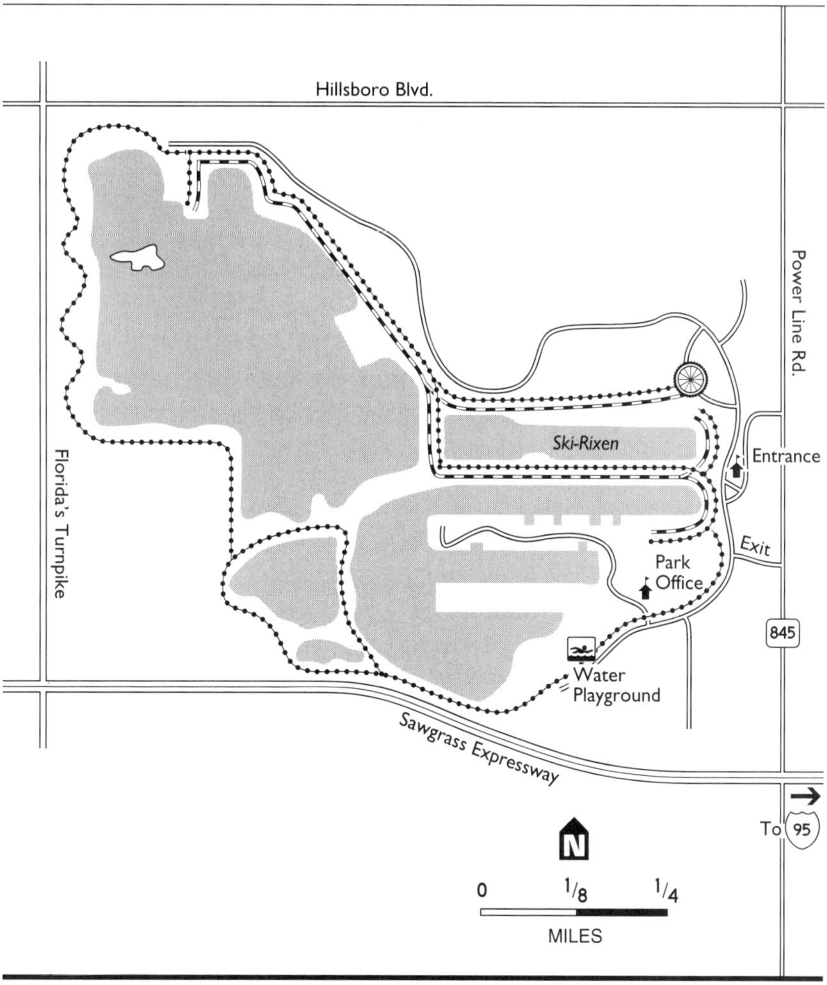

right. After paying the entrance fee and picking up the map, turn right at the dead end shortly after entering the park. You can park in the lot on the left near the ski course and pick up the paved bike path, which runs along the southern shore of the ski course.

Sources of additional information:

ClubMud
c/o West Broward Bicycle Center
13612 State Road 84
Davie, Florida 33325
(954) 424-9394

Quiet Waters Park
401 South Powerline Road
Pompano Beach, Florida 33073
(954) 360-1315

Notes on the trail: Pick up the paved bike path inside the park and ride it between some of the not-so-quiet waters of the cable-skiing area at Ski-Rixen. Continue riding it toward the boat rentals, looking for the gate behind which the double-track leads to the single-track sections. The single-track is well worn, and the existing area for the trail inside the park is not too spread out, making it easy to stay found (as opposed to lost). The last section of single-track (providing you ride it counterclockwise) becomes very narrow as it goes between the fence (Sawgrass Expressway is the highway you see) and a drop-off. You will probably want to return the way you came after reaching Splash Adventure, the water amusement park, but begin another counterclockwise lap by riding the paved path back through the cable-ski area.

RIDE 57 · Southern Trail

AT A GLANCE

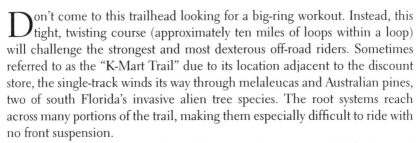

Length/configuration: 10 miles of loops

Aerobic difficulty: Low to moderate

Technical difficulty: Challenging to very challenging; a tight, windy single-track with several steep areas, especially challenging when wet or when met by unaware on-coming riders

Scenery: Australian pines and melaleucas

Special comments: A popular spot located beside a K-mart

Don't come to this trailhead looking for a big-ring workout. Instead, this tight, twisting course (approximately ten miles of loops within a loop) will challenge the strongest and most dexterous off-road riders. Sometimes referred to as the "K-Mart Trail" due to its location adjacent to the discount store, the single-track winds its way through melaleucas and Australian pines, two of south Florida's invasive alien tree species. The root systems reach across many portions of the trail, making them especially difficult to ride with no front suspension.

This has not, however, affected its reputation among rigid-forkers and racers alike. Despite its popularity among off-road riders, its future as a mountain bike destination is bleak. Zoned for future development, many feel it is only a matter of time before bulldozers push this scenic area into a burn pile.

It would be too bad. Southern Trail shows the great demand for such off-road destinations in this area of Florida. On a weekday evening, there must have been 50 people on the trail at one time. The parking lot by the gardening section was full of vehicles sporting bike racks. You could hear laughter

RIDE 57 · Southern Trail

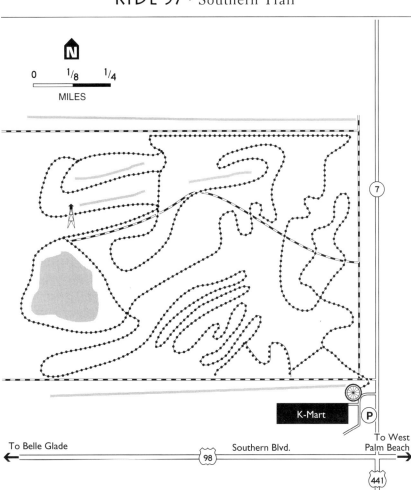

in the woods as people tried riding through the swampy area, and some folks stood around their cars discussing the future of this biking site. One guy finally spoke up and said, "Well, I don't know if it will help or not, but I'm going to join the bike club and either help keep this trail open or help them build some more like this." Now there's an idea.

General location: This trail lies a quarter mile northwest of the traffic signal at the junction of US 98 (Southern Boulevard) and US 441/FL 7.

Elevation change: Short but difficult ascents can be ridden along the canal banks. Other than those, the only significant elevation changes happen along the numerous roots from the exotic melaleuca.

Season: Areas near the lake hold water and create mucky yet rideable mud-holes. Rains also tend to make the roots slick to ride, so it's tricky to stay upright.

Services: A wide variety of goods and services are nearby.

Hazards: Numerous bikers use this trail. Expect to meet some riding in the opposite direction of the recommended counterclockwise route. Narrow, steep pathways and root-like stairs create a technical challenge few will meet without being unseated. Make sure you have a safe passage up and down the canal banks; walk if necessary.

Rescue index: Until you become familiar with the general layout of the main loop, you could find yourself disoriented and miles from the way out. You would be quickly found—probably—by one of the many mountain bikers using this trail.

Land status: This is private land currently not posted as such. The owner could elect to forbid use at any time, although the consensus is that it will not happen. Less sure is the land's future as a shopping mall or housing development.

Maps: The map in this book has been drawn from my notes, not those from a global positioning system.

Finding the trail: Take US 98 west for 9 miles to where US 441 joins, coming in from the south with FL 7. Turn right onto FL 7, going north until the paved entrance to K-Mart's garden department. Park on the right, facing the fence and forest. The trailhead for the single-track is inside the fence where the westbound and northbound double-track meet.

Source of additional information:

West Palm Beach Bicycle Club
P.O. Box 16764
West Palm Beach, Florida 33416
(561) 842-7414

Notes on the trail: Although no signs indicate it, most ride this trail counterclockwise, taking a right over the asphalt heap a few yards into the single-track. The first mile or so provides a warm-up for the more technical demands later on. Take a left onto the double-track leading along the canal behind a row of houses. On your left about 8 houses down, take the single-track back into the forest. Just inside, the trail splits. The left turn carries you to some climbing on the interior of the main loop. A right bypasses most of the highly technical riding required along the banks of several canals. Pay particular attention at the wide and sandy intersection near the last canal: double-track cuts across the single-track, which runs to the left (south). Steep and technical single-track lies to the right of the double-track intersection. The conspicuous orange (sometimes green) blazes and arrows mark the remainder of the trail around the lake in the southwestern quadrant of the loop. By cutting this part of the ride out (approximately one-half mile), you can also avoid some of the wetter spots on the trail. Of course, many people search out the mud, preferring a ride in the slippery stuff. If you're one of those, you can loop around the lake as many times as you need to meet your particular slop quota.

The remainder of the ride occurs in a series of switchbacks through the melaleuca jungle, nearly doubling back on itself in a few spots. Log ramps provide 3 or 4 chances to practice jumps before the single-track dead-ends into the double-track across the canal beside K-Mart.

RIDE 58 · Markham Park

AT A GLANCE

Length/configuration: 3 loops over a 7-mile area

Aerobic difficulty: Low to moderate; beginner trails are flat, but the more intermediate routes have some nice hills

Technical difficulty: Easy to moderate: novice loops are double-track service roads while the intermediate single-track trails have some uphill switchbacks

Scenery: Lakes, ancient coral head rising 30 feet above the double-track

Special comments: There are a variety of recreational options close by (boating, shooting, horseback riding, and more). New trails have been added

This Broward County park has an off-road double- and single-track trail system that makes three loops over a total distance of approximately seven miles. Two novice loops stay mainly on the flat, double-track service roads along the shores of the park's lakes. The intermediate route climbs the hills and knolls found on the single-track.

Did I say hills? Yes. This 665-acre park sits on the eastern edge of the Everglades, but it wasn't always that way. A long time ago, before there was a Miami, a swamp, a conquistador, or even a priest, ancient coral reefs grew large enough to raise some trees. Brightly colored and exotic fish swam on both sides of the coral head wall, until rising into the picket of mangrove roots. Now, after the waters have fallen and shifted, other brightly colored creatures, *Cyclus montanea*, climb these walls.

Since its opening in 1973, Markham Park has been the center of many activities for the heavily populated southern Florida coast. Camping and picnicking,

The trail at Markham Park features something unusual to discover on a trail bordering the Everglades—hills with switchbacks!

of course, are primary attractions. However, that's just the surface. There's also a sports field and courts for the ball-minded; water for the boaters, fishers, and swimmers; a target range for shooters; trails for bikers, hikers, and horseback riders; a landing strip for model airplane pilots; even an observatory and telescope for contemplators of the universe.

General location: Markham Park is located approximately 10 miles west of Fort Lauderdale, near the Sawgrass Expressway (FL 869).

Elevation change: Ancient coral heads rise 30 feet above the double-track roads below. On one climb, 30 feet is gained along 25 yards, with a quick switchback to the right near the top.

Season: Most of this trail seems to stay high and dry for the most part, even during the summer's traditional rainy season. There are, however, some muddy and boggy spots that crop up after a good rain, no matter what time of year it is.

Services: Fort Lauderdale, a few miles to the east, offers complete services. The park has the basics: camping, showers, and rest rooms.

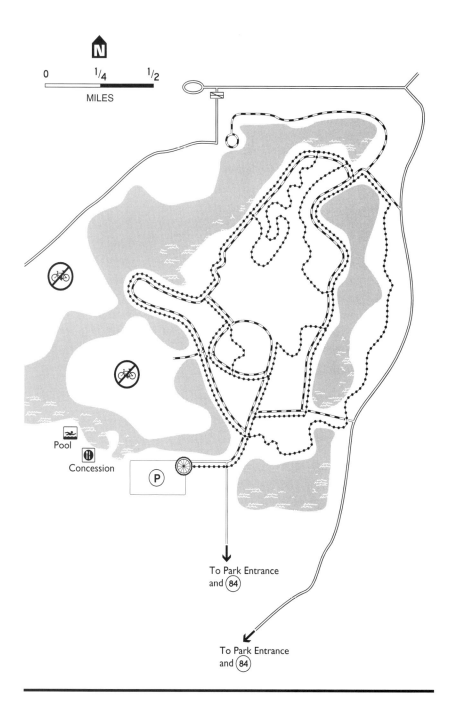

N

0   1/4   1/2

MILES

Pool

Concession

P

To Park Entrance
and 84

To Park Entrance
and 84

Hazards: Prepare yourself for a feature you won't find on many Florida trails—rocks! No, they weren't carted in and dumped to make it more like a mountain. They pop up after rains, remnants of the coral that formed the hills long ago. If you're making a long trip to ride Markham (and many do), call ahead for trail and/or park conditions. Concerts are occasionally held here, and a popular draw could make parking and traffic more than you want to contend with.

Rescue index: This is a fairly small park in an urban setting. Rescue should be easy.

Land status: Markham Park is one of the 7 regional parks managed by the Broward County Commission, Community Services Department, Parks and Recreation Division.

Maps: Maps made by ClubMud, a local off-road bike and social club, can be picked up at the entrance station or main office (near the observatory).

Finding the trail: Enter Markham Park by exiting Interstate 595 onto FL 84 and traveling less than a mile to where the signs announce the turn. Go straight for approximately a mile, following signs indicating bike rentals. You can park in the lot closest to the concession stands (the first left) or take the next left into the parking lot, where I'm sure you'll see vehicles with bike racks on the back, and bikers beginning and returning from rides. The trail-head is reached by biking to the service road that splits two bodies of water.

Sources of additional information:

Markham Park
16001 West State Road 84
Sunrise, Florida 33326
(954) 389-2000
fax (954) 389-2019

West Broward Bicycle Center and
ClubMud
13612 State Road 84
Davie, Florida 33325
(954) 424-9394 (ask for Dan)

Notes on the trail: Whether you're taking the novice route or the intermediate, plenty of signs mark intersections. Basically, the beginning loops follow the dirt roads along the lakes, and the single-track serves the more advanced sections. In any case, you should sample each of the loops. The intermediate is not too difficult; even the rank beginner can pedal much of it. Sections that can't be safely ridden—both downhill and up—can be pushed until the necessary skills and strength are developed. Likewise, with the novice loops, advanced bikers should use them for sprint training or cooling down from the workout on the interior single-track.

RIDE 59 · Hugh Birch State Park

AT A GLANCE

Length/configuration: A 1.5-mile paved loop and
a 2-mile (total) out-and-back

Aerobic difficulty: Low; mostly flat terrain

Technical difficulty: Easy; one spot where exposed
roots require some maneuvering and concentration

Scenery: High tree canopies, Australian pines,
views of the intracoastal water

Special comments: There's plenty of beach to bum around on after
riding

These secluded acres of intracoastal hammock retain a small piece of what
was once the dominant ecosystem along the south Florida coast.
Although some of the cycling on the park grounds occurs on the mile and a
half of paved service road looping the interior of this barrier island, you can
also ride about two miles total out-and-back double-track. Most of the riding
follows the exercise course, which has stations directing the participant to do
a certain number of repetitions of, say, deep knee-bends.

Although it is probably not over a couple of hundred of yards long, one
single-track route takes the rider under an ancient canopy. The exposed roots
from these monsters are high enough that the rider needs to concentrate on
making the maneuvers required to go up and over. If this is too demanding,
the paved route inside the park safely allows the rider to share the shady and
breezy circle with hikers, rollerbladers, and slow-moving vehicular traffic.

I enjoyed riding the double-track section cutting through the forest by the
picnic pavilions on the north end. Although it is a despised exotic tree, the
thick stand of Australian pines, whose evergreen boughs remind me of the
taller and more graceful white pines of my native north Georgia, have deposited
a thick layer of blonde needles underneath. It is hard to think of it as an invasive pest when you pass through this section. These trees pale in comparison to
the stately, huge banyan tree near the southern picnic pavilion, where I saw a
young girl—father coaxing one moment, scolding the next—who had overes-
timated her tree-climbing skills and was stranded in one of its crooks.

Although it's not a long loop, I saw something different and amusing each
time I made one of my five laps. If it wasn't the raccoons trying to mooch or
sneak a meal in broad daylight and bolting across the path in front of me as
I caught them in the act, then it was a crab that had walked out on dry land,
or a yacht in the intracoastal, moving quietly except for the wave rolling in
front of it. And when I finished riding, I walked over to the beach at Fort

This tree inside Hugh Birch State Park has nearly created its own forest.

Lauderdale and played beach tourist for an hour or so. You can see a lot of strange things in 90 minutes on a south Florida beach.

General location: Hugh Taylor Birch State Recreation Area is located in Fort Lauderdale.

Elevation change: No elevation change of consequence, except in an overgrown area of the forest on the northern end, near the picnic pavilions. Off to the left—just after beginning a section of double-track—you can see a bank that rises to the size of a fairly tall dune.

Season: This all-season trail occasionally gets some standing water in places.

Services: This is a recreation area with all the attendant facilities. No camping is permitted except by groups. Other services can be found in Florida's Atlantic coastal communities.

Hazards: Traffic shares the paved portions of the service road.

Rescue index: This trail can be the site of a quick rescue.

Land status: This is part of Florida's state park system.

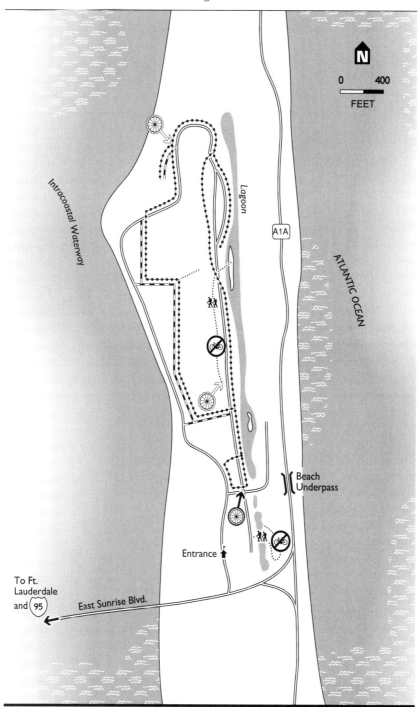

Maps: The park entrance station has copies of the map for Hugh Taylor Birch State Recreation Area, although the nature trails and existing double-track are not indicated completely. I made notes on the trails and used these to make the additions to the map in this guide.

Finding the trail: Exit Interstate 95 onto Sunrise Boulevard, County Road 838, headed east. Look for the entrance to Birch Park just prior to running into the ocean. Park in the lot just west of the southern nature trail.

Source of additional information:

> Hugh Taylor Birch State Recreation Area
> 3109 East Sunrise Boulevard
> Fort Lauderdale, Florida 33304
> (954) 468-2791

Notes on the trail: Continue north on the park's paved road and investigate each trail you see going off to the right and left. There aren't that many trails, and the possibility of getting lost inside this park is slim to none. On the northern end of the island, a hiking trail (only) heads to the left. Go down to this trailhead and turn right for the short single-track paralleling the main road. The forbidden trail goes to the interior and the site of the primitive youth camp (or is it youth primitive camp?). Look for the gated double-track on the inside of the loop on the northern end of the island. Don't forget to be a beach bum after you're finished riding.

RIDE 60 · Oleta River State Park

AT A GLANCE

Length/configuration: 6 total miles of various loops on an out-and-back

Aerobic difficulty: Low to high, depending on which trails you travel

Technical difficulty: Easy to challenging; loops for all levels; the expert single-track route has narrow chutes, natural obstacles, and sharp turns at the finish of steep descents and climbs

Scenery: Spacious woods

Special comments: Among the top trail systems in Florida; ask about additional trail mileage

North of Miami, the Oleta River drains a portion of the Everglades into Biscayne Bay. Between these two bodies of water, over six miles of trail have been developed for whoever chooses to roll off-road: slightly more than

Oleta River State Park has single-track so tight and rolling, you'll barely be able to squeeze through.

a mile of expert single-track, a half-mile of intermediate single-track, almost three miles of novice single-track, and (as if that isn't enough) more than two miles of paved pathway. They all connect in what essentially is an out-and-back, but various loops of different lengths and difficulties can be ridden off the main out-and-back. And don't be surprised when more mileage is added.

After hosting a race in the spring of 1996, Oleta River State Park established itself among the top trails anywhere in Florida. Many of the riders in that competition had come unprepared for the difficulty of the expert single-track. Built on top of what used to be ancient coral heads and reefs, the most common obstacles come from plenty of broken chunks of bone coral in the way.

Those alone would not be so hard to avoid, but the trail designers created a route demanding strength and finesse. Some of the toughest moves require tight turns at the top of 45-degree, six-foot climbs. Those are followed by equally sharp drops. At the bottom, a 90-degree turn must take place in three bike lengths before taking on another six-foot wall. If you could accomplish these moves at sufficient speed (I can't), you would look like a tugboat pitching

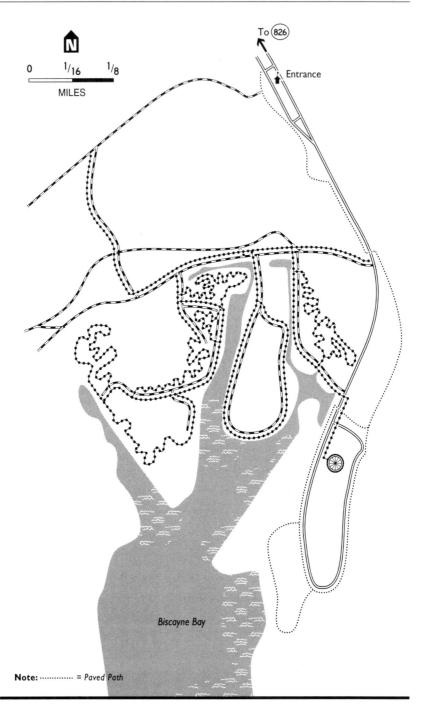

and yawing in a typhoon. Future plans, however, call for moderating some of these chutes so that the steeper climbs don't follow tight turns.

General location: Oleta River State Park is located slightly north of Miami.

Elevation change: There are no long, extended climbs here—but plenty of the short and dramatic type.

Season: This is an all-season trail.

Services: The state park has all the services you would expect of a top-notch park. Miami is 10 miles south, but you won't have to travel that far to find what you need.

Hazards: The expert route has plenty of hazards—rocks, roots, steep drops, and narrow turns.

Rescue index: This is a popular biking destination, so you shouldn't have to wait long for help to arrive.

Land status: This land is managed by the Florida state park system.

Maps: At the entrance (where you can expect to pay at least $3.25 to enter) ask for the map of the single-track Oleta River Bike Trails.

Finding the trail: Exit Interstate 95 by following the signs to Oleta River State Park, final destination County Road 826 (N.W. 167th Street) headed east. After crossing US 1, look on the right for the entrance to the park. Park in one of the spaces in the big lot on your left after entering the park and driving approximately one-quarter mile. Just as the pavement splits, look to the right for an information station on posts by the paved bike path. You should see the green, blue, or red blazes marking the entrance to the single-track sections, which first follow a novice double-track.

Sources of additional information:

Oleta Shore State Recreation Area
c/o Oleta/North Shore GEOpark
3400 N.E. 163rd Street
North Miami Beach, Florida 33160
(305) 940-7439

ClubMud
c/o West Broward Bicycle Center
13612 State Road 84
Davie, Florida 33325
(954) 424-9394

Notes on the trail: Each biker can choose whichever course is appropriate to the individual's skills. As you get better, you can graduate from the paved, out-and-back path from 163rd Street to the swimming area and ride on the double-track just across (west) from the entrance station. It leads to where the bulk of the single-track can be ridden. From the parking lot, however, ride north toward the entrance and look left for the information station. The novice double-track begins here. Follow the signs and adhere to the suggested direction of ride. I guarantee you don't want a head-on meeting anywhere on the tight expert stuff, and the intermediate track—in places—is just as tight—but also just as fun.

RIDE 61 · Shark Valley

AT A GLANCE

Length/configuration: 15-mile loop through the Everglades

Aerobic difficulty: Low to moderate; hills in places

Technical difficulty: Easy; the wide loop is paved

Scenery: Tree islands, sawgrass prairie, and every kind of wetland wildlife one can imagine (including alligators)

Special comments: A trip to the top of the 65-foot observation tower for a view of this incredible landscape should not be missed

In 1946, Mobil Oil built the first half of what became a 15-mile, paved, flat loop through the Everglades, a service road used for exploring the possibilities of discovering oil. If the Everglades survives in its natural form—a "river of grass"—then it will be partly due to there being only muck—and not oil—below the surface of the shallow waters. Of course, it didn't hurt this unique environment's chances when 460,000 acres acres were set aside by Congress in 1947 as the Everglades National Park. This vast sawgrass swamp has expanded several times since then and is now 1,509,000 acres and is still an awesome place to visit.

Tree islands dot the horizon of sawgrass prairie. Great white egrets and ibis rise into a blue sky broken by dark, tall thunderheads. Closer to your front tire, Louisiana herons stalk shallow waters, oblivious to all but the hunt. Small alligators float in pools. A water moccasin's head moves slowly just above the waterline, keeping close to cover unless a stray osprey or kingfisher swoops down. This is the Everglades.

The trip on the tramway has an added treat for energetic bikers at the halfway point. A 65-foot-tall observation tower can be climbed to get a vulture's-eye view of an amazing landscape. While you're up there, look to the southeast, where the eye of Hurricane Andrew blew through with 165-mile-an-hour winds on the morning of August 24, 1992.

General location: Shark Valley Visitor Center is south of Tamiami Trail (US 41), approximately 30 miles west of Miami.

Elevation change: Few people know there is 65 feet of elevation change in the middle of the Everglades, and it's yours for the climbing at Shark Valley.

Season: Summer rains can flood sections of the trail. Check at the Visitor Center for current water levels.

RIDE 61 · Shark Valley

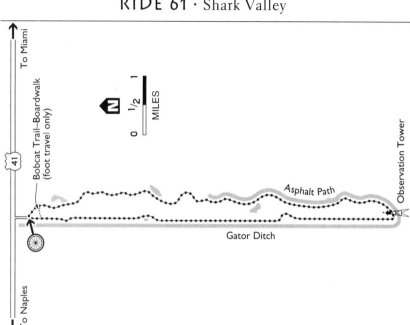

Services: Basic services can be obtained at the Miccosukee Indian Village; otherwise, a 30-mile-plus trip to Miami will be necessary for more specialized needs.

Hazards: Visitors are warned to stay at least 15 feet away from alligators basking on banks or floating in the water. Alligators can reach land speeds of 30 miles an hour; in the water, they are amazing acrobats. As Pam, Jared, and I came back to the trailhead, after hearing a constant chorus of gator-grunts, we saw a 6-footer staring at us from the opposite bank. As soon as we returned its stare, it submerged slowly. A trail of small bubbles rose to the surface in the middle of the canal. Pam said, "Watch! He's coming to the top!" Sure enough, now facing the bank it had left from moments ago, the alligator breached in an explosion of tail and snout. Its tail flipped a 2-pound bream 2 feet out of the water. As the fish disappeared into the dark water, the gator swished back around to resume its original position. Its expression seemed to say, "See what I can do?"

Although the park reports only one documented record of an alligator attacking a human, it happened on the same day we saw the gator throw the fish in the air. The story released by the National Park Service stated a

This paved trail at Shark Valley poses unique challenges—among them, real, live gator backs.

7-year-old Brazilian boy lost control of his bicycle and tumbled into the canal where alligators cross the path. Apparently, the normally shy creature either became enraged or was convinced it could make the small boy a meal. In any case, the parents were able to catch the gator and pry the boy loose before he suffered too much damage. The gator? An "investigation" was held and the attacking gator was found and relocated.

Rescue index: Regular tram rides are given on this trail. Consequently, you won't have to wait long for help to arrive. Even in the off-season—the summer—trams come by every 2 hours.

Land status: This path lies in Everglades National Park.

Maps: The Everglades Official Guide and Map can be picked up at the entrance station.

Finding the trail: Take Tamiami Trail (US 41) west out of Miami. Watch for the turn on the left to Shark Valley approximately 15 miles west of Tamiami's junction with FL 967. You will be getting close after you pass into the Miccosukee Indian Reserved Area, where the speed limit drops to 35 mph.

Source of additional information:

Everglades National Park
40001 State Road 9336
Homestead, Florida 33034-6733

(305) 242-7700 or 221-8455 (Shark Valley Tram Tours)
(305) 221-8766 (Shark Valley Visitor Center)

Notes on the trail: You're on the wrong trail if you're not on asphalt. Recommended travel direction is counterclockwise, which gives a 7-mile ride to the observation tower, with the remaining 8 miles on the twists and turns on the loop's back leg. If you're having a hard time of it, you can elect to return the way you rode in, saving yourself a mile.

RIDE 62 · Old Ingraham Highway

AT A GLANCE

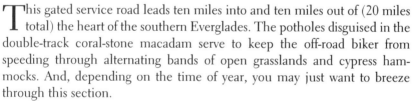

Length/configuration: 20 miles total of service road

Aerobic difficulty: Low to moderate; some slight changes in elevation

Technical difficulty: Easy; dirt double-track

Scenery: Open grasslands, cypress hammocks, mangrove

Special comments: This spot is known for its hordes of hungry mosquitoes and deer flies

This gated service road leads ten miles into and ten miles out of (20 miles total) the heart of the southern Everglades. The potholes disguised in the double-track coral-stone macadam serve to keep the off-road biker from speeding through alternating bands of open grasslands and cypress hammocks. And, depending on the time of year, you may just want to breeze through this section.

"I've got a friend who mountain bikes," a ranger at Shark Valley told me. "He says you have to go at least 17 mph in order to outrun deer flies." The ranger looked at my riding shorts and short-sleeve shirt and asked, "Do you have long pants and a long-sleeve shirt?" I shook my head, no. It was 90 degrees—time to shuck 'em if you got 'em.

When I arrived at the gate, the mosquitoes hovered in gauzy gray clouds; deer flies dove angrily and pinged against the glass. Horse flies big enough to ride off into the sunset circled overhead in their ceaseless search for blood. My blood, I knew, would do just fine.

I slung my cameras around my shoulders and put my bike over the gate. Small stains of blood had already formed on my shirt where the salt marsh mosquito had drawn a full measure. I shook like a wet dog trying to dislodge any remaining bloodsuckers and pedaled down what looked like an endless road.

Reeds—from 12 to 15 feet tall—stood between me and the canal running alongside the road. The wind knocked the reeds together, sounding like an

Old Ingraham Highway leads straight into the heart of the Everglades. Despite its benign appearance, it can be a difficult ride.

angry wood stork or a frog with a stutter. As I reached a cruising speed of approximately ten miles an hour, I heard animated rustling in the grasses on the edge of the road.

In the middle of the road, thousands of harlequin grasshoppers wobbled with their mates in a tango of procreant urge. I tried to miss as many as I could, but the snap and crackle of carapace filled the morning air. Then they disappeared. It was about this time that I began to feel a deer fly's snout penetrate the flesh behind my ear. Safe in the eddy, the rascals drilled me like a dentist.

A gator grunted and splashed into the canal as I passed by on my return trip. An osprey flapped its six-foot wings and took off from the top of a bald cypress. A twisted black limb lay in the road; I hadn't seen it on the way in. Then it came alive and slithered quickly into the canal. I snuck a peek through an opening in the mangrove along the bank of the canal and saw an alligator snapping turtle swimming in the middle.

As I made one of the few turns in the road, I startled a raccoon foraging

RIDE 62 · Old Ingraham Highway

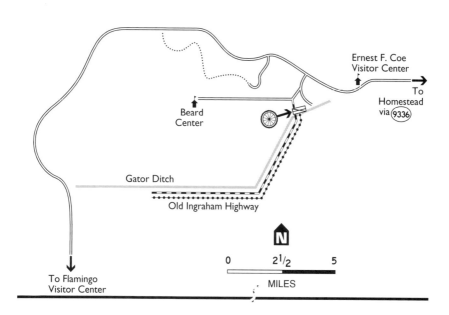

next to the road. Its first reaction was to run, which allowed me to document the speed of a racing coon—eight miles an hour. When I got back to my car and began putting down notes, I realized that the summer is supposed to be the slack time for wildlife sightings. Hard to imagine what this place looked like in the days when the Miccosukee were the only ones around.

General location: Old Ingraham Highway is near the Royal Palm Visitor Center, southwest of Florida City, whose sign announces "City of Florida City City Limits."

Elevation change: Most of the negligible elevation change occurs between the road and the bottom of the canal that was dug to build the road.

Season: Summer rains can—and should—inundate this trail. Also, a flood of insects, both on the ground and aloft, will challenge your summertime enjoyment. However, should you opt for a Dog Day Ride in the 'Glades, you might come prepared with an insect hood attached to your lid.

Services: Miami is located 30 miles to the northeast and provides complete services; Homestead and Florida City are about 10 miles away.

Hazards: Natural conditions which may be dangerous are present, among them insects and reptiles. It's a good place to ride with someone else.

Rescue index: It is unlikely you'll receive assistance quickly. Normal equipment repair—say, from a punctured tire caused by running over a snail shell shard (left over from a meal of the snail kite)—takes on added urgency when you're being sucked dry by a horde of mosquitoes and deer flies.

Land status: The 1.5 million acres in Everglades National Park are the setting for this ride.

Maps: The Everglades Official Map and Guide is provided at the entrance station at Ernest F. Coe Visitor Center.

Finding the trail: After entering the park, stay on the main road until you come to the first paved road to the left, toward Royal Palm Visitor Center and Beard Center. Take the right fork and continue straight at the next intersection, where a road to the right leads to Beard Center. The gate blocks the road shortly after passing the sign on the left for Hidden Lake Environmental Education Center.

Source of additional information:

Everglades National Park
40001 State Road 9336
Homestead, Florida 33034-6733
(305) 242-7700

Notes on the trail: There's not much trick to staying on this wide, hard surface. You'll find a canal on your right headed out and on your left coming back in. Ingraham Highway makes one turn headed out: from southwest to west. You can't miss it. At this turn a primitive camp spot (Ernest Coe) can be used by registering at the park headquarters. The most noticeable change in the terrain comes from the sawgrass prairies that give way to hardwood hammocks.

RIDE 63 · Bridal Trails, Key West

AT A GLANCE

Length/configuration: Less than a mile (total) out-and-back

Aerobic difficulty: Low; flat terrain

Technical difficulty: Moderate; some narrow tight turns on the single-track that winds through mangrove tunnels, and other spots that require root-hopping

Scenery: Mangrove hammocks

Special comments: Take some time to explore the town

The southernmost point of the continental United States—Key West—has everything, including a network of out-and-back single-track (less than a mile total) on either side of Key West International Airport. Surprisingly (if that can be said about anything Key Westian), the narrow tunnels bored through mangrove hammocks demand a skilled sense of balance while executing the tight turns. It is not your traditional off-road Florida trail.

But tradition plays a very small role on Key West. In fact, it seems that the entire East Coast's eccentricities have dripped down the seaboard and been distilled along these mangrove and shell islands called "keys," reaching their strongest and most potent form in Key West.

Formerly a collection point for the spongers who grappled the coral reefs growing offshore, Key West has much to offer the biker willing to explore parts of the old city. The culture viewed from the downtown sidewalks could well be Florida's most unusual natural history.

While I was stopped at a red light, a young man in an old pickup made the turn onto Flagler Avenue. Clinging to his left shoulder, a red and blue macaw reached outside and grabbed hold of the rain gutter until the truck straightened out, then let go and resumed its normal cruising posture inside the cab.

My aunt had told me, "Key West is for the birds," but I thought she was kidding until I was stopped in traffic waiting for a chicken to cross the road. Actually, it was a rooster, resplendent with its red comb falling rakishly over an eye, iron-red tail upright and jerking with each slow and deliberate strut it made. A woman on the sidewalk watched the fowl disappear in the shrubs behind a key lime tree, then turned to me and asked, "Why did that chicken cross the road?"

General location: The single-track lies just north of Smathers Beach. Key West is found at the dead end of US 1.

Elevation change: I was told once in a Boynton Beach bike store that Key West has some old bomb shelters which bikers climb. I located one such structure—padlocked and behind fencing—with a 20-foot-tall mound. Other than that, expect elevations to vary somewhere between sea level and a couple of feet.

Season: Less mud will be present in the mangrove flats and salt ponds during the winter months.

Services: Key West caters to every need of the visitor to the Conch Republic, including a bike shop: Bicycle Therapy (305) 293-8479.

Hazards: The single-track requires technical hops over mangrove roots. The mud is insidious and can quickly accrete on a tire in a slimy, gray mess. Surprisingly, the single-track had numerous hikers (all males, all unescorted) on it the day I was there.

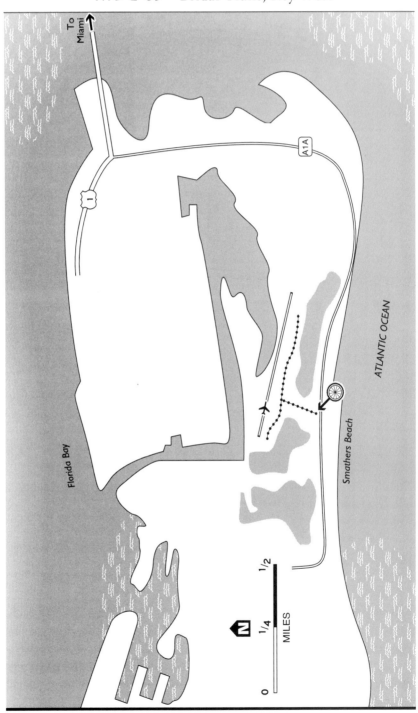

To Miami

A1A

Florida Bay

ATLANTIC OCEAN

Smathers Beach

N

MILES

0   1/4   1/2

This bike hints at the eccentric experiences found in Key West.

Rescue index: You can be easily reached on your Key West ride.

Land status: The single-track lies on public land associated with Little Hamaka Park and the salt ponds.

Maps: The only map I know of indicating these trails is found in this book.

Finding the trail: After crossing the bridge onto Key West, turn left toward the airport. Go past it and the East Martello Fort. A line of trees sits off the road, hiding one of the interior's large salt ponds. About 200 yards before reaching the hotel, look to the right, where a wide double-track lies on the other side of some coral heads blocking vehicle access.

Source of additional information:

The Florida Keys and Key West Convention and Visitors Bureau
P.O. Box 866
Key West, Florida 33041-0866
(305) 296-1552 or (800) 352-5397
www.fla-keys.com

Notes on the trail: I explored the single-track leading both to the right and left of the main double-track. The trail to the right stays close to the high fence separating Key West International Airport from the mangrove flat. The trail cuts through the mangroves, never leading far before dead-ending. You'll find out before long if this is your kind of trail.

SOUTHERN GULF RIDES

This section of Florida's gulf coast, beginning with Brooksville in the north and going south to Naples, roughly follows the path of railroad builder Henry Plant. Few states have been affected as dramatically as Florida by a rail system. Flagler's extensive rail network settled the east coast, and Plant's brought the country to the west. Although the degree of development has not hit this side of Florida as hard as the Atlantic seaboard, large metropolitan areas like Tampa–Saint Petersburg, Sarasota, Port Charlotte, and Fort Myers sprawl nearly uninterrupted along 150 miles of coast.

It's difficult to pick up on the atmospheres of some parts of the country with just a quick trip; however, the people on the western side of Florida seem to approach life with a more low-key manner than their east coast cousins' frenetic and charged energy. These western Floridians hail from all sorts of cultural backgrounds, with large Eastern European populations having arrived in the 1930s and earlier when Tarpon Springs was the undisputed sponge capital of the world.

Much of wild Florida can still be encountered on the southern gulf coast as the Green Swamp, the Myakka River, and the Peace River flow seaward. Farther south, the Big Cypress National Preserve joins the Everglades as a vast swamp, or series of strands—like the Fakahatchee and the Kissimmee Billy—which drains the huge Lake Okeechobee to the north receptacle for much of south Florida's 60-plus inches of annual rainfall.

Much of that water leaves Florida in the slow-moving sheet reaching Florida Bay through a thick jumble of ten thousand or so mangrove islands. A gradual mix of fresh and sea water occurs here, growing strange and beautiful creatures such as the manatee, Florida panther, and crocodile. This is the land where another strange and beautiful creature, the off-road biker, can catch a glimpse of places like nowhere else on earth.

Sources of additional information:

University Bicycle Center
1220 East Fletcher Avenue
Tampa, Florida 33612
(813) 971-2277 or 977-8317

SWAMP (SouthWest Association of
Mountainbike Pedalers)
9401 Takomah Trail
Tampa, Florida 33617
(813) 985-5021
cdalekid@gte.net

Ft. Myers Schwinn Cyclery
1941 Courtney Drive
Ft. Myers, Florida 33901
(941) 939-2899
www.mudcutters.org
closed Sunday and Monday

RIDE 64 · Croom Trails, Withlacoochee State Forest

AT A GLANCE

Length/configuration: 12-mile loop and 35-mile
loop; total trail length with connectors is more than
55 miles

Aerobic difficulty: High; some major ups and
downs

Technical difficulty: Moderate to challenging;
gatorbacks, stumps, sand, and tight turns keep this
single-track difficult and interesting

Scenery: Woods

Special comments: For single-track fans

Some estimate that there are over 140 miles of single-track loop both north and south of Croom Road in the Withlacoochee State Forest east of Brooksville, but according to the SouthWest Association of Mountainbike Pedalers the official single-track trail inside the state forest comes closer to 55 miles. The 400-member SWAMPers from Tampa volunteer their time to help maintain and keep the trails in good shape, and from what I saw, the rest of the country can take its cue from the hard work these riders are doing.

The course does have the reputation for getting a bit sandy in places, which makes 8-Mile Hill (so-called because it's right around the eight-mile mark in the upper loop) especially tough. Not far from there, the excavation from an abandoned phosphate mine provides the site for some serious up-and-down that'll cause you to inflate the airband in your helmet.

General location: This part of the Withlacoochee State Forest is located east of Brooksville, which is approximately 45 miles north of Tampa.

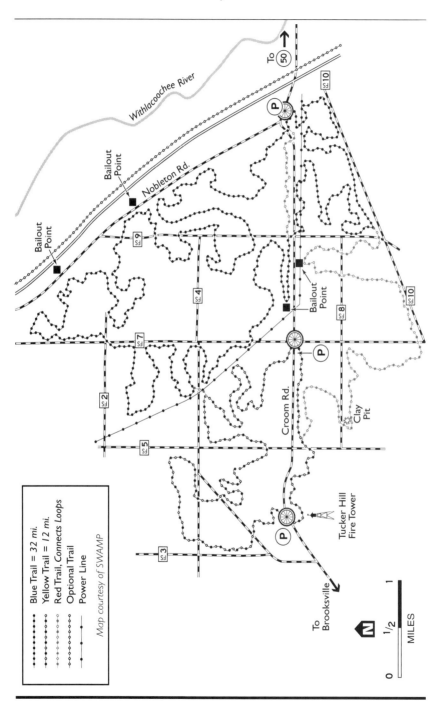

Jack and Bill cruise near 8-Mile Hill on part of the Croom Trails.

Elevation change: Due to prehistoric conditions that shaped this land, relative peaks rise to over 130 feet above sea level at the Tucker Hill trailhead. Some descents take on true mountainous degrees.

Season: Hunting closes this area to bikers on or about the second Saturday in November until approximately the first Saturday in December. Pray for rain to pack the sand down. When I was here, it rained Sunday afternoon and the sand was no problem on Monday morning.

Services: Brooksville, where the basics can be had, is about 10 minutes from the trailhead. Tampa is an hour's drive to the south.

Hazards: Plenty of gatorbacks and stumps will keep you on your toes. Sand and narrow turns make a slippery combination.

Rescue index: The forest seems more remote than it is; you're pretty near civilization—a school bus comes up to Tucker Hill Trailhead.

Land status: This land is managed by the Florida Department of Agriculture and Consumer Services, Division of Forestry.

Maps: Contact the Visitor Center in Brooksville for an updated map of the trail system.

Finding the trail: Leave Brooksville headed north on US 41. About a mile out of town, Croom Road turns to the right. About 2 miles after the pavement ends, at the top of the hill (lookout tower on the right), slow down and look on the left 50 yards below, where a bulletin board and water spigot are set back from the road. The trail begins here.

Sources of additional information:

SouthWest Association of Mountainbike Pedalers
9401 Takomah Trail
Tampa, Florida 33617
(813) 985-5021
cdalekid@gte.net
www.swampclub.org

Withlacoochee State Forest
Recreation Visitor Center
15003 Broad Street
Brooksville, Florida 34601-4201
(352) 754-6896
boltonl@doacs.state.fl.us

Notes on the trail: A double-track gridwork of roads (3, 5, 7, and 9 run north-south with Roads 2, 4, 6, and 8 going east-west) borders the single-track looping inside the grids. The unofficial direction of travel is counterclockwise on weekends and other high-use times. If you want to ride some of the smooth stuff on the Withlacoochee State Trail, you can join it via the intersection of Nobelton Road and Road 6, also called Croom Road, in the southeast corner of the trail system.

RIDE 65 · Richloam in the Withlacoochee State Forest

AT A GLANCE

Length/configuration: 30-mile loop of service road

Aerobic difficulty: Low; flat terrain

Technical difficulty: Moderate; this double-track can be really tough during dry weather

Scenery: Wetlands and forest

Special comments: The best time to ride is after a big rain the night before

A long loop (approximately 30-plus miles) of double-track service road begins in the Richloam tract of the Withlacoochee State Forest. The 49,000-plus acres of Richloam comprise more than a third of the total state forest's 128,471 acres, and it is full of biking adventures.

Don't expect to be tested for your hill-climbing skills on this ride; it is a part of what makes up the large and wild Green Swamp, a wetland catching the tributaries of the Withlacoochee River, not to be confused with its name-sake in southern Georgia. This is not only a land rich in nutrients for the cypress that grow here, but a land rich in biking potential.

Let your imagination run wild in this untamed region between Tampa and Orlando, as wild as the ancestors of the ponies and cattle seen grazing in the pastures. The first of the small horses came with the Spanish in the 1500s as the first of Florida's west coast explorations were made. As the cattlemen moved in to raise large herds, they used the ponies to run the ranches. With not too much effort, you can almost hear the cowboys whistle and the whips crack.

General location: The Richloam tract of the Withlacoochee State Forest is located east of Brooksville, halfway between Tampa and Orlando, on both sides of County Road 471.

Elevation change: Elevation starts at around 86 feet above sea level and pretty much stays there.

Season: Stay away during hunting season.

Services: Brooksville has many of the services you'll need. What you lack can be found in either Tampa or Orlando.

Hazards: Natural conditions that can be dangerous are present; additionally, there are hunters at certain times of the year.

Rescue index: This is a remote route. Plan accordingly for self-rescue.

Land status: This land is managed by the Florida Division of State Forestry.

Maps: A good map can be acquired at the Withlacoochee State Forest office in Brooksville; just ask for the Withlacoochee State Forest Mapguide.

Finding the trail: Take Exit 61 off Interstate 75 and head east on FL 50 until it dead-ends into County Road 471. Turn right onto CR 471. You can begin your ride by turning onto any of the following 4 dirt roads on the left: River Road, Fish Hatchery, Center Grade, or South Grade. Or you can explore the western section by taking one of the first 5 dirt roads to the right: North Carter Pond Road, South Carter Pond Road, Clay Sink Road, Center Grade, or South Grade.

Source of additional information:

Withlacoochee State Forest
Recreation Visitor Center
15003 Broad Street
Brooksville, Florida 34601-4201
(352) 754-6896
boltonl@doacs.state.fl.us

Notes on the trail: Several loops of various lengths can be put together in Richloam alone, but by incorporating the Van Fleet State Trail, more

RIDE 65 · Richloam in the Withlacoochee State Forest

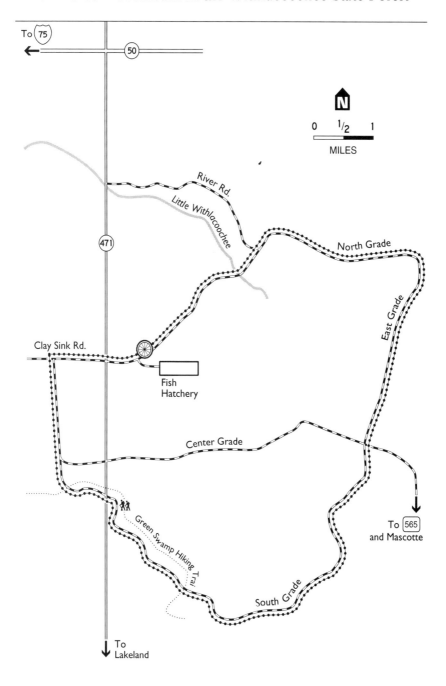

To (75)

(50)

N

0   1/2   1
MILES

River Rd.

Little Withlacoochee

(471)

North Grade

East Grade

Clay Sink Rd.

Fish Hatchery

Center Grade

Green Swamp Hiking Trail

To (565)
and Mascotte

South Grade

To Lakeland

The Withlacoochee
State Forest offers plenty
of double-track solitude
for the solo cyclist.

mileage lies in the immediate riding area than you can easily cover in an entire weekend. For a representative route, begin at the fish hatchery (after first stopping by to check it out) in a clockwise direction. Head northeast and cross Little Withlacoochee River before the intersection with River Road coming in from the left. Bear right on North Grade. It turns south (and changes its name to East Grade), crosses Center Grade (which you can take west for a shorter loop), and turns back north along—you guessed it—South Grade, which closely follows the Green Swamp Hiking Connector (foot travel only) for the last 3 or so miles before crossing FL 471. Take the dirt road north to its intersection with Center Grade on the right. It dead-ends into Clay Sink Road, where you turn right to get back to the fish hatchery, but not before first recrossing FL 471.

RIDE 66 · Withlacoochee State Trail

AT A GLANCE

Length/configuration: 46-mile paved out-and-back
(92 total miles)

Aerobic difficulty: Low; fairly flat terrain

Technical difficulty: Easy; typical rail-trail

Scenery: Woods, occasional highway intersections

Special comments: Also used by hikers and
rollerbladers

When I arrived at the Ridge Manor trailhead of this trail (a 46-mile, paved out-and-back—92 miles total) on a Thursday morning, there were over 20 cars in the parking lot. Not only were bikers using this linear state park, but rollerbladers and hikers strolled and skated on the 12-foot-wide crumb-rubber surface, made from over 10,000 tires plucked from the Polk County landfill. I like that idea of the rubber meeting the road. We should expand on it and take all the used tires in the world, shred them up into crumb rubber, and pave state trails everywhere.

I met an older gentleman who kindly endured my odd questions concerning his knowledge of the Withlacoochee State Trail. He said, "The Withlacoochee is the best rail-trail in the state, maybe anywhere!" He went on to describe all the aspects of cruising the former rail bed of Henry Plant's West Coast Route, whose tracks were laid to rail out the huge phosphate deposits in the ground nearby.

I enjoyed the conversation and decided to follow up on his suggestion to find Jack at Awesome Cycles. After talking to Jack for the second time (at the Croom Trails), I discovered my intentions had been misunderstood by the elderly gentleman. "You know that guy you talked to at Ridge Manor the other day?" Jack asked.

"Yes. I got lots of good information from him."

"Well, he came in the shop later on and told me," Jack said, "that he had been talking to a guy claiming to be doing research for an off-road biking guide. But he thought the guy was really trying to rip off his bike rack."

I shook my head. Such is the image of a well-traveled bike guide.

General location: The Withlacoochee State Trail, open since 1992, is located a few miles east of Brooksville.

Elevation change: There isn't much change in elevation, other than going over some highways.

Season: Although the pavement makes this an all-weather surface, hunting

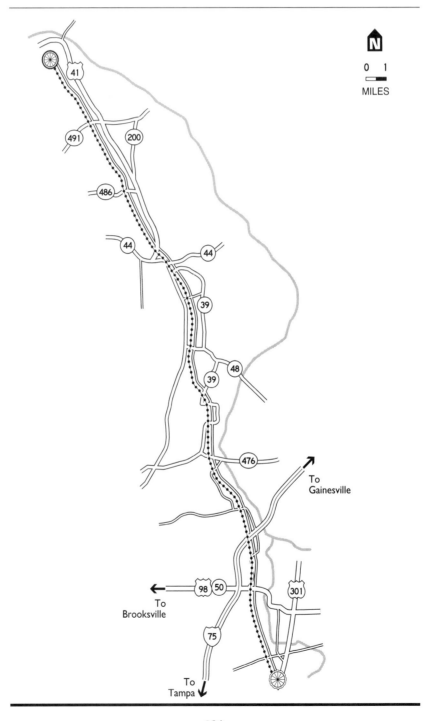

N

0   1
MILES

41

491   200

486

44   44

39

48
39

476

To
Gainesville

98 50

To
Brooksville

301

75

To
Tampa

does occur in the deeper, darker recesses of the trail. Firearms are not allowed on the trail, but it is my understanding that hunters can — and do — get very close to the trail during hunting season.

Services: Brooksville does a pretty good job of meeting all the basic needs; for the more specialized goods and services, head to either Tampa or Orlando.

Hazards: Motorized, vehicular traffic can pose a hazard at certain intersections on this trail.

Rescue index: Some sections are remote, but you can get a quick rescue on most of the trail due to its popularity and proximity to towns.

Land status: This linear state park is managed by the Florida state government.

Maps: You can obtain a map of the trail at Suncoast Bikes in Inverness.

Finding the trail: Exit Interstate 75 at Brooksville onto FL 50 headed east. Look for the entrance on the left about 1 mile away. If you travel under the trail's overpass of FL 50, you have gone too far.

Sources of additional information: Rails-to-Trails of the Withlacoochee meets on the third Thursday of each month at 7 p.m. at the Lakes Region Library in Inverness. If it can't wait, contact either of the following:

Withlacoochee State Trail
12549 State Park Drive
Clermont, Florida 34711
(352) 394-2280

Rails-to-Trails of the Withlacoochee
P.O. Box 807
Inverness, Florida 34451-0807
(352) 726-2251

Notes on the trail: Beginning at the northern terminus at Haitian Avenue and Citrus Springs in Citrus Springs, Florida, fairly remote areas can be ridden approximately 15 miles south to the development in Inverness. Wallace Brooks Park and Fort Cooper State Park are located within 3 miles of each other, where FL 44 goes over the trail. Inside Withlacoochee State Forest (past Floral City, Istachatta, and Nobleton) the Florida Trail can be accessed by foot only. Croom Trails, sites of enduro races, are considered among the best off-road biking opportunities in this part of the state for those wishing for the more technical obstacles of single-track riding. Silver Lake Recreation Area is the last stop inside the forest before you reach Ridge Manor West, but you may be in a hurry to leave the tire-hum of Interstate 75 behind. The southern terminus occurs at US 301 just after the trail crosses over County Road 575.

RIDE 67 · Van Fleet State Trail (in the Green Swamp)

AT A GLANCE

Length/configuration: 29-mile out-and-back (58 total miles), rail-to-trail conversion

Aerobic difficulty: Low; flat, straight, and paved

Technical difficulty: Easy

Scenery: Green Swamp, wetland wildlife

Special comments: Connects up with an unpaved trail in Withlacoochee State Forest and another at Green Swamp Trails

The 29-mile out-and-back (58 miles total) of this rail-to-trail conversion follows a pretty route—pretty straight and pretty apt to stay that way. The one turn in the trail occurs in the southern section, not too far from where Van Fleet crosses Dean Still Road. You may want to slap on some slicks if all you're riding is this paved path, but since Van Fleet does allow access to the rougher riding on the roads in the Withlacoochee State Forest and the Green Swamp, it makes sense to keep your fat tires on.

Van Fleet may have the distinction as the remotest of the rail-trails. One length of approximately ten miles in the heart of this swamp is uninterrupted. It is long enough to make a human feel like a minority, as far as living things go. The day I was there, love bugs alone were thick enough to have strangled a gasping biker. You say you don't know love bugs? Then visit Van Fleet in mid-September when the goldenrod turns dark with a mass of these profligate propagators, most of which fly joined at the tip of each other's abdomens. The female soon swells to twice the nearly dessicated male's size as she literally drains her mate of his vital juices.

But you'll see much of the other swamp life, too, including birds of nearly every rank and distinction. Bats and owls patrol the dusky skies, and early morning rides will likely have a reptile of some persuasion stretched out across the trail. As the Green Swamp begins to take back its natural state, trees will grow over the former route of Seaboard Coast's "Old Straight Arrow" freight line, and the chugging of locomotives will be replaced by the deep breathing of bikers.

General location: Van Fleet State Trail's southern terminus is located in Polk City. The northern trailhead lies 30 miles north-northwest on FL 50 at Mabel.

Elevation change: The relatively high elevation (approximately 105 feet above sea level at Mabel) changes little over its 29 miles, although the intersection of

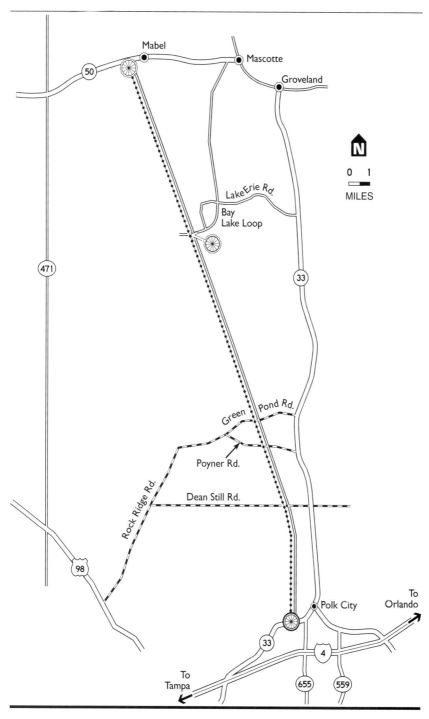

Mabel

Mascotte

Groveland

50

N

0   1
MILES

Lake Erie Rd.

Bay
Lake Loop

471

33

Green Pond Rd.

Poyner Rd.

Rock Ridge Rd.

Dean Still Rd.

98

Polk City

To
Orlando

33

4

To
Tampa

655   559

Fussell Road and FL 33 north of Polk City (and a half mile east) does reach nearly 140 feet above sea level.

Season: The pavement allows Van Fleet to be easily ridden year-round; however, the remote ride through the Green Swamp during hunting season is not recommended.

Services: Polk City can provide the basics, but the more specialized needs must be met in Lakeland or Auburndale, and possibly even Orlando or Tampa.

Hazards: Horses ride a parallel path and should not be a problem, but give the skittish animals a wide berth and an early greeting. Some hunters in hunting season, overcome by the testosterone surge brought on by the discharge of gunpowder and the possibility of blood, have been known to shoot quickly at anything that moves in the woods, thereby prompting the manufacture and distribution of camo toilet paper.

Rescue index: This is a remote trail. Despite being paved, it carries the possibility of a lengthy rescue.

Land status: Van Fleet is public land managed by the Florida state government.

Maps: Request "General James A. Van Fleet State Trail in the Green Swamp," the map showing trail shelters and intersections.

Finding the trail: The southern terminus lies in Polk City at FL 33 and FL 655.

Source of additional information:

General James A. Van Fleet State Trail
12549 State Park Drive
Clermont, Florida 34711
(352) 394-2280

Notes on the trail: A useful feature of this trail enables a long, off-road loop to be made with the Withlacoochee State Forest (WSF) and the Green Swamp Trails. An 8.5-mile out-and-back (17 miles total) can be ridden from the northern trailhead to the intersection with FL 655. If you'd like to ride on something looser than pavement, hang a right (west) here to hook up to the Richloam tract of the WSF.

RIDE 68 · Green Swamp Trails

AT A GLANCE

Length/configuration: 4 loops totaling 40 miles

Aerobic difficulty: Low; flat terrain

Technical difficulty: Easy

Scenery: Headwaters of the Hillsborough and With-lacoochee Rivers, cypress domes, sawgrass marsh, quicksand, and swampland wildlife

Special comments: One of the wildest places to ride in the state

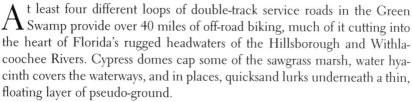

At least four different loops of double-track service roads in the Green Swamp provide over 40 miles of off-road biking, much of it cutting into the heart of Florida's rugged headwaters of the Hillsborough and Withlacoochee Rivers. Cypress domes cap some of the sawgrass marsh, water hyacinth covers the waterways, and in places, quicksand lurks underneath a thin, floating layer of pseudo-ground.

And, as you would expect around so much water, plenty of fowl can be seen: eagles, osprey, herons (great blue and green-backed), egrets, spoonbills, warblers, cardinals, towhees, ducks, anhingas, moorhens, and the ubiquitous vultures. But plenty more of Florida's wild side can be viewed from the stealth of a bike saddle: turtles (from tiny baskers to the giant alligator snapping turtles), snakes, gators, otters, deer, armadillos, and practically everything else, including a bigfoot-type creature described in local swamp lore.

General location: The Green Swamp is located between Tampa and Orlando.

Elevation change: There is not much change.

Season: Do not venture into the Green Swamp after periods of heavy rain. Also, hunting season is not the time to be in this wild and woolly Florida frontier.

Services: Brooksville has the basics and Tampa has the specialties.

Hazards: Although hunters may be present at times, horses are not allowed. Be on the lookout for hikers using portions of this double-track network, although they will most likely stay on the nearby Florida Trail.

Rescue index: Be prepared for self-rescue.

Land status: This land is managed by the Southwest Florida Water Management District.

Maps: Request the Recreational Guide to Southwest Water Management

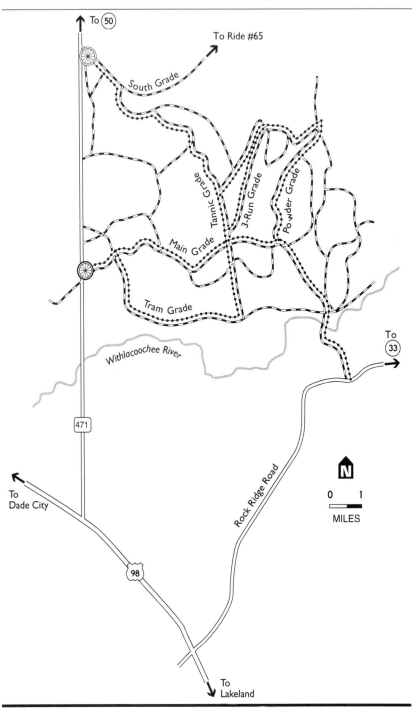

To (50)

To Ride #65

South Grade

Tannic Grade

3-Run Grade

Powder Grade

Main Grade

Tram Grade

Withlacoochee River

To (33)

471

N

0   1

MILES

To
Dade City

Rock Ridge Road

98

To
Lakeland

The Green Swamp may be the wildest place to pedal in the state.

District from their offices; no maps were available at the trailheads when I was there.

Finding the trail: Take the Brooksville exit off Interstate 75 and head east on FL 50 to Tarrytown. Turn south onto County Road 471 and drive approximately 15 miles. Turn onto the dirt road after Richloam's South Grade, on the east side of 471.

Sources of additional information:

Southwest Florida Water Management District
Land Resources Department
2379 Broad Street
Brooksville, Florida 34609-6899
(904) 796-7211

For camping permits, contact
Florida Game and Freshwater Fish Commission
3900 Drane Field Road
Lakeland, Florida 33811
(813) 648-3203

Notes on the trail: The service roads in the Green Swamp, which are used for the bike trail, provide the central link connecting two other nearby off-road trails: Richloam (in the Withlacoochee State Forest) and the Van Fleet State Trail. Although the roads in Green Swamp can be ridden in various configurations and lengths, depending on the mood you're in, an interesting combination of the three trails can be put together. Begin in the Richloam tract on South Grade heading southeast. Look for Tannic Grade, a dirt road turning to the right and leading into Green Swamp. Take the next left on Bull Barn Road, go a little over a mile and a half and turn left onto Levee Road. The next intersection, approximately 3 miles later, occurs at Main Grade; take a left. Continue straight past Ellis Grade (on the right), Tannic Grade (on the left), and Powder Grade (on the left shortly before Main Grade turns to the south) and turn onto Rock Ridge Road. Take Rock Ridge east to the Van Fleet State Trail via Green Pond Road (the north fork) or Poyner Road (the south fork). Head north on Van Fleet, taking its straight, flat, paved route to the intersection with County Road 565 approximately 13 miles away. Turn left (west) until you come to East Grade in the Richloam tract of the Withlacoochee State Forest. You can either continue straight on Center Grade, eventually coming to FL 471, or turn south onto South Grade, which brings you directly back to the trailhead, making the loop.

RIDE 69 · Morris Bridge Park

AT A GLANCE

Length/configuration: Various loops totaling over 20 miles

Aerobic difficulty: Low to moderate, depending on where you ride

Technical difficulty: Easy to moderate; the main double-track trail is perfect for beginners; the single-track offers challenge by way of root systems and gatorbacks

Scenery: Nice woods

Special comments: This is a great place to get lost via sand pits that will eat up trails at intersections; thankfully, it's easy to find your way out

A combination of single- and double-track creates various loops of over 20 miles inside this park outside Tampa. Most of the single-track is easily ridden, although lower parts along the Hillsborough River with cypress knees and downed trees create a technical challenge. Gatorbacks, exposed root systems of the sabal palm, can also prove difficult to cross over upright.

The double-track serves as the "main trail" that all beginners should have no difficulty with, other than dealing with outcrops of shifting loose sand. The pits in the southern section of the trails offer extra practice for your extreme sand moves. My favorite parts are those sections of single-track that slip in and out of stands of saplings and shrubs, even though they can be a little disorienting.

There's no telling what you may find on some of Florida's trails.

Apparently, this disorientation is all part of the experience. I talked to two young women who had just finished doing a loop and told me, "We always get lost somewhere in the middle, but we always find our way back." Encouraged, I struck out with a biker from Bartow who had never ridden these trails, and, sure enough, we wound up somewhere on the other side, not really lost, but not knowing which way was out. But by following trails we didn't recognize, we returned to the trailhead by the pits. This is a good trail network to try confused cycling on, but if you prefer a map, they are available at local bike stores.

General location: Morris Bridge Park is located a few miles northeast of Tampa near Interstate 75.

Elevation change: You can get in a little hill work here . . . but not much.

Season: Some sections of the trail are under water at certain times of the year and should not be ridden.

Services: Tampa has whatever you need and is only a few minutes from the trailhead.

Hazards: Exposed roots and slick spots, in addition to sandy areas, can pose some problems if you're not expecting them. Disorientation, while normal, could create a longer ride than you prefer, so come equipped for staying in the woods for several hours.

Rescue index: This is a popular site, so should you have any problems, you

RIDE 69 · Morris Bridge Park

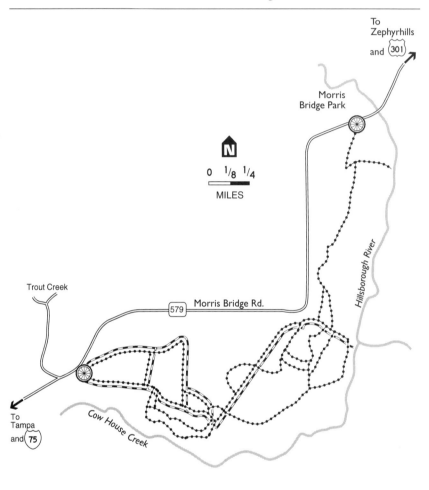

will probably be quickly seen or heard. Providing you know the way, either of the 2 trailheads is relatively close.

Land status: This public land is owned by the Southwest Florida Water Management District and managed by Hillsborough County Parks and Recreation.

Maps: A detailed map—"Off-Road Biking Trails of Morris Bridge County Park"—can be picked up at area bike shops or through SWAMP.

Finding the trail: Exit Interstate 75 at Fletcher Avenue and head east on what immediately changes names to Morris Bridge Road. Trout Creek Park is less than a mile across the road from the southern trailhead. The northern trailhead is farther up the road at Morris Bridge Park before you cross over Hillsborough River (4 miles).

Source of additional information:

SouthWest Association of Mountainbike Pedalers
c/o Wes Eubank
9401 Takomah Trail
Tampa, Florida 33617
(813) 985-5021 or 988-6435
www.swampclub.org

Notes on the trail: White diamonds with a biker emblazoned on them mark the main trail. Blue blazes mark the more difficult single-track. Most of the mileage can be found south of the power lines and north of Cow House Creek. Some sections will be closed depending on the time of year and the water level. Make sure you do not ride on any closed trails. It would have been nearly as impressive to see any type of rock, but I was surprised to discover chert, a hard rock used for making arrow points, scattered on sections of trail.

RIDE 70 · Pinellas Trail

AT A GLANCE

Length/configuration: 35 miles out-and-back (70 miles total)

Aerobic difficulty: Low; flat terrain

Technical difficulty: Easy

Scenery: Rollerbladers and other bikers

Special comments: Florida's most popular recreation trail which accounts for the numerous amenities and services you'll come across during your ride

It's not single-track, but it's Florida's most popular recreational trail—35 miles out-and-back (70 miles total), slicing through Florida's west coast urban-hood on what used to be the Orange Belt rails. The only wildlife you'll see on this trail will be pushing pedals, walking, or rollerblading. And there's plenty of it, too.

Everyone should be so lucky! A bike trail reserved just for bikers, hikers, and skaters that begins at your back door and goes to the back door of your friends. You want to meet for lunch? Pick the spot. There are places to eat every two or three miles and motels just about as often if you want to make it an overnighter (no riding at night, though).

RIDE 70 · Pinellas Trail

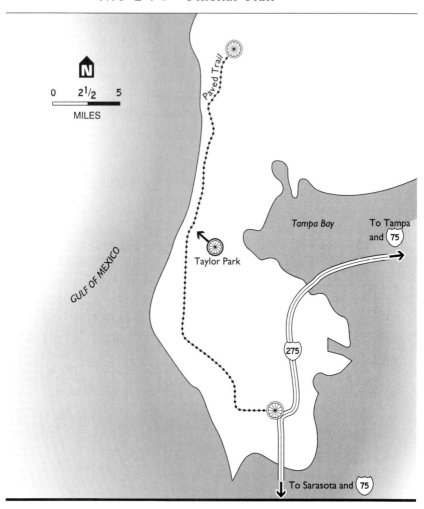

Plenty of parks along the way have facilities available, but the one park you should be sure to visit is Taylor Park, where the headquarters for the Pinellas Trail rangers is located. A mixture of residential and industrial areas makes up the other neighborhoods of the Pinellas Trail.

General location: Pinellas Trail is located between Tarpon Springs (in the north) and St. Petersburg (in the south).

Elevation change: The overpasses contain the only significant elevation changes.

Season: This is an all-season trail—during daylight hours only.

Services: There are services at just about every pedal stroke.

Hazards: The biggest hazard is other trail users.

Rescue index: You will have little trouble getting aid on Pinellas Trail.

Land status: This land is managed by the Pinellas County Park Department.

Maps: An excellent map can be found in the *Pinellas Trail Guidebook*, put out by the Pinellas County Planning Department.

Finding the trail: Although there are numerous access points, the best spot to start from may be Taylor Park. Head toward St. Petersburg from Tampa via Interstate 275. Exit onto Ulmerton Road (FL 688) and travel approximately 10 miles to the intersection with 113th Street; turn right. Then turn left onto 8th Avenue S.W., taking note of the Pinellas Trail as you cross it one block west.

Source of additional information:

Pinellas County Planning Department
14 South Fort Harrison Avenue, Suite 2000
Clearwater, Florida 33756
(727) 464-4751
(727) 549-6099 (trailhead information)
fax (727) 464-4155

RIDE 71 · Myakka River State Park

AT A GLANCE

Length/configuration: 20 miles total out-and-back, horse trails and fence line can be ridden to add miles

Aerobic difficulty: Low; fairly flat terrain

Technical difficulty: Easy; paved double-track service roads

Scenery: Open prairie, sawgrass marsh, Upper Myakka Lake

Special comments: Watch out for the feral hogs!

PART ONE: NIGHT RIDE ON A BLACKTOP

Sleep escaped me the night I camped inside this wilderness preserve, and so I did what any sleepless-in-Myakka biker would do. I rode part of the approximately 7 miles (14 miles total) out-and-back paved service roads, some of which skirt the southern banks of the Upper Myakka Lake. It was late, and thinking the only vehicle I might possibly see would be the park ranger's truck, I kept my lamp off and navigated by starlight.

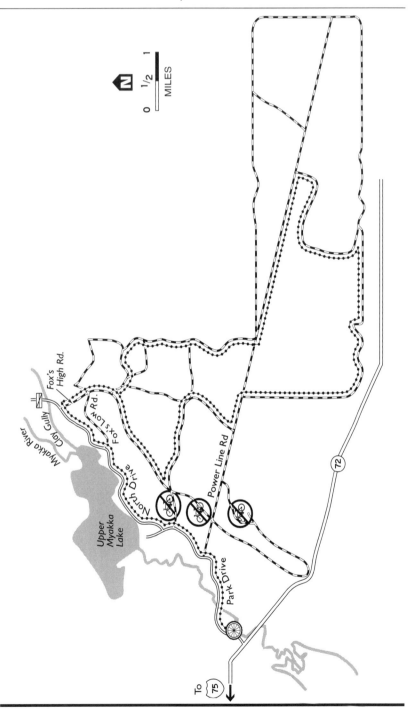

Signs of feral hogs are apparent on parts of the trail inside Myakka River State Park.

I also took my shirt off, and as I pedaled into the dark tunnel under the canopy of live oaks, mosquitoes swarmed bike-level in the swamp air. They randomly hit my legs, arms, and chest. I got a small pleasure out of knowing I was doing my part to control the blood-sucking bugs. I realized, however, that I could ride all night taking out mosquitoes and not come close to the burgeoning billions I had probably caused to propagate by offering my rich biker blood.

I heard noises ahead on the trail. Deer, I thought, but it was too dark to tell. I was glad the animal went into the thick trees, instead of coming out. After riding for over an hour and spying several coons crossing the road ahead of me, I began to think how good a shower and some sleep would feel. I set a course back to the campground, ready to ride off-road at dawn.

PART TWO: PEDALING THE PRAIRIE AS MORNING BREAKS
ON THE MYAKKA

Some may wonder why I didn't just take off through Myakka's 12 miles of looping double-track back roads at night. Although it is feasible for a group of riders to head into unfamiliar territory at night armed only with biker brazenness, it is not wise for a solo rider bent on self-preservation to try such a trip.

Some of the noises I heard the night before were made by shy and harmless creatures like the raccoon, armadillo, and deer. Some were probably made by those black tuskers, feral pigs, whose sign could be seen in many places the next morning. Though small, an enraged boar is still more than a match for a peace-loving cyclist. So are the lengthy (approximately six feet) reptiles (especially diamondbacks and water moccasins) that make their living in the cool of the summer night.

My dawn ride was early enough to catch the last of these feeders heading toward shade to wait out the day's heat in bush and den. A covey of 15 quail exploded off a sandy opening in the marsh. Although seeing and hearing these birds in flight does not provide the same adrenaline rush you get from descending a steep downhill, it comes close. I saw two more coveys and an osprey nest in the top of a dead pine before I reached the road under the power line, where—for some reason—a flock of vultures still sat on their night roosts: 50-foot-tall metal stanchions bespattered with the pungent products of the previous day's digestion.

General location: Myakka River State Park is located approximately 20 miles due east of Sarasota.

Elevation change: Approximately 3 feet of height separates the Myakka Lakes (13 feet above the Gulf of Mexico) from the surrounding land.

Season: You would not want to ride off-road here in the wetter times of the year. The pavement, however, provides a pleasant route in all but the severest floods.

Services: Few services other than basics can be found before reaching Interstate 75, 10 miles to the west. Camping is provided inside the park, but you have to go all the way to Sarasota, or perhaps Tampa, to acquire more specialized services.

Hazards: During daylight rides, there are no extraordinary hazards. Night rides, however, come with a long list of potentially damaging obstacles.

Rescue index: Much of the ride occurs in the open prairie and sawgrass marsh, where sound travels long and well. A strongly blown whistle should grab the attention of someone driving on either Park Drive or FL 72. However, for this ride, you may want to take your cell phone with you.

Land status: This land is managed by the Florida state government.

Maps: The entrance to the park has maps showing the many miles of biking opportunities.

Finding the trail: Exit Interstate 75 onto FL 72 heading east. Approximately 9 miles later, look for the entrance on the left marked by a sign.

Source of additional information:

Myakka River State Park
13207 State Road 72
Sarasota, Florida 34241-9424

(941) 361-6511
www.myakka.sarasota.fl.us

Notes on the trail: I warmed up for my cross-marsh ride by pedaling pavement from the campground to where I picked up the trail behind a wire gate just south of the park's north entrance. I bypassed the short spur leading left to Mossy Hammock Campsite, going straight until I reached the intersection with Power Line Road. I turned right under the power lines, listening to their 60-cycle hum overhead. An additional 12 miles of loops created for horseback riding can also be used by bikers, who continue straight at this intersection. In addition to all these miles, the fence line can be ridden—all 30-plus miles of it.

RIDE 72 · Sanibel Island

AT A GLANCE

Length/configuration: 50 miles total of paved out-and-back paths

Aerobic difficulty: Low; flat terrain

Technical difficulty: Easy

Scenery: A mixture of condos and beach

Special comments: A prime spot for shell-collecting

Off the coast of Fort Myers, the crescent-shaped Sanibel Island can be ridden by the off-road biker for over 25 miles (more than 50 miles total) on asphalt out-and-back paths. Nearly all the routes run parallel to the main island roads on Periwinkle Way and Sanibel-Captiva Road. Other paths run along West Gulf Drive and Casa Ybel Road, which allow beach access to shell collector's destinations such as Tarpon Bay Road Beach and Gulf Side City Park.

Indeed, if Sally were to go down to the seashore to collect seashells, she would find no better place to gather mollusk homes than Sanibel. Much of the reason so many high-quality shells can be found here is that instead of being aligned parallel to Florida's west coast, the island is perpendicular to the coast, thereby catching the current and a large number of shells deposited along its southern shore.

Although the trail on Sanibel stretches the definition of an off-road ride somewhat, the ride to Captiva Bridge and Blind Pass does much to make you forget you're not on narrow single-track screaming down a mountain slope. I was able to end my ride here just as the sun began burning on the light chop of the Gulf of Mexico. I took my boots off and wiggled my toes in the sand while the last pelican made its run home down the beach. Now how can you not tell someone about a ride that ends like that?

General location: Sanibel Island is located west of Fort Myers in the Gulf of Mexico.

Elevation change: There is no elevation change here.

Season: This is an all-season trail.

Services: Sanibel Island's stores and shops can provide nearly all you need. Whatever's lacking can be acquired across the bridge in Fort Myers.

Hazards: Take care not to run into other bikers, hikers, and vehicular traffic.

Rescue index: You could set the world's record for quickest rescue here.

Land status: This is municipal property managed by the Sanibel Island government.

Maps: Stop at the Chamber of Commerce to pick up your map and guide to Sanibel Island.

Finding the trail: Leave Fort Myers on County Road 867 (McGregor Boulevard) and follow the signs to Sanibel Island. Be prepared to pay at least $3 for the toll bridge at the end of the Sanibel Causeway.

Sources of additional information:

Sanibel-Captiva Islands Chamber of Commerce
1159 Causeway Road
P.O. Box 166
Sanibel, Florida 33957
(941) 472-1080
fax (941) 472-1070
e-mail: Islands@coconet.com
www: http://www.coconet.com

Fort Myers Schwinn Cyclery
1941 Courtney Drive
Fort Myers, Florida 33901
(941) 939-2899
www.mudcutters.org
closed Sunday and Monday

Notes on the trail: Sections of path can only be accessed by riding on the main roads. For example, if you begin riding from the Chamber of Commerce, a short pedal on Periwinkle Way is necessary to get to the bike path. Remember, all bikers must follow all traffic laws in Florida while on Florida roads, e.g., turn signals, speed limits, etc. Don't forget to include a ride to Ding Darling National Wildlife Refuge sometime during your stay in the neighborhood; it's on the right of Sanibel-Captiva Road, approximately 5 miles west of the Chamber of Commerce.

RIDE 72 · Sanibel Island
RIDE 73 · Ding Darling Trail

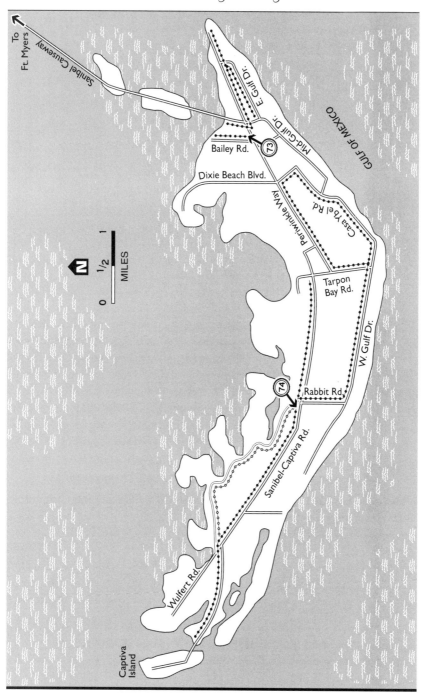

RIDE 73 · Ding Darling Trail

AT A GLANCE

Length/configuration: 5-mile out-and-back (10 miles total)

Aerobic difficulty: Not much up and down here

Technical difficulty: Easy; crushed limerock surface makes for good grip on the trail

Scenery: Gulf waters and seaside wildlife in abundance

Special comments: A good place for a family trip: nice hiking and canoe possibilities close by

The 5,000-plus acres in the Ding Darling National Wildlife Refuge offer a five-mile out-and-back (ten miles total) ride on a wide, crushed limerock surface. It isn't difficult, which is good because the inclination here is to rubberneck while you pedal. And who can blame you? The west Florida seascape has been preserved here in all its attendant glory.

Spoonbills live here, swishing their odd-shaped bills through the water and waiting for that slight touch of something finned to trigger their lightning-fast jaws. Pelicans circle and patrol the smooth gulf waters, stalling out before throwing their wings back and diving on top of fish. Insects, too, are plentiful; at times it seems there's a proboscis for every pore of your body.

In the shade of a gumbo limbo tree you might observe anoles, whose flashing dewlaps remind me of teenagers standing on street corners, blowing bubbles of unconcern. It's an infectious feeling. If you're like me, you'll find yourself pedaling from one end of Ding Darling to the other without a care in the world.

General location: Ding Darling is located on Sanibel Island, just across from Fort Myers.

Elevation change: There is no appreciable elevation change.

Season: This is an all-season trail, except for Friday, when it is closed for a gator's day off.

Services: Sanibel Island makes its living catering to the needs of the vacationing public. Chances are you'll find what you need on the island; however, you may have to make the trip back to Fort Meyers to get some specialty items.

Hazards: Motorized traffic, but it usually progresses slowly.

Rescue index: This is among the easier sites to arrange a rescue.

Land status: This land is managed as a national wildlife refuge.

Maps: Maps of Ding Darling National Wildlife Refuge can be obtained from the refuge's office.

Finding the trail: Leave Fort Meyers headed southwest on County Road 867 (McGregor Boulevard), following the signs to Sanibel Island. Prepare to pay at least $3 to cross the toll bridge onto the island. Take a right onto Periwinkle Way headed to Captiva Island. Look for the entrance on the right, approximately 5 miles from the Chamber of Commerce.

Source of additional information:

J. N. "Ding" Darling National Wildlife Refuge
One Wildlife Drive
Sanibel, Florida 33957
(941) 472-1100

Notes on the trail: What this trail lacks in technical challenge is more than equaled by the sights. Park the bikes at the westernmost entrance to Indigo Trail and hike down 4 miles total of out-and-back. Bikers are requested to pay an entrance fee of (at least) $1 per person. If you're staying on Sanibel or Captiva for a couple of days, you may also want to rent a canoe and explore the unique waterways.

RIDE 74 · Loop Road

AT A GLANCE

Length/configuration: 52 total miles

Aerobic difficulty: Low; very flat

Technical difficulty: Easy; wide service road; the only technical acrobatics required is pothole-hopping on damaged parts of the trail

Scenery: Swamp, cypress, and Everglades wildlife

Special comments: This is an unreliable ride during periods of intermittent rain, but if you manage it without confronting any trail floods, absorb the serene and leisurely experience

Big Cypress Swamp—all million and a half acres of it—has nearly half of that set aside in the multi-use Big Cypress National Preserve. The 26 miles one way (52 miles total) of open, wide, flat service road won't get points for its technical requirements. It does, however, rack them up for allowing exploration of this vast area.

As you would guess, cypress are abundant along the route. They stand like sentinels guarding the entrance to the swamp. Anhingas perch on stumps,

This pool inside
Big Cypress Preserve
is guarded by—what
else—big cypress trees.

holding out their wings like Batman as the sun dries their sodden flight feathers. The lucky fry from bass and bluegill dart nervously near the submerged stalks of bulrushes, safe for the moment from the anhinga's dive.

Mysterious splashes occur in the distance. Fish, bird, amphibian, reptile, mammal? It could be any of these. I spotted turtles lined up on logs. They fell into the water like fighter planes, peeling off in formation, wiggling their flippers, and twisting their necks. Black snakes dropped headfirst, straight as ropes—disappearing under banks and among roots.

Vultures reluctantly interrupted their feast of an alligator carcass as I pedaled slowly toward them. Their great wings stirred a stench of gator tail being steamed in 90 degree heat. An otter slipped off a stump, swimming to a quieter spot in the swamp to fish. The unmistakable roar of an airboat could be heard in the distance. When I reached the smoother pavement just before Forty-Mile Bend, I found the big ring on my bike and left the deer flies behind, taking with me memories of the wild side of the Everglades.

General location: From Forty-Mile Bend on Tamiami Trail (US 41), Loop Road begins in Dade County, goes into Monroe County, and ends in Collier

RIDE 74 · Loop Road

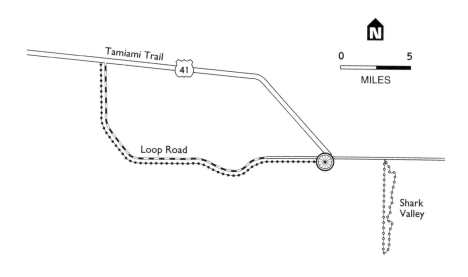

County, hooking back into Tamiami Trail approximately 5 miles west of the Oasis Visitor Center.

Elevation change: It starts out low and goes lower, barely.

Season: Loop Road could very well be closed during the summer. Heavy rains have washed away portions of the paved surface, leaving behind significant potholes. It could wash away a biker as well. Hunting is also a possible hazard during the traditional fall and spring months.

Services: Don't expect much in the way of services way out in Big Cypress Swamp. Anything out of the ordinary will need to be picked up in Miami or its outlying communities, an hour or so east of the Forty-Mile Bend trailhead.

Hazards: This road is not gated; expect to see an occasional vehicle (slow-moving, probably, due to the frequent potholes that are real axle breakers). Along with other natural conditions that can be hazardous, you could find yourself on a dry road starting out and a flooded road later—especially during the traditionally wet summer.

Rescue index: Be careful. It would take some time to effect a rescue or provide assistance.

Land status: This land is in Big Cypress National Preserve, managed by the National Park Service.

Maps: Loop Road shows up on the Everglades Official Map and Guide, available at any of the Visitor Centers.

Finding the trail: Head west on Tamiami Trail (US 41) until you pass the Miccosukee Cultural Center on the left. As the highway goes to the right a couple of miles down the road, turn left onto Loop Road. A wide, graveled pull-off on the left makes a good parking spot and beginning.

Source of additional information:

> Big Cypress National Preserve
> HCR 61, Box 110
> Ochopee, Florida 33943
> (941) 695-4111
> www.nps.gov/bicy

Notes on the trail: Getting lost on this road will not be a problem. The entire 52 miles may be more than you would like to ride in a single day, however. For that reason, you may want to set up a shuttle at either end of the road. Loop Road comes back into Tamiami Trail at the Monroe Check Station, where you can safely leave your vehicle. You'll know the intersection by the swamp buggies locked up behind a fence, 5 miles on the left after passing the Oasis Visitor Center. Bring plenty of water and snacks. This is a good route to take your time on and absorb the experience. As I rode along, I met 2 rangers surveying sites where new drainage culverts will help divert the destructive floodwaters that seasonally wash away the roadbed. Some of the hops over potholes can be spectacular. Do not, however, attempt to hop over a basking gator's back. Should the beast become motivated enough, it could easily catch and dispatch bike and biker.

RIDE 75 · Fakahatchee Strand Preserve

AT A GLANCE

Length/configuration: 15-mile out-and-back (30 miles total)

Aerobic difficulty: Low; flat

Technical difficulty: Easy; paved with no intersections

Scenery: Big cypress trees and a Royal Palm hammock

Special comments: If you can see through the clouds of deer flies and horse flies that are following you, you may catch a glimpse of a rare native Florida panther.

RIDE 75 · Fakahatchee Strand Preserve

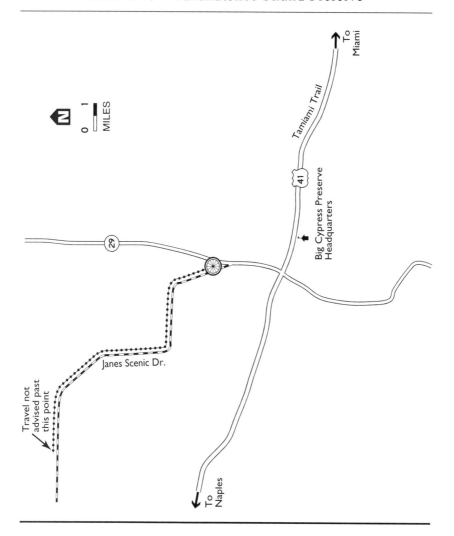

The 15-mile out-and-back (30 miles total) on the limestone double-track inside Fakahatchee Strand State Preserve takes the off-road biker into one of the few remaining primitive areas of the Everglades accessible by two wheels. Although you will see many of the typical swamp creatures—gators, snakes, coons, and such—you may also be one of the last to ever see one of the 30 to 50 remaining Florida panthers in their native habitat.

You'll also see the big cypress trees on this preserve. Although they are impressive, they are just slightly half the age of the 800-year-old giants that were trammed out of here by the Tidewater Cypress Company. One of my favorite Florida trees, the Royal Palm, has a hammock here that preserves the world's largest wild stand of these trees. Its bottom trunk looks like a sturdy stone sculpture, and its rough elegance gives way to a green bark that shines smoothly under the shade of large fronds.

General location: Fakahatchee Strand State Preserve is located southeast of Naples.

Elevation change: There is no elevation change unless you get off the former tramway and into the strand.

Season: The summer is often touted as the season *not* to ride here due to the heat, the bugs, and the frequent lightning storms. But guess what? I happened to be here in summer and found this to be a great ride in all respects but the bugs.

Services: Bring all your necessities with you to the trailhead, and carry enough water to get you there and back and then some. Naples can provide many of the off-trail services you need.

Hazards: Although the Fakahatchee has many of the hazardous natural conditions found in Florida, the deer flies and horse flies present the most formidable, consistent hazard that I experienced. The little suckers have a knack for congregating in large numbers in the air eddies behind your ears—delivering *en masse* a simultaneous drilling to your epidermis. And, no, it is not likely you can outride them. They are speedy demons who nearly caused me to wreck 5 times on this trail alone.

Rescue index: This is remote country, and depending on the time of year you ride, it may be days before someone happens along to offer assistance.

Land status: This is state managed land open to the public.

Maps: You can get a map of Fakahatchee Strand State Preserve at the state preserve ranger station on Janes Scenic Drive, 0.25 mile east of Highway 29.

Finding the trail: Head east on US 41 (Tamiami Trail) out of Naples until you come to State Road 29 at Carnestown. Turn left (north) and go approximately 2.5 miles. On your left you'll see Janes Scenic Drive. Park here.

Source of additional information:

Fakahatchee Strand State Preserve
P.O. Box 548
Copeland, Florida 34137
(941) 695-4593
www.dep.state.fl.us/parks/District_4/Fakahatchee.Strand/index.html

Notes on the trail: As you would expect on a paved out-and-back with no intersections, this is an easy trail; however (and this is a big however), at the end of the out-and-back, a large grid of paved roads (for a subdivision that never caught on) stretches as far as you can see. These are not to be explored without the aid of a professional guide and/or a global positioning system. Consider the bridge the end and return the same way you rode in.

RIDE 76 · Bear Island

AT A GLANCE

Length/configuration: 7-mile out-and-back (14 miles total)

Aerobic difficulty: Low; flat terrain

Technical difficulty: Easy

Scenery: Cypress trees, swamp vegetation and wildlife

Special comments: A truly remote ride

North of Alligator Alley, near the Okaloacoochee Slough, a network of off-road vehicle trails in Big Cypress National Preserve offers swamp cyclists another primitive destination. A 7-mile out-and-back (14 miles total) takes a flat route on double-track near the last remaining habitat of the Florida panther. Although you may be one of the privileged few to see the endangered cat, it is unlikely. You will know them by their radio collars and ringworm-infested coats.

Big Cypress is home to the snail kite, bald eagle, wood stork, and red-cockaded woodpecker, endangered species all. You're much more likely to see a clapper rail instead or hear an oak toad croaking its midday melody. And you may also hear the internal combustion roar of swamp buggies (ORVs) or air boats as they come through maidencane and cattails. If you happen to be near the Black Hole when you hear one approaching, pull over and watch it cross the deep, long hole. Better yet, see if you can hitch a ride to the other side. Do not, however, be tempted to tag along with one of the gators you're likely to see.

General location: This trail system is north of Interstate 75 (Alligator Alley) and east of State Road 29 behind the gate on Bear Island Road.

Elevation change: There is very little elevation change.

Season: The summer rains can be more than a nuisance and a hindrance. Ditto for the bugs, reptiles, and summer humidity. Hunting is allowed in season within the Big Cypress National Preserve.

Services: The closest services lie to the west near Naples on the Tamiami Trail.

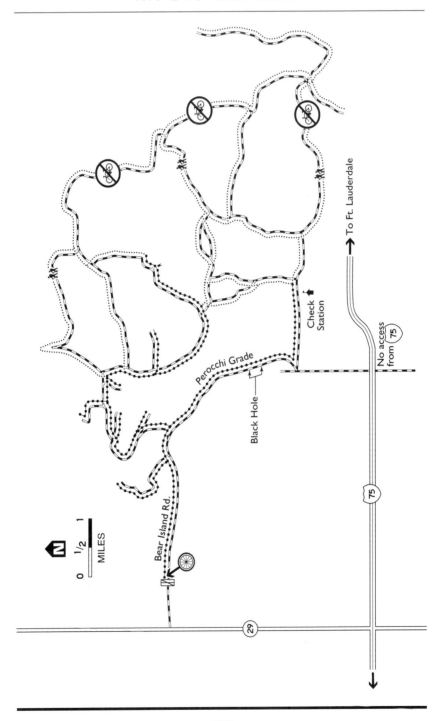

Hazards: You may have to share the trail with an ORV, and in season hunters may be slopping through the sloughs and strands in search for that stray deer or hog.

Rescue index: Prepare for self-rescue. It is a bona fide boonie-ride.

Land status: This is part of Big Cypress National Preserve.

Maps: The Oasis Visitor Center has detailed maps of all trail systems in the preserve. Ask in particular for the Bear Island Off-Road Designated Trail System. In addition, ask for the Big Cypress map.

Finding the trail: From Naples, take I-75 to SR 29 and exit north. After a little more than 4 miles, look for the gated access road on the right to Bear Island. Pull off to the side of the road and park.

Sources of additional information:

Superintendent
Big Cypress National Preserve
HCR 61, Box 110
Ochopee, Florida 33943
(941) 695-2000
www.nps.gov/bicy

Oasis Visitor Center
HCR 61, Box 11
Ochopee, Florida 33943
(941) 695-4111

Notes on the trail: Hardrock Trail, blazed with green, is but 1 of the 5 different trails in the Bear Island network. Clearly marked, numbered intersections allow for easy exploration into the wild side of Florida's Big Cypress Swamp. At intersection 24, a left leads to the longer, yet easier, route. A right connects to Turner River Road and the check station, but not before crossing what the ranger at Oasis called "the Black Hole," 200 yards of chest-deep water. In the future, a bridge at this point will make this section easier to cross. Also, as it stands, no loop can be legally ridden; 2 separate out-and-backs exist instead of the 10-mile loop that would be made by allowing passage along part of the red trail (intersection 13 to intersection 11A).

MISCELLANEOUS TRAILS

I t's an exciting time to be riding off-road in Florida. Trails and plans for new track are being developed at an unprecedented rate. But the down side—at least so far as this guide is concerned—comes from being unable to present a complete list of information for some of these in-process routes. But enough information exists to get you there, or to connect you to people who are more than willing to give current updates on the following trails (in addition to those that will surely come in the near future), so you can easily add any of these miscellaneous trails to your repertoire.

RIDE 77 · Gold Head Branch State Park

AT A GLANCE

Length/configuration: Fire lines and service roads (mileage unknown)

Aerobic difficulty: Low

Technical difficulty: Easy

Scenery: Rolling sandhills

Special comments: The sand service roads are disked through the year and are quite soft

I thought I had uncovered a gem of a ride after talking to a representative of a Jacksonville bike shop about riding possibilities at Gold Head. I heard reports of steep sections of single-track inside this park's hiking trail system.

Alas, when I called the park, I was told that the hiking trails are for foot travel only. However, there are fire lines and double-track service roads that the off-road biker can ride on this small 2,100-acre site, which got its start in the 1930s when the Civilian Conservation Corps constructed the facilities around a deep ravine among the rolling terrain of central Florida's sandhills.

General location: Gold Head Branch State Park is located 40 miles southwest of Jacksonville.

Elevation change: Although the hiking trails have some steep sections, it sounds as though the double-track is not quite as steep.

Season: This is an all-season trail.

Services: The park has all the modern facilities befitting a Florida state park. The small community of Keystone Heights has the basics; Palatka may have more specialized goods and services.

Hazards: Unknown.

Rescue index: You should have no trouble getting rescued here.

Land status: This land is managed by the state of Florida as a state park.

Maps: Ask for the map of Gold Head Branch State Park.

Finding the trail: Exit Interstate 295 on the south side of Jacksonville and begin driving southwest on FL 21. The park is located on the left just before Keystone Heights.

Source of additional information:

Gold Head Branch State Park
6329 State Road 21
Keystone Heights, Florida 32656
(352) 473-4701

RIDE 78 · Dyer Park, Palm Beach County

AT A GLANCE

Length/configuration: Paved loop (mileage unknown)

Aerobic difficulty: Low; flat

Technical difficulty: Easy

Scenery: Woods

Special comments: Construction of a 2-mile single-track loop is planned

Not all of Florida's off-road trails are flat. Some have descents that require a high degree of expertise.

This former landfill has been developed into a county park where a paved asphalt loop (approximately ten feet wide) goes around one of the filled cells; in addition, some true off-road single-track of perhaps a two-mile loop will be constructed in partnership with the West Palm Beach Bicycle Club. The property was given to the Department of Palm Beach County Parks and Recreation by the Solid Waste Authority. A BMX track and horse trails are also in the works for this east coast urban park.

General location: Dyer Park is located west of Haverhill Road and east of Florida's Turnpike, just west of West Palm Beach.

Elevation change: There is little elevation change.

Season: This is an all-season trail.

Services: The park has all the modern conveniences you would expect. Florida's nearby east coast provides all other goods and services.

Hazards: There will be other users on the trail.

Rescue index: This is an easy place to effect a rescue.

Land status: This land is managed by Palm Beach County.

Maps: Maps will be made available by the Department of Parks and Recreation; ask for Dyer Park map.

Finding the trail: Call for directions.

Sources of additional information:

West Palm Beach Bicycle Club
P.O. Box 16764
West Palm Beach, Florida 33416
(561) 842-7414

Palm Beach County Department of
Parks and Recreation
(561) 966-6600

RIDE 79 · Long Pine Key Trail

AT A GLANCE

Length/configuration: 6.8-mile out-and-back (13.6 total miles)

Aerobic difficulty: Low; flat terrain

Technical difficulty: Easy

Scenery: Wetlands landscape and wildlife

Special comments: Best to avoid this ride during summer months

This out-and-back of 6.8 miles (13.6 miles total) in Everglades National Park was built primarily with hikers in mind, but bikers received permission to use this wide, flat trail as well. Series of walking trails lead off this main out-and-back, beginning from the Long Pine Key campground at gate G4. On the day I arrived at the trailhead, it was 90 degrees at 10 a.m. I had already seen researchers from the Daniel Beard Center who were dressed like those people in the bug repellent commercials, hoods and all exposed skin covered. Since I had made my way through the Everglades on bike earlier that same morning and was still stinging from my bouts with the deer flies, I did not ride this trail.

General location: Long Pine Key is located in the heart of Everglades National Park.

Elevation change: Little elevation change occurs.

Season: I avoided riding this during the summer months. During the winter, this should be the place to ride off-road.

Services: The campground has drinking water, rest rooms, grills, and picnic tables. Other services may be acquired in Homestead or Florida City.

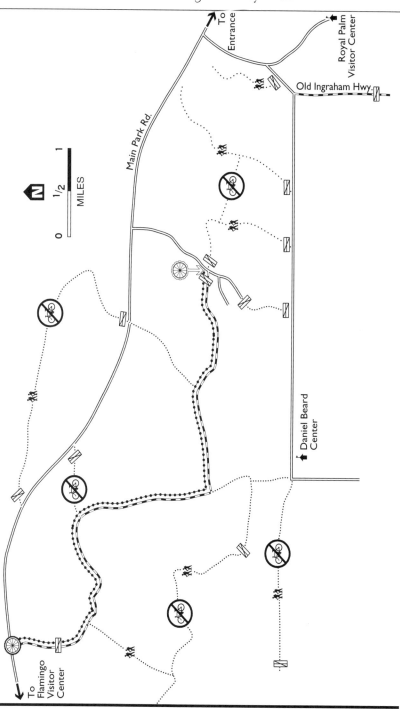

Hazards: The hazardous natural conditions found in the Everglades are formidable and plentiful, mainly composed of reptiles and insects.

Rescue index: Plan on self-rescue here.

Land status: This is part of Everglades National Park.

Maps: I used the map of Pinelands Trails to show the route here. You can get a copy at the Ernest F. Coe Visitor Center.

Finding the trail: Enter Everglades National Park and turn left about 4 miles down the main park road. You should see the sign for and road leading to Long Pine Key campground on the left. The last road on the right (it's gated) is the beginning of Long Pine Key Nature Trail.

Source of additional information:

Everglades National Park
40001 State Road 9336
Homestead, Florida 33034-6733
(305) 242-7700

Notes on the trail: Beginning at the campground, you will notice a 1-mile hiking-only connector on the right about a mile and a half into the ride. Slightly over a mile later, the trail cuts north at an intersection with another footpath, and Long Pine Key Trail maintains a northerly direction for nearly 2 miles before curving to the west. You'll notice another foot-travel-only trail turning to the right at the intersection where it changes direction. Almost a mile and a half later, before reaching Pine Glades Lake, you'll see a foot trail going to the left. The gate across the trail signals the remaining half mile to the main park road.

RIDE 80 · North Port

AT A GLANCE

Length/configuration: 7-mile loop

Aerobic difficulty: Moderate to high; short, steep, abrupt changes in elevation

Technical difficulty: Moderate to challenging; steep concrete drainage area may be suitable only for expert riders; single- and double-track combined with some paved roads

Scenery: Subdivisions and forest

Special comments: Night rides are very common

This seven-mile loop in Port Charlotte's water retention management area has sections requiring fairly advanced skills. Some paved subdivision roads are incorporated with single- and double-track, best completed by going on one of the regular Friday night rides organized by the good folks at Fort Myers Schwinn. That's right; night rides are the most frequent time for taking on this trail. The steep sides of the concrete drainage areas, which are part of the ride, can be more challenging than what a beginning or intermediate biker may want. Call for complete details.

General location: North Port is located in Port Charlotte.

Elevation change: Some dramatic elevation change occurs, but it is short-lived.

Season: Since this is part of the water management program, it can be under water during certain periods.

Services: Port Charlotte has a wide range of goods and services.

Hazards: Unknown.

Rescue index: You could be rescued fairly easily here . . . if you're riding with some local riders.

Land status: This is part of the land managed by the Southwest Florida Water Management District.

Maps: No maps are available.

Finding the trail: Call for information.

Source of additional information:

Fort Myers Schwinn Cyclery
1941 Courtney Drive
Fort Myers, Florida 33901
(941) 939-2899
www.mudcutters.org
closed Sunday and Monday

RIDE 81 · Boyett Park

AT A GLANCE

Length/configuration: 35 miles of loops

Aerobic difficulty: Low to high, depending on which trails you ride

Technical difficulty: Easy to challenging; double-track for beginners, and intermediate single-track that connects to expert trail

Scenery: Dense vegetation, lake

Special comments: Something for everyone here, though it can be a slow ride through the undergrowth that is slowly taking over the trails

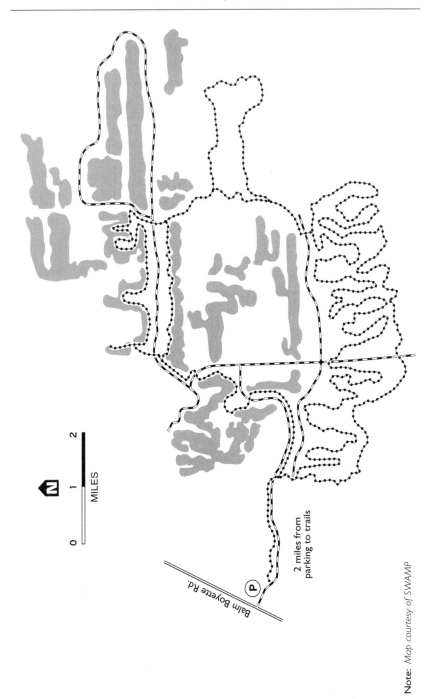

MILES

2 miles from
parking to trails

Balm Boyette Rd

P

Note: *Map courtesy of SWAMP*

The SouthWest Association of Mountainbike Pedalers has done it again. Approximately 35 miles of single- and double-track make a series of loops in an old phosphate mine south of Tampa. For the beginning biker, 13 miles have been blazed along what is mainly double-track. An intermediate course of nearly 9 miles of single-track connects to the expert trails.

General location: Boyett Park is located south of Tampa.

Elevation change: There are some sections of considerable elevation change in line with what you would expect from a former phosphate mine.

Season: This is an all-season trail.

Services: Tampa is the place to go for your specialized needs. The basics can be found nearby.

Hazards: Dense undergrowth along sections of the expert course make the going slow. "The best of the riders," says Wes Eubank of SWAMP, "cover trail no faster than 4 miles an hour."

Rescue index: Rescue is not a big problem at this park.

Land status: Managed by the Hillsborough County government.

Maps: SWAMP used its global positioning system out on the trail in order to make an accurate map.

Finding the trail: Call SWAMP for updates.

Source of additional information:

SWAMP (SouthWest Association of Mountainbike Pedalers)
9401 Takomah Trail
Tampa, Florida 33617
(813) 985-5021
www.swampclub.org

RIDE 82 · Gran Canyon

AT A GLANCE

Length/configuration: 10 miles of single-track
Aerobic difficulty: High
Technical difficulty: Moderate to challenging
Scenery: Farm with former phosphate pit
Special comments: Farm owner charges a day-use fee

The approximately ten miles of single-track in this former phosphate (also called limerock) pit can be as difficult as any in Florida. This trail is located on a privately owned farm whose owner charges at least $3 per day. This is not a trail for the weak of heart or leg.

General location: Gran Canyon is located near Brooksville.

Elevation change: Substantial descents are found here.

Season: This is an all-season trail. Call for reservations.

Services: Limited services are available on-site. Brooksville has the basics. Tampa—to the south—can meet specialized needs.

Hazards: Hazards are what you would expect in a former phosphate mine. Helmets are required.

Rescue index: It should be easy to get rescued here.

Land status: This is private property; call first.

Maps: No maps are available.

Finding the trail: Call first, but you'll be in the neighborhood by taking FL 50 toward Brooksville. Turn right on Mondon Hill Road. Turn right again onto Cooper Terrace. No signs announced the entrance when I arrived on a weekday.

Source of additional information: Phone John Bennefield at (352) 796-8955.

GLOSSARY

This short list of terms does not contain all the words used by mountain bike enthusiasts when discussing their sport. But it should serve as an introduction to the lingo you'll hear on the trails.

ATB
all-terrain bike; this, like "fat-tire bike," is another name for a mountain bike

ATV
all-terrain vehicle; this usually refers to the loud, fume-spewing, three- or four-wheeled motorized vehicles you will not enjoy meeting on the trail — except, of course, if you crash and have to hitch a ride out on one

bladed
refers to a dirt road which has been smoothed out by the use of a wide blade on earth-moving equipment; "blading" gets rid of the teeth-chattering, much-cursed washboards found on so many dirt roads after heavy vehicle use

blaze
a mark on a tree made by chipping away a piece of the bark, usually done to designate a trail; such trails are sometimes described as "blazed"

blind corner
a curve in the road or trail that conceals bikers, hikers, equestrians, and other traffic

BLM
Bureau of Land Management, an agency of the federal government

buffed
used to describe a very smooth trail

catching air	taking a jump in such a way that both wheels of the bike are off the ground at the same time
clean	while this may describe what you and your bike *won't* be after following many trails, the term is most often used as a verb to denote the action of pedaling a tough section of trail successfully
combination	this type of route may combine two or more configurations; for example, a point-to-point route may integrate a scenic loop or an out-and-back spur midway through the ride; likewise, an out-and-back may have a loop at its farthest point (this configuration looks like a cherry with a stem attached; the stem is the out-and-back, the fruit is the terminus loop); or a loop route may have multiple out-and-back spurs and/or loops to the side; mileage for a combination route is for the total distance to complete the ride
dab	touching the ground with a foot or hand
deadfall	a tangled mass of fallen trees or branches
diversion ditch	a usually narrow, shallow ditch dug across or around a trail; funneling the water in this manner keeps it from destroying the trail
double-track	the dual tracks made by a jeep or other vehicle, with grass or weeds or rocks between; mountain bikers can ride in either of the tracks, but you will of course find that whichever one you choose, and no matter how many times you change back and forth, the other track will appear to offer smoother travel
dugway	a steep, unpaved, switchbacked descent
endo	flipping end over end
feathering	using a light touch on the brake lever, hitting it lightly many times rather than very hard or locking the brake
four-wheel-drive	this refers to any vehicle with drive-wheel capability on all four wheels (a jeep, for instance, has four-wheel-drive as compared with a two-wheel-drive passenger car), or to a rough road or trail that requires four-wheel-drive capability (or a one-wheel-drive mountain bike!) to negotiate it

game trail	the usually narrow trail made by deer, elk, or other game
gated	everyone knows what a gate is, and how many variations exist upon this theme; well, if a trail is described as "gated" it simply has a gate across it; don't forget that the rule is if you find a gate closed, close it behind you; if you find one open, leave it that way
Giardia	shorthand for *Giardia lamblia,* and known as the "backpacker's bane" until we mountain bikers expropriated it; this is a waterborne parasite that begins its life cycle when swallowed, and one to four weeks later has its host (you) bloated, vomiting, shivering with chills, and living in the bathroom; the disease can be avoided by "treating" (purifying) the water you acquire along the trail (see "Hitting the Trail" in the Introduction)
gnarly	a term thankfully used less and less these days, it refers to tough trails
hammer	to ride very hard
hardpack	a trail in which the dirt surface is packed down hard; such trails make for good and fast riding, and very painful landings; bikers most often use "hardpack" as both a noun and adjective, and "hard-packed" as an adjective only (the grammar lesson will help you when diagramming sentences in camp)
hike-a-bike	what you do when the road or trail becomes too steep or rough to remain in the saddle
jeep road, jeep trail	a rough road or trail passable only with four-wheel-drive capability (or a horse or mountain bike)
kamikaze	while this once referred primarily to those Japanese fliers who quaffed a glass of sake, then flew off as human bombs in suicide missions against U.S. naval vessels, it has more recently been applied to the idiot mountain bikers who, far less honorably, scream down hiking trails, endangering the physical and mental safety of the walking, biking, and equestrian traffic they meet; deck guns were necessary to stop the Japanese kamikaze pilots, but a bike pump or walking staff in the spokes is sufficient for the current-day kamikazes who threaten to get us all kicked off the trails

loop	this route configuration is characterized by riding from the designated trailhead to a distant point, then returning to the trailhead via a different route (or simply continuing on the same in a circle route) without doubling back; you always move forward across new terrain, but return to the starting point when finished; mileage is for the entire loop from the trailhead back to trailhead
multi-purpose	a BLM designation of land which is open to many uses; mountain biking is allowed
ORV	a motorized off-road vehicle
out-and-back	a ride where you will return on the same trail you pedaled out; while this might sound far more boring than a loop route, many trails look very different when pedaled in the opposite direction
pack stock	horses, mules, llamas, et cetera, carrying provisions along the trails . . . and unfortunately leaving a trail of their own behind
point-to-point	a vehicle shuttle (or similar assistance) is required for this type of route, which is ridden from the designated trailhead to a distant location, or endpoint, where the route ends; total mileage is for the one-way trip from the trailhead to endpoint
portage	to carry your bike on your person
pummy	volcanic activity in the Pacific Northwest and elsewhere produces soil with a high content of pumice; trails through such soil often become thick with dust, but this is light in consistency and can usually be pedaled; remember, however, to pedal carefully, for this dust obscures whatever might lurk below
quads	bikers use this term to refer both to the extensor muscle in the front of the thigh (which is separated into four parts) and to USGS maps; the expression "Nice quads!" refers always to the former, however, except in those instances when the speaker is an engineer
runoff	rainwater or snowmelt
scree	an accumulation of loose stones or rocky debris lying on a slope or at the base of a hill or cliff

signed	a "signed" trail has signs in place of blazes
single-track	a single, narrow path through grass or brush or over rocky terrain, often created by deer, elk, or backpackers; single-track riding is some of the best fun around
slickrock	the rock-hard, compacted sandstone that is *great* to ride and even prettier to look at; you'll appreciate it even more if you think of it as a petrified sand dune or seabed (which it is), and if the rider before you hasn't left tire marks (from unnecessary skidding) or granola bar wrappers behind
snowmelt	runoff produced by the melting of snow
snowpack	unmelted snow accumulated over weeks or months of winter—or over years in high-mountain terrain
spur	a road or trail that intersects the main trail you're following
switchback	a zigzagging road or trail designed to assist in traversing steep terrain: mountain bikers should *not* skid through switchbacks
technical	terrain that is difficult to ride due not to its grade (steepness) but to its obstacles—rocks, roots, logs, ledges, loose soil . . .
topo	short for topographical map, the kind that shows both linear distance and elevation gain *and* loss; "topo" is pronounced with both vowels long
trashed	a trail that has been destroyed (same term used no matter what has destroyed it . . . cattle, horses, or even mountain bikers riding when the ground was too wet)
two-wheel-drive	this refers to any vehicle with drive-wheel capability on only two wheels (a passenger car, for instance, has two-wheel-drive); a two-wheel-drive road is a road or trail easily traveled by an ordinary car
waterbar	an earth, rock, or wooden structure that funnels water off trails to reduce erosion
washboarded	a road that is surfaced with many ridges spaced closely together, like the ripples on a washboard; these make for very rough riding, and even worse driving in a car or jeep

whoop-de-doo	closely spaced dips or undulations in a trail; these are often encountered in areas traveled heavily by ORVs
wilderness area	land that is officially set aside by the federal government to remain *natural*—pure, pristine, and untrammeled by any vehicle, including mountain bikes; though mountain bikes had not been born in 1964 (when the United States Congress passed the Wilderness Act, establishing the National Wilderness Preservation system), they are considered a "form of mechanical transport" and are thereby excluded; in short, stay out
windchill	a reference to the wind's cooling effect upon exposed flesh; for example, if the temperature is 10 degrees Fahrenheit and the wind is blowing at 20 miles per hour, the windchill (that is, the actual temperature to which your skin reacts) is minus 32 degrees; if you are riding in wet conditions things are even worse, for the windchill would then be *minus 74 degrees!*
windfall	anything (trees, limbs, brush, fellow bikers . . .) blown down by the wind

INDEX

STEVE JONES left his home-town of Marietta, Georgia, shortly after his first shaving accident. Since then, he has milked cows, pumped gas, been shipped across the Pacific on a U.S. Navy tug-boat, and flown across the Atlantic in the belly of a 747. He once flirted with respectability by becoming an English teacher, even receiving a college degree from the University of Tennessee. His parents now answer the ques-tion, "What's Steve doing these days?" with sidelong glances and coughs, but when pressed finally tell the truth: "He's a writer who spends his days riding a bike and his nights tapping out stories." Steve has had articles published in state and national magazines.

Steve's other books include *Mountain Bike! The Deep South*, *Mountain Bike! The Southern Appalachian & Smoky Mountains*, and *The Nuts and Bolts of Mountain Bike Technique*. When he's not finding, riding, or writing about single-track, you will likely find him home in Dahlonega, Georgia, with his wife and son.